SURVIVING POWER

SURVIVING POWER

The Experience of Power— Exercising It and Giving It Up

Xandra Kayden

THE FREE PRESS
A *Division of Macmillan*, Inc.
NEW YORK

Collier Macmillan Publishers
LONDON

The Free Press
A Division of Macmillan, Inc.
866 Third Avenue, New York, N.Y. 10022

Collier Macmillan Canada, Inc.

Printed in the United States of America

printing number
1   2   3   4   5   6   7   8   9   10

Library of Congress Cataloging-in-Publication Data

Kayden, Xandra.
    Surviving power / Xandra Kayden.
        p.   cm.
    Bibliography: p.
    Includes index.
    ISBN 0–02–917231–4
    1. Power (Social sciences) 2. Control (Psychology)
3. Politicians—Psychology.   I. Title.
JC330.K39   1990
303.3—dc20   89–16939
                                                          CIP

Credit Acknowledgments

Grateful acknowledgment is made to the following:

"The Disillusionment of Success: How Women View the Work World," by Jane Meredith Adams, November 10, 1986. Reprinted courtesy of The Boston Globe.

Hardball: How Politics Is Played. © 1988 by Christopher J. Matthews. Reprinted by permission of Summit Books, a division of Simon & Schuster, Inc.

"He's staying on as Attorney General, but many other Justice officials may not," by Ruth Marcos, November 28–December 4, 1988 National Weekly Edition, © The Washington Post.

"Life After Salomon Brothers," by William Glaberson, October 10, 1987. Copyright © 1987 by The New York Times Company. Reprinted by permission.

"New Frontier of Women's Psychology," by Judy Foreman, September 22, 1989, Boston Globe Magazine. Reprinted courtesy of The Boston Globe.

Tip O'Neill with William Novak, Man of the House: The Life and Political Memoirs of Speaker Tip O'Neill (New York: Random House, 1987), © 1987.

"Politics as an Ego Trip," by Daniel Golden, December 20, 1987. Reprinted courtesy of The Boston Globe.

Reprinted by permission of The Putnam Publishing Group from The Power Lovers, by Myra MacPherson, © 1975 by Myra MacPherson.

Shelley Ross, Fall from Grace: Sex, Scandal, and Corruption in American Politics from 1702 to the Present (New York: Ballantine Books, a Division of Random House, Inc., 1988), © 1988.

To Bill, Ellery, and Jim

Contents

PART ONE

1. The Powerholder's View of Power   3

What Power Means to Those Who Have It   4
Power and Influence   7
Power and Authority   11
The Culture of Power   13
Cultural Changes   20
Power as a Temporary Phenomenon   22

2. Crossing the Border   25

How Far the Journey   25
Realizing Power   27
     The Gap Between Winning and Knowing You
       Have Won   27
     Victory and the Spoils of Victory   29
Relationships with Others   33
     New Neighbors   33
     An Irreducible Barrier   34
     A Different Standing   35
Standing Alone   40
     Realizing the Need for Restraint   41
     Recognizing the Limitations   42
     Re-Ordering the Universe   43
     There Is No Going Back   45

3. **Exercising Power—the Unexpected Experience**   47

The View from the Battlements, Looking Down   47
  Trust   48
  Structuring Self-Reliance   51
The View from the Battlements, Looking In   56
  The Good Stuff   56
  A Sense of Competence   58
  Picking Your Own Team   59
The Daily Grind   61
  Focus on Process   61
  Favors   62
  Ritual and the Public Role   63
The Frustrations of Power   65
  Limitations   65
  Vulnerabilities   69
  Getting Tired   71

4. **The Structures of Power: The Context in Which It Exists**   77

The Ways That Power Is Achieved   78
  Legislative Power   79
  Executive Power   84
  Staff Power   88
Autonomy and Objectives   91
  Public versus Private Structures   92
Borrowed Power: Appointees and Rainmakers   95
  Influence from the Inside: the Appointees   95
  Influence from the Outside: the Rainmakers   98
Conclusion   101

5. **Men and Women**   103

Expectations   103
The Experience of Power   107
  Different Fears   107
  Differences in Attitudes About Deference   111
  Different Organizational Styles   117
  Different Relationships/Different Needs   120
  Responding to Pressure   123

Sex Roles and Power   124
Women and Power   127

6. **Private Relationships**   131

Family Life   137
Friendship   141
Illicit Relationships   143
The One-Night Stand   146
Aberrational Behavior   148
Conclusion   150

PART TWO

7. **Losing Power**   157

How One Loses Power   159
The Things That Are Lost with the Loss of Power   162
The Awkwardness of Incompetence   166
Financial Security   169
Transition: the Actual Pain of Loss   172
Conclusion   176

PART THREE

8. **Surviving Power: Life After Power**   181

Age: the Physical Determinant of Expectations   183
Experience in Losing   184
Letting Go   186
Private Options   191
Staying in the Arena: Influence   194
Using the Skills   195
Private Person/Public Image   197
Private Person/Private Image   202

Notes   209
Acknowledgments   215
Index   217

PART
ONE

■

CHAPTER

1

■

The Powerholder's View of Power

This is a book about power—not what people do with it, but what it does to people: what it is like to get it and use it, and what happens when it is lost. Power does not have án existence in its own right. When it comes, it is wrapped into the character of the individual who holds it, and when it goes, it bares an identity that has been changed by the experience. Those who hold power do not all share the same experience of it, partly because there are degrees of power and success, and partly because of the differences between individuals in character and background. It is also likely that, as society changes, the culture of power shifts, and the experience of power must be as varied as all of the experiences of life. But there are commonalities, and they are what I would explore, for the sake of those who go through the experience, and for the sake of the organizations and structures of society over which they hold sway. Although the focus of the book is on political power, I have interviewed persons in the private sector for the same reason: to explore the commonalities and the differences.

The book is divided into three parts: the experience of power; losing it; and surviving it. It is based primarily on interviews I have held with many of those who have gone through the process. Some have survived the loss of power better than others, because they had a stronger sense of who they were when they came into power, or because of other circumstances of life that were more favorable: the times were better for using power; or they were younger; had a better place to go when it was over; or they had other interests or just a better understanding of what was to come. Most had problems surviving the loss of power because it is a transitional stage in life, but one to which we do not pay sufficient attention. It is an area, I believe, that deserves some consideration.

WHAT POWER MEANS TO THOSE WHO HAVE IT

Definitions of power, however varied, always reveal the nature of one's approach to the subject. Those inclined to view society in structures and institutions, see power as a systematic phenomenon. Those who study the individual, see it in terms of the intention and control of individuals. Most see it from the perspective of the powerless.

The question of what power means came up frequently in the interviews I did with those whom the world considered to have exercised it. Most of these former powerholders found little in the traditional definitions to help them understand either the behavior of those around them, or their own experience. For example, if you think about power as being about control and intentions, it sounds right in the abstract, but means relatively little to those who are trying to achieve an objective because their control over others—or even their own environment—is almost invariably less than what they thought they needed to reach their goal. The experience of power is not so much about control as it is about trying to exert control and achieve goals; except, perhaps, where it comes to their own autonomy and command over their own lives in both the public and the corporate worlds.

There is "real" power in the world, but—from the perspective of most of those who experience significant power—it would be more accurate to say there is probably more powerlessness. John Buckley, a former sheriff in Massachusetts, said that when he thought of power *per se*, he thought about the old sheriffs he used to meet in the South:

> They would walk through their institutions and their officers and inmates would greet them like—God, like I've gone back 100 years! The inmates wouldn't even look at them. They had to keep their eyes down. And someone dared to speak to him, and the sheriff would say, "Where did you get the nerve to speak to me?" And the officers would sit there saying, "Yes, sir. Yes, sir." And I said this must be what power really is. First of all, they obviously didn't come through very often, but when they did, it was clearly the signal for everyone to bow low—the Great One, the Holy One is passing by.

"Of course," he went on to say of these southern sheriffs, "They've lost touch with reality."

Power of that sort—naked, ultimate, undiffused, measured by abject obedience—is not real for most of those who wield power in our complex world. What remains of that image that is real, however, is the sense of exhilaration that comes with the exercise of power, and the achievement of an objective that may or may not come from dominance over others. There are times when the sense of being the white knight charging off into the sunset (feeling good, knowing there is purpose behind one's actions) feels empowering, but it is a highlight in a more mundane landscape. "What in life is ever this black and white?" a former powerholder said of his exhilaration in the old job:

> That we were right, that there were beneficiaries, there was satisfaction in getting the bad guys ... what is ever going to provide this degree of satisfaction? Now, that's almost turning up on its head the constraints, the grayness of being a mayor, or a governor, or a state rep. And the trade-offs, the concessions, and the compromises—the shared power, and all the things that are typically endemic to federalism and democracy. I didn't suffer from them. Yes, the legislature got in my way when I wanted to hire new people, and there were some minor constraints. But no, I didn't suffer from the excesses of democracy.

Most powerholders feel exhilarated from time to time. They feel like creative entrepreneurs who can accomplish great things, but they rarely feel they have the power to do everything they would like to do. More often, the powerholder is aware that someone else has more power, or, if not more, that other individuals are beyond the powerholder's control. While powerholders are usually more conscious of their limitations than they are of their power, there is also a peculiar discontinuity between power in the abstract and power in practice in the experience of making something happen. What actually induces an individual to behave in a certain way (casting a vote, doing X instead of Y) may be the result of a maximum effort on the part of the powerholder, or something entirely minimal or extraneous. What is measured by the outside world is the change, not the effort that led to the change. What is remembered by the powerholder is the effort, particularly if it was a great effort. And if there was no effort, it may not even be recalled as power at all.

It is human nature to be more conscious of those who have power over us, and to spend relatively little time looking at those over whom we have power (with the exception of those who are driven by pathologies of one sort or another). A teacher who has the capacity to determine a student's career rarely thinks of it as power. A vote cast for or against a piece of legislation may determine the lives of thousands of individuals, but so large a number of people becomes an abstraction, and the legislator is more apt to be aware of the compromises that had to be made along the way to pass the legislation in the first place. We are all familiar with the consequences of the limits of separated powers when it comes to the executive branches of government. A president may want to pursue a particular course of action but is constrained by Congress and the laws it has enacted, and frequently—fairly frequently, it seems, judged by the tendency in recent years for the White House to take on the work of the executive agencies—a president is stymied by his own government agencies, that are manned by civil servants and watched over by interest groups who were there before he came and will be there long after he goes.

Frustration comes from the expectation that having power means being able to achieve something, that doors would open, that others would bend to the powerholder's will. Although few who attain great power are naive enough to believe others will automatically bend to their will, the experience of power is very much associated with the expectation that it will yield more satisfaction than it does. This is not a universal verity, but it is a characteristic of democracy in general and of the United States in particular, both of which owe their origins to a driving need to limit power.

An educator once remarked to me that today's students have managed to control their enthusiasm for history. We all have, and probably always will. It appears to be a characteristic of Americans (if not of everyone else) to assume that our world is new and modern, designed specifically to satisfy our current needs. We suffer a collective loss of memory when it comes to understanding the origins of our institutions, particularly our political institutions. But most if not all institutions developed as ways to distribute power. They are, in fact, defined by the distribution: a monarchy is a hereditary control of single power at the top; an aristocracy a sharing of responsibility among a group at the top; and a democracy, the further devolution of power based on the assumption that power rests with the many and no one should have too much of it. Democracy in the United States has led to an amazingly diffuse power structure, and public powerholders are purposefully bound by constraints against the free exercise of their will. Frequently, of course, we say we would rather it were otherwise, but, more frequently, we are content with what we have wrought.

The limitations of power notwithstanding, power is a finite commodity in all organizations and social structures. Some possess more and others possess less. The larger the institution, the greater the likelihood that power will be diffused among a larger number of individuals. But the larger the institution, the greater the formality of its exercise and the greater the status affiliated with it. It is something of a paradox, and often someone with maximum status—like the president of the United States—is left among the most circumscribed in every aspect of his life. He can exercise enormous influence, but the direct exercise of power usually follows very prescribed paths and requires accommodations by others.

If status is one of the greatest assets of a powerholder, the notion of power becomes like beauty: it is something perceived more in the eyes of the beholder than experienced by the possessor. The impact of power rests in the relationship between the powerholder and the powerless. Although it is a genuine relationship for both sides, most of the attention has been focused on the impact of power on the powerless. This book is an exploration of the impact of power at the other end: on the power-holder.

POWER AND INFLUENCE

There is a tendency to use the words "power" and "influence" inter-changeably, although we know there is a difference. The former presumes the ability to act purposefully; the latter the capacity to have access, to guide, to be involved in the process. Many of those we think of as having power hold their positions through their appointment to office by some-one to whom they are accountable. They have responsibility for, and relative autonomy over, specific areas (health, defense, the production of shoes). Others who are perceived to be powerful are further away, often outside the institution, having influence rather than responsibility. They may be called upon to offer advice in a crisis, or, in less troubled times, they may make recommendations about who should be appointed to office. The smallest number of powerholders are those who hold their power directly, accountable to no one, or to everyone, i.e., to the voters. Properly speaking, only this last group—those who answer to no one—could be said to hold power.

Former Speaker of the House Tip O'Neill tells a story that draws a nice contrast between power and influence. In 1959, a man named Frip Flannigan, who was the Washington representative of the W.R. Grace Company, and a friend of O'Neill's, came to see him about the opening of the St. Lawrence Seaway. A Grace ship, that they hoped would be the first trans-Atlantic passenger ship to make port in Chicago, was being out-maneuvered by two Dutch ships, and they wanted some way to recoup the public-relations battle:

I took Frip with me to see old Tom O'Brien, the head of the Chicago delegation and the former sheriff of Cook County. . . . Whenever Daley needed a vote, it was Tom who passed the word to the other members from Illinois. When Frip told him about the Grace ship, he put in a call to Mayor Daley. "Mr. Mayor," he said, "I've got Tip O'Neill here. Tip is one of the leaders of the New England group, and whenever you want something for Chicago, he always delivers New England for us. Maybe you could help him out."

"What the hell does he want?" growled Daley.

"Let me put him on," said Tom.

I explained the situation to Daley, and then I put Frip on the phone. Daley asked a couple of questions and told Frip he'd get back to us in twenty minutes.

When the mayor called back, he said to Frip, "The first Dutch ship is going to arrive tonight around ten o'clock. The second one will arrive around three in the morning, and your ship is due in around six. All three ships will be forced to stay out in the harbor while the health authorities run an inspection.

"At nine in the morning, your ship will be the first to come in. To celebrate the occasion, tomorrow will be a special holiday in Chicago. We'll have a big parade with high school bands and the whole works, and W. R. Grace will receive worldwide recognition for having the first ship to make the trip to Chicago without a stop."[1]

O'Neill had influence: he knew who to call, and he knew they "owed" him; Daley, on the other hand, had power.

In our world, and for my purposes, this book is about those who have played a critical role in significant institutions. These are the persons to whom others show deference and who attain important standing in our eyes. These are the persons who are apt to be changed by the experience of their roles. There may well be a difference at the very top of the mountain between those who have power and those who have influence. It is likely to be true that the powerful—as F. Scott Fitzgerald said about the very rich—"really are different" from the rest of us, but both power-holders and influence wielders can develop an enlarged sense of their roles and their identities. Both are part of the peer group of the powerful, while others are on the outside looking in. Still, there are differences between power and influence, and it would be well to consider them.

Power, unlike influence, has a root source. Elective power comes from the citizenry in a democratic society and is possessed for a specific period of time. It is renewed every two, or four, or six years in the United States, and it cannot be taken away easily. It is a formal, legitimate license, and as Kevin White, the former mayor of Boston noted:

> It was immediately won when I was elected. I was given this power by law. It was quickly defined whom I could appoint and whom I couldn't appoint. Who I had to share the appointing process with. Who I had to say I can't tell you until I get approval from the legislature. . . .
> Men can expend it, but there is a certain limit by which it cannot contract. It cannot contract because it is based on constitutional power which is the most stable of all public powers. You can delegate it, but you can't contract it.

Influence, on the other hand, is a reflected power that depends on somebody else. It can be given to you through appointment to office, or earned in a variety of indirect ways. One can gain influence through knowledge, or experience, by birth or association, or even by accident of proximity. If decisions are made by those who happen to be in the room at the time, and you happen to be in the room, you are apt to have an influence on the decision.

The significance of access/that can be influential/that can be powerful is seen in the arrangement of offices in every organization. They are literally positioned according to their degrees of influence with the Final Authority: those that are nearest having the most influence; those that are farthest away generally having the least.

Lacking the root source of power does not mean that influence is necessarily less valuable. A cabinet secretary has more status than a sheriff and, usually, more than a mayor. A cabinet secretary also usually has an impact on the lives of many more people, although the power of a sheriff to incarcerate others is clearly a superior force. Some (perhaps most of those I interviewed) preferred influence over a larger number rather than power in a smaller world, because there is greater status attached to larger institutions and more of an opportunity to make a difference in the world. Others might trade off standing in the larger world for greater control over a smaller environment

One reason many aspire to influence rather than to power is because influence lasts longer, just because it is not fixed in a term of office. As Eunice Howe, a former Republican National Committeewoman put it, "Having a career doesn't matter too much to me. It is having influence that matters. A title gives you access to power, but jobs come and go." There is an entire world of individuals who think of themselves as going in and out of public service and who value their reputations for being persons of influence. The key to their success is access. One trouble-shooter for a governor observed that "access for people like me is power. The fact that at any point that I want to I can literally—within 24 hours or less—talk to the governor, or his top policy advisor, or his chief secretary, is power." Influence, in his view is "psychic income, which is no less important than anything else." Another man put it even more succinctly: "That's what it's all about—just collecting access. That's all I do." One can have influence with a wide spectrum of powerholders, whereas power is held for one office, for a limited period of time.

The aspect of influence that goes beyond psychic rewards, and has an impact on the behavior and attitudes of others, is that which exists—like power—almost entirely in the eyes of others. One must be perceived as being influential in order to really be influential. Once one is accepted into the "inner circle" of the influential elite, there is very little heavy lifting. As Ms. Howe noted, "It takes energy to establish it, but, once established, you don't have to do anything."

One Republican woman recalled a time when she was asked by a Rockefeller family lawyer to attend an affair at a college in another state. Although supportive of Nelson Rockefeller, she had never thought of herself as a member of his circle. The trip would be a long one and she told the attorney that she was surprised she was being asked to attend. He responded by pointing out things that Nelson Rockefeller had done for her over the years—rewards she had never traced to his influence—and, acknowledging the debt, she got into her car that Sunday and drove to the distant school.

Influence can be lost if one ignores it, or if it is abused, or if there is a change in administrations. John Ehrlichman described an incident early in his career as an aide to President Nixon in 1969:

> Joe ——— phoned and asked if he could bring a client in. He was the president of ——— Company. They had absolutely nothing on their minds. He didn't want to talk of any substance at all. So after about fifteen minutes, Joe said thank you and they got up and left. And I said to my secretary, "What was all that about?" And she said "Joe was proving to his client that he could get in."

In the political world, those who can gain access in the administrations of both parties are viewed as statesmen. It is clearly a lofty status to which many aspire, although the route to achieving such standing is neither clearly marked nor assured.

POWER AND AUTHORITY

There are other distinctions about power that have bearing on the experience. Power comes with the office, but individuals vary considerably in their capacity to exercise it. Some refer to this as the distinction between power and authority, although occasionally the meanings of the terms are reversed. For our purposes, let us accept the notion that "authority" refers to the legal responsibilities associated with the office, and "power" to the ability of the individual to exercise it.

To a large extent, an individual's power in office depends on his or her ability to internalize the role: to understand its uses and limitations; to come to think of it as part of one's self. Without that, process of internalization, there is likely to be a conflict that cannot help but lead to an irrational or unconscious use of authority that, in turn, has the potential to undermine the position as well as the individual who holds it. If the exercise of power is not conscious, it clearly cannot be linked to an objective. If it is not clearly linked, there is a risk of squandering the control of the power holder and, ultimately, the integrity of the organization. It is not uncommon, for instance, to hear someone say, "I don't have any power, I'm just concerned with the process." Or, "I'm just doing my job, I don't have any power." Those who fail to understand that process is power, or that their jobs are perceived by others to be powerful, are likely to handle it badly, failing to understand those over whom they do, in fact, hold power.

On the other hand, "authority," as one former powerholder noted, "gives you the opportunity to exercise power, but you may not exercise it." Ehrlichman aptly described the weakness of the link between power and authority in terms of his experience:

There were occasions when I would call and say I am calling on the President's express instructions to tell you to do this, and it didn't happen. And there are bureaucracies, particularly in the military, where that is not an automatic junction. . . . There are all kinds of obfuscations, resorts to Congress, and all that stuff to try to stop a presidential instruction from being carried out. . . . It was months and months and months of hard work to get them to believe that we meant it.

But sometimes, I didn't even need to say "The President wants." All I had to do was call up and say this is me and why don't you fellows do this? And they were galvanized at that. Other times, I'd call and say "Richard Nixon, your Commander in Chief, wants you to do this," and they'd immediately set to work to figure out how to frustrate me.

While the fusion of power and authority can be irresistible, it does not occur automatically, particularly when changes in administration mean an entirely new set of powerholders, as is the case in the United States at all but the most local levels of government. Those who are not apt to be "galvanized" into action by a phone call from the White House are likely to have an alternative power in mind, whether based in the law, in members of Congress, or in a strong interest group. They are likely to be committed to another course of action that would be threatened by a new direction, and, most of all, they are likely to believe that the link of power and authority is weak in that powerholder.

While it is important to combine power with authority to be an effective powerholder, it is possible to have power without authority. A man with a gun can have power over us, can make us do almost anything, but he would not have authority—the right of office—to make us act in any particular way.

There are other ways of having power without the authority of office that are more meaningful. There is personal power that is not necessarily linked to office in intelligence, knowledge, and experience in a specific area. Power can be conveyed by one's demeanor: a deliberative manner of expression, or a way of holding one's self in public. Physical attributes of the actor make a difference. Kevin Harrington, a former president of the Massachusetts State Senate, is 6'9", and communicates a sense of power just by being there. He noted, however, that he consciously added to the illusion of his stature by a number of strategies, including not smiling when he walked down the halls of the State House.

The converse of that is the difficulty of presenting yourself as a serious person if you are small and look young. Women's magazines frequently include advice on appearing powerful, that runs the gamut from not smiling, to "dressing for power." Many years after I had worked for Elliot Richardson in the Department of Health, Education and Welfare, he told me that whenever we met, he had to concentrate very hard on what I was saying because he could not get it out of his head that I was not 15 years old (I was 30 or 31 at the time). I hesitate to imagine what others thought who did not so carefully focus their minds on me or the issues with which we were concerned. Although this is a problem more likely to be faced by women, it certainly affects men who do not fit the standard mold.

While these physical factors of stature are easy to trivialize, they are often real and significant determinants of success because there are fairly clear cultural expectations of physical ideals and what we want our leaders to represent in relation to them. There are always exceptions to the rule, but the popular prejudice works in favor of those who suit the norm and against those who do not. An identity based on physical attributes is something that is confirmed and reconfirmed throughout one's life, and, unlike power, it is not a temporary phenomenon. When looking young becomes part of one's identity, it will remain so well beyond the early years.

It would be an interesting academic exercise to test the hypothesis that having power makes a person look powerful by measuring how often the subjects of the experiment can identify a powerful person in a crowded room. Short of undertaking the experiment, however, I would speculate that when power is linked to authority, it is conveyed in the non-verbal language of one's bearing (possibly even overcoming physical determinants not associated with power) and it is easily recognizable by strangers.

THE CULTURE OF POWER

There is a world—a culture—to which those who exercise power and those who hold influence belong. Elliot Richardson, often described as the best that the Boston Brahmin world had to offer, made the observation that, above all, it is a civil world. A world where niceness counts, he said, and "the bastards don't last, unless they have a very independent base. No one can survive in Washington who isn't nice."

There may have been times when civility was not the order of the day in the world of the elite, in Washington and other centers of power elsewhere in the country. It is likely that the characteristics of elite cultures—as of all cultures—change over time. It seems at first blush, however, that civility, or politeness, characterizes the acme of social intercourse. It is a world where only gentle people exist, and one to which only those who know and care about each other belong. They do not necessarily have to like each other, but they do have to behave in a respectful manner toward each other. It is a world of acts born out of preference rather than need. Deference is paid by choice and everyone has his or her place. Ann Wexler, a highly regarded Washington lobbyist and former White House aide, described the sense of it this way:

It has to do with home life, a good education, a good background. It has to do with being real.... Some people do it naturally and others don't Some people crave power and want to be like Elliot Richardson, but never can be because they don't quite know how, or it never comes through with their personalities. They can't move from one niche to the next.

Psychologists, sociologists and, doubtless, linguists have a great deal to say about the nature of social intercourse at elite levels, but it comes down to the meaning of polite society. As another participant in that world put it,"People with real power tend to be very accessible, gentle people." Another noted that such people were "generally compassionate and ... more generous with their time." A fourth pointed to returning phone calls as a characteristic of the civility.

There is an argument that the function of civility is to instill self-constraint in the individual.[2] It would follow from this, that those most civilized, i.e., those at the elite level of society, would also be the most self-constrained, the most polite. They would be "nice." Conversely, those who are not polite have not internalized the appropriate restraints, do not represent the best of the culture, and are not worthy of inclusion in the world of the elite.

The epitome of civility is society at court: a world that, by definition, has no other profession but manners.[3] Although our democratic culture does not support the notion of courtiers *per se*, the tradition of civility at the elite level appears to remain relatively constant. There is always an elite, but what makes the difference between a democracy and other political structures is the relative openness of the elite world to those who prove themselves worthy. Because democratic elites are more accessible to those who merit inclusion by reason of their accomplishments rather than by reason of their birth, it does not mean that our elite lacks structure or coherence. There are some who are definitely members of the court, and most who are definitely not.

Recognition of one courtier by another is based on civility. Lack of civility while in power is often used as an explanation for the dramatic fall of some powerholders. Had they been nice, it is inferred, they would have been protected. And, by the same token, an unusually civil person is sometimes saved from the dire consequences of a fall from power because other elites will gather round.

An interesting anecdote on the value of personal consideration was told to me by a number of people several years ago about Jeane Kirkpatrick and an ambassador from an Arab country at the United Nations. According to the American Ambassador, she and the representative were negotiating on a resolution at her official residence in the Waldorf Hotel in New York. "He was notorious for being difficult and was being hard as nails," she said. When he left her suite, he got into the elevator which dropped twenty floors. Later, Kirkpatrick said,

> I've always thought falling in an elevator must be a horrible experience . . . and he thinks the United States is hopelessly anti-Arab anyway. . . . I thought, Oh, God, and here we had the elevator falling! So I wrote him a note and said I felt really badly to hear about it and that he must feel awful. I asked one of the security guards to take it down to him in his suite at the Waldorf. And the next morning, he smiled at me and thanked me.
>
> This is only important because of the very tough guy that he is. He's described as a tough, cold, unsmiling, hard-as-nails person. . . . We were able to establish—at least temporarily—for the rest of those negotiations—a kind of a human dimension in a relationship which maybe helped a little in diplomatic relationships.

Examples of the lack of civility exist in the centers of power as well, but they are often pointed to as the exception that proves the rule. One observer, wise in the ways of Washington, cited crude behavior as a factor in the number of charges brought against some of the Reagan appointees, noting a specific case against a friend of the President's who was a former aide in the Reagan White House:

> I think there are a lot like ———— who came in thinking they had so much power they could do whatever they wanted to. They forgot about civility. And they forgot about collegiality—which is the other thing in government. . . . He thought he was one of the most powerful people in the world. He played favorites . . . and he made a lot of enemies. He emerged in a blaze of glory when he started his business with clients. He knew what the rules were. He just violated them, knowingly. He thought he could get away with it because he was who he was. It's a classic abuse of power and he did it because he thought he was different. He was being totally unrealistic. . . . He lost his sense of balance completely, In fact, I don't think he ever had it. And on the other hand, I think Ronald Reagan probably understands the use of power better than anybody.

The same explanation of lack of civility could be applied to John Tower's failed bid to become Secretary of Defense in the Bush Administration. For all the arguments posed against him (drinking, womanizing, even conflicts of interest), the most damning factor in the long run appears to me to have been the fact that he was not liked in the Senate because he had abused his power when he was there. The pundits pointed to the rare refusal of the Senate to confirm a Cabinet nominee—but it was really a rare thing for the Senate, that most exclusive of clubs, not to have approved one of their own.

Many have argued that the most salient characteristic of our politics in the last quarter century has been its anti-establishment nature. The implication (and often the practice) is that those who are alienated feel morally superior to those in power and, therefore, feel no obligation to be polite to those who exclude them. Whether or not that puts more pressure on the "Establishment" to be polite to its own kind, it certainly helps draw a line between those who are "in" and those who are not.

This attitude of moral superiority carries beyond the under classes to those who would be their champions in the very centers of power. There is a sense of outrage, a presumed need to slap the wrists of the power-holders, and a rush to correct past evils by ignoring those persons who block the paths to righteousness. Both the Carter and the Reagan presidencies reflected the disdain they felt toward the Washington elite, and charges abound that their White House staffs were rude, keeping their distance from the establishment as a measure of their imperviousness to its seductive lure. Not only did they not play by the rules, they did not want to learn the rules. Both these presidents came to office on the wings of an essentially anti-establishment campaign, and although the principals were not themselves charged with impoliteness, it is not surprising that many of their aides were.[4]

It would be carrying this particular argument too far to suggest that crudeness and lack of personal regard by one side necessarily influences the behavior of the other. Those who have power and prestige want to be thought of as having it by virtue of birth, background, talent, intelligence, or accomplishment. Charles A. Vigeland provides the perfect description of a member of the elite in this sketch of a treasurer of Harvard University—one of the most established and elite worlds in the United States:

> He intimidated certain people, not because he was wealthy, not because he was intelligent, not because he believed and acted as if manners mattered, and not because he was good at what he did, but through the genuine impression he conveyed of a person who was supremely content, whose happiness came not from the satisfaction of doing his job but of living his life. His good cheer

and abundant energy frightened others. He seemed invulnerable to the common concerns of his fellow men. He was disinterested; the trick for [him] wasn't so much in what he had but in how he used it. He seemed unafraid to admit an ignorance, to acknowledge a debt, to make a new acquaintance. His involvement in the moment was total, his concentration on what was at hand complete. George Putnam was in love with his world.[5]

The assurance of virtue and belonging of the haves, however, is exactly what angers the "have nots," and encourages them to believe that the "haves" are unfeeling and that their politeness is a sham and a means of exclusion. What makes the political culture different today—at both the mass and elite levels—is the rejection by the "have nots" of the rights of the "haves," and the expectation that there ought to be equality.

Current values have an impact on an individual's sense of right and wrong, as well as on his behavior and sense of identity. It is a problem of varying acuteness for those who succeed to power from the ranks of the powerless, particularly for women and minorities. The capacity of a minority person in power to internalize being in a position of power is, in great measure, affected by that person's ability to identify with both sides, and to accept himself as an empowered individual who comes from a powerless class.

Believing that you belong among the elite can also be a problem for individual members of the dominant group among the powerful, because insecurity can strike anyone. To the extent that you doubt your right to exercise power, to that extent your insecurity will affect your behavior towards others, and, ultimately, your capacity to rule. The scandals of aberrational behavior on the part of great powerholders that emerge from time to time suggest something of the nature of the pressure that power exerts on an individual who is not comfortable in the role.

There is another factor in the culture of power, especially as it relates to Washington, that bears mentioning. Presidential administrations and congressional elections notwithstanding, there are communities of power made up of persons who have known each other for many years, and who survive because they are protected by civil service, because their electoral bases (or those of their bosses) are secure, because they represent stable interests, or just because they have become institutions themselves, with their own independent bases in money, associates, or talent.

There are communities of elites formed around spheres of activity: foreign affairs, intelligence, the military, welfare, and so on. They wield enormous influence, if not power in the most direct sense. And those who would seek to have influence upon them, need to conform, at least to some extent, to their expectations of behavior.

Who they are and what they value are partly the result of the age cohort they represent in the population. There is, for instance, a group of persons who came to Washington with the New Deal in the 1930s: they rose far in the bureaucracies, stopping just short of the top political positions. They share a knowledge of each other, of how their agencies work, a commitment to the ideals of their youth, and a strong sense of public service. Most have retired now, but they made government function smoothly for many years. Harry McPherson, who is a generation younger, knew them well in his years in Washington as an aide to Lyndon Johnson, and as a practicing attorney. He thought that the Johnson administration was the last to know they existed and the last to rely upon them to make things happen:

> Many of the people were there in the Nixon administration, but the people in the White House didn't know them. And that's important. I think it is, anyway. That the President have around him some people who know the bureaucracy, know the people. And have some sense, not just of how it works . . . people who know the kind of person out there—by name. Can call them up and say, "I don't know where this is in your department, but maybe you can help me find it. I really don't trust what I'm getting here on paper and I need your help, and can you . . ." And doing that can be enormously beneficial.

An argument can be made that ignorance of that world led to a number of the White House scandals we have gone through in the past several years, because those in the White House did not know how to make the agencies conform to their interests. Of course, there is an alternative view—that knowing what buttons to push in the agencies is not necessarily sufficient to overcome the sense of those who actually have their fingers on the buttons, if they believe the buttons should not be pushed. Peter Woll and Rochelle Jones have argued that the federal bureaucracies frequently carry out their own policies in opposition to White House directives because they are accountable to Congress or the courts as much as they are accountable to the President. "In the final analysis," they suggest, "the expertise, continuity, and political ties of the permanent civil service severely limit the ability of any President to alter bureaucratic practices through his appointments."[6] To the degree that an agency is politically independent of the White House, to that degree it can and will apply its own standards and standard operating procedures to actions proposed by the Chief Executive. If the Internal Revenue Service, or the Federal Bureau of Investigation, or the Central Intelligence Agency chose not to respond to Nixon's requests because it did not suit their purposes or their sense of correctness, there was very little the president could do about it. The same sense of frustration seems to have impelled much of the activities summed up in the Iran/Contra scandal a decade later, even when the head of the C.I.A. was as much or more involved in seeking action as those in the White House itself.

The bureaucracies aside, there are many communities of power in Washington, each with its own mores, values, and shared experience. Many are bound together as an age cohort, dependent on when they came to Washington—whose administration, what issue. The New Deal made the greatest impact, if only because of the rapid and extensive growth in the size of the federal government in the 1930s and 1940s, but there are others who came of age politically under Kennedy, Johnson, and Nixon. The Reagan legacy is also apt to be strong, given the efforts of the administration and its supporters to fill middle-level as well as top-level positions.

It comes down to an "us" against "them" mentality, with "them" being the new boys on the block (or the old guard, depending on your frame of reference). The sense of embattlement encourages an insider culture and often makes a virtue of personal regard for fellow members of the group. The more embattled one is from the outside, the more valuable it is to be on the inside, in the warmth and caring of one's fellow combatants. The unusually large number of marriages in the Reagan administration, between the young men and women who represented the administration in the various agencies, has been explained by the sense of isolation these individuals felt within their agencies, and the great comfort with the few others they could find in government who shared their conservative views.

The marriages notwithstanding, the sense of us against them is a continuing characteristic of power elites in their relationships with the world of the non-elite. It would be true in all cases where power is held by one group over another. The differences between elites and non-elites are exaggerated now—in the last quarter of the twentieth century—because of the sense of moral outrage on both sides that characterizes the increased ideological nature of American politics; but there would be differences regardless—each side with its own sense of proper behavior—just because there are separate and identifiable cultures of power and what might be called cultures of "anti-power."

CULTURAL CHANGES

The culture of power reflects the society in which it exists, and as societies change, so, too, will the dynamics that make up all of its cultures. The world of power in the early part of the century, for instance, appears to have been characterized by much greater formality than it is today, and it may well be that the personal concern today's power elite tend to show toward associates is an alternative way of maintaining the civility required for the exercise of power within a confined world, while eliminating the strictness associated with the rigid adherence to rules. Shirley Williams, a former president of the Social Democratic Party in England, recalled her mother's experience during and after the First World War, noting that the women who held power then—a smaller minority than today—had to demonstrate that they were as correct as the men:

> Women were extremely formal. The hospital matron was the most formal of people: rigorous—more male than the males. . . . They were famous for being martinets . . . in a power structure which was unforgiving. Things like being told that you couldn't have leave when your brother's best friend died—even a day—because that was not permitted. You might have if he died—for just a day—but you couldn't for his best friend. That was an inconceivable thing.
>
> She came back after four years in a military hospital, and the first thing that the principal of Somerville said to her—because she had broken her degree course and gone off to the war and come back again—she said, "Well, Miss Britain, you've wasted four years. How do you think you are going to make up for that?"
>
> Now, that was the style, and the principal was just living by the values of a strictly academic society in which serving in the war was neither here nor there. Just nothing to do with scholarship, consequently a total waste of time. Like getting married. These things were just a waste of time.

It is tempting to suggest that the consequences of affirmative action in the past fifteen years have had some impact in changing the elite environment, but, in all likelihood, the women and minorities who have made it to the top are accepted in large part for their ability to resemble and adjust to the dominant culture—as is expected of all candidates for inclusion, whether or not they come from a minority. Still, there have been changes due to the acceptance of the *idea* that these outside groups ought to be part of the process.

Organizations and cultures need to be flexible enough to respond to changing values and external pressures if they are to survive. In the case of the disequilibrium caused by the recent civil rights, peace, and feminist movements, various institutions have responded by redirecting resources, and sometimes by co-opting dissidents and bringing them into the process. In the past few years, both strategies have been applied because power elites have accepted the argument that equality requires participation in the process in order to secure an equitable allocation of the resources. This solution may not be necessary to the maintenance of social structures, but the approach has been linked convincingly; at least, we are willing to accept its legitimacy as a tactic to achieve equality.

The consequence of bringing outsiders in is that it changes the world of the decision-makers. However great the problems of the persons who serve as tokens, including a desire to blend in as much as possible, token outsider representation is not too serious a danger for the dominant culture as long as the outsiders are tokens—because they help draw those of the dominant culture closer together, often exaggerating dominant traits in the process.[7] (In the case of the Reagan administration marriages, curiously, it would suggest that ideological differences transcend gender differences in terms of defining the group.) Once a group goes beyond tokenism in its inclusion of minority representatives, however, the minority values begin to have an impact. As Anne Wexler noted of the Washington world:

> If you look at Washington in terms of how power is manifested—as opposed to ten years ago—we look at old-time lobbying like it was some kind of neanderthal, quaint custom. Most of the new members of Congress don't go off and play golf. Sure there are some vestiges of people who like to go out with their lobbyist friends to Burning Tree and drink and play golf, but every time there is a new Congress, and a new generation—not only does the makeup change, but the commitment to the way of life changes.

One reason golf has fallen by the wayside as *the* social sport of decision-makers is that women are less likely to play it; another is that today's young decision-makers prefer more active sports to keep themselves in shape. They are also likely to work harder and have less time for a sport that requires as many hours as does golf. Ms. Wexler went on to remember a conversation on the subject:

> I was talking to Congressman ———— last year and he was complaining that he had to work so hard. And he was saying, "You

know, I heard the Speaker talking ... about how, when they used to come to Washington, they'd come to organize Congress in January and then they'd go away. They'd go to Florida and play golf until the 1st of April, and then they'd come back and they'd dilly around the first year and pass some laws the second year. It was very relaxed. This year they came to organize the Congress and they went to work!" This is something fairly new for these guys.

One reason Congress works harder is that there is more competition for positions of leadership, no longer assumed by heirs apparent, nor passed on entirely through seniority. Interest groups are better organized, communications are more extensive, technological changes are rapid, and, of course, if some work harder, they set a standard for others to follow or be left by the wayside. The same changes in life style and competition exist in the private world as well. Everyone works harder, everyone is more conscious of competition as the United States—and probably all of the other developed nations in the West—come to terms with the implications of an economically, socially, and technologically-linked global economy. Changes in the world outside have some impact on the inside, and similarities in the external experience have similar consequences on the individuals who share them, whether in the world of politics proper, or in the private spheres of corporate and voluntary associations.

POWER AS A TEMPORARY PHENOMENON

Although most individuals spend years working towards the achievement of power, it is not a prize that is won and held for the rest of time. In public life, power is usually limited by a term (even many terms) in office. It can be lost in the gamble of leaving one office to seek a higher office. It can be lost outright in an election that may, or may not, have had any bearing on the behavior of the powerholder. In corporate life, it used to be possible to retain power until retirement, but take-overs—and the fear of take-overs—have changed that certainty of independence forever in most publicly-owned institutions.

Knowing something will happen, and being prepared to deal with that eventuality, however, are two different things. The temporary nature of the prize makes some hold their power ever more dearly; some spend considerable time preparing an escape to another power venue, and some absolutely refuse to look at what awaits them tomorrow.

Many try to stay in power because they fear the unknown. Many lose themselves in the role, and know they will lose a big part of their identity if they lose the role. These fears and anxieties of powerholders can be costly to the organizations they control. If nothing else, they work to create stress in the powerholder's identity with the role, increasing the separation of power and authority because the private identity is threatened. A few forget that power is temporary and behave as if they will always be there, treating inferiors as if they were inferior, in which case, their behavior can be costly to themselves when they lose power and find themselves among the "inferior."

If power is temporary and influence is borrowed, those who succeed best at either game are those who realize the ephemeral nature of their situation. It may well be that, for most, the greatest power they ever exercise rests in their capacity to appoint others whose participation in an organization will ensure the memory of their role. Long-range objectives will always be attained by others.

Those who succeed best at power are those who have the greatest awareness of its nature and of themselves. Some part of power will always be wrapped in mystery, dependent on the specific components of its exercise. But some of the experience is merely a haze that can be lifted, if we look. The following chapters seek to explore the experience, analyzing the unexpected, and putting it into the context of the lives of the individuals who went through it.

Many of us know individuals who have power, or have held power, whom we consider ego maniacs at best, and fools at worst. As great leaders, they are not necessarily great human beings. We make allowances for those we like, or for those with whom we agree. We disparage others with ease, and often—very often—with a measure of scorn. One might argue that some of those represented here are less than perfect human beings, but this book is an attempt to see the circumstances of their lives from their perspective. It is an effort to climb inside their minds and see how the world has treated them, more than it is to see how they have treated the world. They understand each other because they have shared something of the human experience not given to everyone.

Of those who come into power, some will leave it blessed with the glow of a job well done and a memory of themselves carved into history. Some will leave it with a feeling of frustration and failure that can reach to the deepest levels of despair. Some will fail in the eyes of others but find a way to look upon it in another light. The experience of power tests the soul, and those who would survive it must grow with it, respect it, and, in the end, must learn to live without it. If the powerholder is to successfully outlive his term of office, he or she must let go of the structure and definition that power provides and learn how to address the world from a smaller, more intimate, more revealing persona. Where, before, a sweep of the hand had broad repercussions, now it only brushes aside that which it touches directly. Where, before, others made room, nothing precedes one but the fading memory of what had been, and the former powerholder must learn to clear his own path.

Not everyone suffers with the loss of power —for some it is a release and an opportunity to pursue private rewards—but for most, at some point in their journey, they must come to terms with the loss of the guideposts that helped them on their way up. The competitiveness that drove them successfully in the past may no longer suit. There are, in fact, a whole host of behaviors and experiences that come with the search and attainment of power that need to be put aside. One must learn to give and take with equality rather than giving or taking with the sense of noblesse oblige that can characterize superior beings. How much of the past came from the needs of the personality and how much from the needs of the time will have a significant impact on how well the former powerholder survives and adapts to a new life. Another factor must surely be how aware the individual is of the experience of power in the first place, and what must come afterward. It is that knowledge that this book seeks to explore and to extend to a wider circle, some of whom expect to achieve power, and some of whom would like to better understand their own experience and themselves. In many respects, having power is like growing up. It is worth striving for. It is worth understanding.

CHAPTER

2

---■---

Crossing the Border

Acquiring power is like entering a new country. Things seem the same at the border, but the more one wanders into the interior, the more one realizes that the language and customs with which one was raised are really from another land, a land that may or may not be seen again. It is not unlike the experience of an American talking to an Englishman: each expects that the other speaks the same language, but the more one comes to understand the other, the more one realizes how different the two languages really are.

Those who enter the land of power find that old friends become strangers. Conversations that used to be easy now pass through a filter, and meaning gets lost in the translation. Everyone looks at you with expectations you only dimly comprehend, and they, in turn, assume intentions where there were none and interpret actions where there was barely any movement at all. Public leaders complain about distortions in the press. Less visible leaders say again and again that they need to learn whom to trust. It is a country made up almost entirely of citizens passing through. One can take up residence for awhile, but in the end, the border must be crossed again, and rarely back in the same direction from which one came.

HOW FAR THE JOURNEY

One reason for the sense of strangeness is that almost all of those I interviewed explained their success in achieving power as a continuing process that was not especially goal-oriented beyond an inchoate desire to make a difference, or do good. They did not set a course to guide them to power. They described themselves as competitive rather than aggressive; as persons likely to want to do as well or better than their peers, but not as people focused on long-range desires to achieve power. Some talked of the challenge of the experience and the opportunity to test their mettle. The more common attitude was expressed by Kevin Harrington: he knew he wanted to be senate president once he was elected to the senate "because it was there—like the mountain."

Some of this competitiveness may be peculiar to the American experience because we imagine ourselves to be a relatively classless society. If all of us are essentially equal, we prove ourselves by competing against our peers. If we were to accept the notion of class, it would be easier to accept the concepts of inherent differences between a leader and those who are led. Idealizing equality, however, means that we do not strive for power; rather, we strive for measures that prove our worth against our equals.

The most obvious consequence of the absence of a long-range goal is that when power is achieved, the individual is likely to be surprised by the experience of it. There is a difference between being better in a group of peers and being its leader. It is much like the difference between being a parent and being a child—ultimate responsibility rests solely with the adult. How close one comes to the achievement of power—and why—will probably always remain within the world of speculation, but one clear consequence of power is that there is a marked difference in the experience between parent and child, leader and group member, and if most people cross those lines because they were focused on out-doing their siblings—rather than emulating their parents—they will be unprepared for what follows.

Another consequence of the focus on competition with peers, rather than on power for its own sake, is that it takes time to re-orient one's self once one reaches the top of the mountain. The senate president recalled that after he had been in office for about a year, there was a column in the *Boston Globe* querying his goals. As he recalled it, the story and his reaction were as follows:

"Harrington has been elected Senate President. He's spent the whole year amassing all of this power, but it's not clear what his agenda is, and what he wants to do with the power." And of course, only I knew that I didn't know what I wanted to do with the power either. I didn't know what I wanted to do with the presidency. I mean I had had the goal to become president of the Senate, and now I was president of the Senate, you know the old cartoon—now what do I do?

A third unexpected consequence of rising because there is a path, rather than because power is a goal in itself, is the necessary shift that is required to move from being the advocate of an idea or a philosophy to being a processor of the ideas and rights of others. The powerholder's job becomes one of making it possible for everyone else to do their job. It is the administrative side of leadership, but it usually comes as a surprise and it is why many who step down from leadership roles say they want to get back to their own research, their own work. Administration is a necessary element of power that orders and secures it, enabling the leader to devote attention to the borders of the realm where he or she seeks to extend it, dealing with peers in the world of power. It is human nature to always view it as getting in the way of doing the job, rather than being part of the job.

There is a darker side to the question of ambition that still fits the image of climbing the mountain because it is there. According to Doris Kearns Goodwin, a noted political biographer:

> Some people run to fulfill an inner lack of self. This kind of person never has a resting point. They won't be satisfied with being senator when somebody they think is no better than they are is running for president. And when they've been elected president, they start worrying about how they will compare with the other 36 or 38 presidents in history. . . . It's a strange thing to seek the applause of millions over the love of one person in bed at night.[1]

"You don't play this game for other people," said a former business executive. "You play this game for yourself. The fact that you have been given more resources is every reason to go out and do more. It doesn't end."[2] Whether it is compensation for inner needs, or whether it is built into the culture of a nation that was founded on the Calvinist notion that success is an outward sign of God's grace, or whether it is built into the biology of a species that requires leadership for survival, how far one wants to go is a major determinant in what the experience will be like along the way.

REALIZING POWER

The Gap Between Winning and Knowing You Have Won

The realization that you have power, whether directly or indirectly, borrowed or possessed, always comes later. It is usually linked to an

action and another person, rather than to the title, or to reflection about
the achievement of attaining the title. What comes before the realization
that you are thought of by others as a powerful person is the sense of
obligation to "get the job done."

Whatever the position, it is usually different than anticipated, with
other responsibilities, unexpected frustrations, and a host of differences
that one could only barely sense when seated on the other side of the
table. Sometimes the realization of power comes as much as a year and
a half afterwards, when the actor catches a glimpse of himself in another's
eye. One chief aide to a governor described it this way:

> I knew I was doing most of the action—but somebody said that
> there is a world out there that thought they had to get to me
> about getting to issues to change the government. You know what
> I mean? I never saw it that way. It was respond, respond, respond.
> But it made me think about it. One day, when I was walking in the
> State House, I saw Joe ———— walking out of the Governor's office
> with a coat (meaning he didn't come there often) . . . and I said,
> "Gee, there must be a perception that I am close to the Governor."
> That never occurred to me, for a couple of years or so.

I suspect that persons who are elected to office—those who actively
and publicly declare themselves to be seeking a particular position (with
all of the risks of loss)—have a stronger sense of where that position fits
into their lives than those who exercise power by appointment, even if
they actively sought the position. As one person put it, "One of the things
that is exciting about our life (in elective office) is that we have made
choices so that we have had varied experiences and we have decided
whether to do it or not do it. There has not been a single track that you
could not extricate yourself from." The willingness to make such choices,
take such risks, and "extricate yourself" from the entanglements of
everyday life may well be more characteristic of those who run for office
than those who are appointed, or it may be that the experience of putting
yourself so openly on the line, and soliciting support, frees one from the
reserve with which we more commonly clothe ambition.

All the elected officials, the staff aides, and the appointed officials to
whom I spoke said that the aides and appointed officials had not thought
very much about the future. The more sophisticated among them recognized their position as temporary and borrowed, but if they thought of
these positions as stepping stones in a career in the abstract, most of
them did not have a specific plan in mind. In contrast, those who ran for

office had some sense of a career goal and of the steps required to get there, even if later events caused them to change direction.

I interviewed a number of people who became senior assistants to presidents or to members of the Cabinet. The sense of power that comes with these positions is easier to perceive in the uprooting and transition that usually accompanies a new administration in Washington, and in all of the ritual and formality of taking office. In most instances, those who filled these roles were older and more sophisticated than the young aides at the state level, but the realization of power was equally remarkable and unfamiliar, and clearly something for which most do not prepare themselves. One man sagely noted that there is no training, no way to plan for a career as "Advisor to the President." It is a role entirely dependent on someone else's reactions. Nonetheless, there were lessons to learn in its uses and its restraints.

Victory and the Spoils of Victory

What comes with accession to office is a sense of victory, not a sense of power. The feeling of power comes later, over time, when other things happen, sometimes long after the winner settles into the job and reflects upon how others have begun to behave differently toward her. There are things others want of you: jobs, favorable decisions, or just to be in the presence of the new leader. When you go from being a supplicant to being a source, as is particularly the case in the transition from being a candidate for elective office to being the office holder, the realization of change comes from two sources: those who can directly ask things of you, and those who are further away in the world at large who begin to treat you in a different way. Ehrlichman recalled both experiences following the Nixon victory in 1968:

> As you go around in the campaign, you don't get a very good
> sense because you are a beggar, you are a supplicant all the time.
> You are trying to get things for your candidate, and you are trying
> to get the schedules worked out and get arrangements made, and
> people to give money and all of that. [After the election] it begins
> to show up in personnel things early. People begin asking for jobs
> and you think to yourself, "My God, what do I have to do with
> that?" And suddenly you realize that you do have something to do
> with it. . . .
>
> And all this kind of secondary reinforcement of your role begins
> to appear, and people start writing articles about where the locus
> of power is in the administration. . . . it begins to create a certain

amount of validity, which might otherwise not be there. I think if you did this sort of thing in a vacuum—you never see a paper, never watch television—you'd have a very different sense of your role and your so-called capacity than doing it with the media creating a lot of this around you.

One comes to understand that absolute strangers feel they know you because they have read about you in the newspapers or seen you on television, but it is something of a surprise to find changes in the world of one's acquaintances and colleagues. When Jeane Kirkpatrick was appointed Ambassador to the United Nations from her position as a professor of political science at Georgetown University in Washington, D.C., she was startled by the reaction of those around her:

> At the very beginning, I was very surprised—truly—at how much of a fuss people made about my appointment. I mean, people who were friendly—a friendly fuss. In how much interest people took in it, the sort of ripple it created. They were the very same people I'd been living with for decades and they could have heard my views any day of the week about almost anything in the world. . . . There is a sort of added enhancement of the image of one's self in others' eyes that comes with an association with power.

The added enhancement in the eyes of others could be predicted, but it is almost always a surprise. It is the difference between knowing something intellectually and experiencing it firsthand.

Of course, the newly ensconced powerholder may suffer just the opposite reaction to his or her elevation if no one notices. Ira Jackson became the Commissioner of Revenues in Massachusetts when Michael Dukakis was elected to his second term. He knew when he took the job that it was not a particularly prestigious or "glitzy" job, especially in the eyes of his associates at the John F. Kennedy School of Government at Harvard, but neither was he quite prepared for the reception he got his first day on the job:

> I thought this is a trench line, invisible job, just like all my friends had told me and I am thrilled because that was exactly what I wanted to test myself. But, OK, so I arrive at 100 Cambridge Street and I look up at the marquee of the building and the Massachusetts Department of Revenue isn't even listed. I am getting this sinking feeling that maybe it's a ten-person office on the 9th floor and we don't even get minor mention.

I went to the guard and I said, "Can you tell me where the Department of Revenue is, please?" And he said, "Why do you want to know?" So, I said, "Well, can you tell me where Taxpayer's Assistance is?" And he said, "Third floor."

I get to the 3rd floor and, again, there are no signs. There are old registry-like wooden benches out in the corridor, and I go up to the receptionist and I say, "Excuse me, can you tell me where the Commissioner's office is?" And she says, "Why do you want to know?" I said, "Because I am the new Commissioner," and she says to this day she is the person who told the Commissioner where to go on his first day on the job!

I get in the office and no one tells you anything. I am sitting at my desk and this career secretary is bringing in reams of paper for me to sign. By the end of the day, the bureaucracy is killing me with paper. There is no transition report. There is no welcoming committee. There is no wise old man who takes you out to the men's room and says, "Hey kid, I know you are scared shitless and don't know what to do, but here's where things are at. . . ."

Although Jackson tells the story with something of the melodrama of a comedy sketch, at the time, he says, "it was frightening, alienating, and isolating."

Once the powerholder is identified to others by name and face, there is a tendency to deny that a change has taken place in the individual. Doubtless this comes from the need to protect one's sense of identity from too much external stimuli, too much change. Often, the new powerholder has not yet come to believe the position is genuinely his. There is a feeling that a mistake has been made or that he or she is somehow a fraud in the post. Such denial has been explored by those who write about the fear of success.[3] "It was the chair. It wasn't me. It was the position that was important. It wasn't I who was important." The recognition that one's identity is changing—as foreshadowed in the behavior of others—is the first and most obvious price to be paid for success and the achievement of power. The new powerholder puts down his or her coin to pay the price, but clasps the purse evermore tightly.

A newly-named president of a record company had a different kind of experience from Jackson's, and it was threatening in a different way. He recalled going to a night club with a friend a few weeks after he was named to the position.

He was the head of my A and R department. A very good looking guy . . . We were watching a group with a girl in it, and after the

show she came and sat on my lap and started kidding around. He
picked me up and said, "Let's leave." And I said "What are you
talking about?" And he said, "She doesn't give a shit about you.
You are the president of the company. She is sitting in the lap of
the president of the company. She is not sitting in your lap." And I
realized what he was saying. I always tried to realize it's not me.
It's the job.

Offers of everything from better tables in restaurants to sexual favors
are almost common to celebrity status in the United States. It may be a
little awkward at first, but it is easy to grow accustomed to such servile
acquiescence. A more subtle, less racy response was described by a
former ambassador who was frequently at odds with the secretary of
state. While attending an embassy affair in another country, the an-
nouncement came that the secretary of state had resigned and, the
ambassador noted, "It was as if the temperature in the room had risen
10 degrees." The fine tuning of status is probably more characteristic of
the State Department than most other spheres of American life, but it is
familiar enough to be recognized elsewhere.

Sooner or later, depending on how much and why one sought the role
in the first place—to say nothing of what the role actually is—the
excitement of success and power do begin to alter one's sense of self. A
former executive described the realization of power with a wonderfully
vivid image:

Like some women shop for baubles and beads, or other men for
investments, for me, I realized all of a sudden that I could
accumulate people, give them power, but always have the right to
pull it back so that it wasn't something that was given away totally.
There were the risks of distributing it. I began not to talk about it,
but sense it—like something going through your veins.

Whether the power is absolutely yours for a given term of office,
borrowed from another authority, or merely an opportunity to exert
influence on a given occasion, at some stage—near the beginning but not
quite at the beginning—it provides a high, and an increased sense of
ability in relation to others. The greater the context in which the power
can be put in terms of morality, or humanitarian interests, or even just
achievement, the greater the sense of personal efficacy.

When you have a case that you think is right—and most others
think is right—you are not off on some kind of crazy, single person

mission, and you're getting press and people are calling you, and you feel you are making a difference. That is an absolute high.

Most people justify the value of their work in one way or another: the world plays on my sneakers; business couldn't live without my staples, etc., but nowhere is the opportunity to find justification in such a large, unambiguous way as there is in the public sector. And when it is unambiguous, the personal satisfaction can be quite intense, enlarging the individual beyond what he or she was before.

RELATIONSHIPS WITH OTHERS

Society is always prepared to accept leaders and those who would be leaders, even though those persons may be slower to accept themselves in the role. If some worlds are foreclosed, others open.

New Neighbors

The new powerholder finds that he has moved up in the world and now lives in the land of the powerful, or at least the famous. Doors open as if everyone is part of a large, happy family and the acolyte is accepted as a peer: asking and giving favors; providing opportunities to spend time together; and all of the myriad activities that pass for social intercourse at the higher levels of our society.

A newly-elected member of the Republican National Committee described her entry into the world of the party elite as resembling Alice entering Wonderland:

> I didn't know what the RNC was all about, but when I got there, I began to get phone calls from all different parts of the country—half of them asking favors—assuming that I could do something about them. Then I began to say, look, this is worth something. That's when I began to learn about things. I got to know people I was reading about in the newspapers and developed a warm relationship with them and I could ask favors of them.

Moving up in the world may be a smaller shift in position if the new powerholder comes from a background associated with power, the way others are raised with great wealth. It is a peculiarity of a democratic society that power and wealth, while often associated—especially in the eyes of others—can be discrete. A number of those I spoke to were raised in political rather than wealthy families and valued the opportunity their backgrounds gave them to prepare for their own careers, especially in the comings and goings of power. One man, who described himself as a troubled youth, conveyed the sense of security and personal efficacy his family's position gave him in coping with the outside world: "It never entered my head that if I went through a light or something—that I wouldn't get out of it." The power of others was not menacing or awesome, but rather something to be respected and dealt with. "As the very rich cannot conceive of money," he said, "the [fear of power by those raised to power] just doesn't enter their head."

"They will know all of the down sides," a mother said of her children's exposure to political power in the family. "They don't yet know the joy and the headiness as much, because I think that's a very personal thing—when you feel power, or accomplishment, or influence. But they certainly know all the pain. They shared that with us. That's probably a good way to do it," she reflected after a while, "if you've heard it at the dinner table every night, it makes it easier to make the decision to go in or not go in."

An Irreducible Barrier

While the new powerholder moves into a new neighborhood, everyone else grows more distant. "You don't understand," an aide kept telling a newly-appointed public official. "Now there is a megaphone inside you. Whatever you say goes through a megaphone." You say the sky is blue and subordinates wonder if you meant cobalt blue or azure blue, or if you meant it as a hint of something else. A woman recalled the distance that made communication difficult because her power became an irreducible barrier that could never be laid down:

> It took me quite a long time to understand that I could say "Listen, you know, I'm nuts. I say this in a purely personal capacity." I could say that I don't know the facts, and that I don't really care. And I could say it is just a personal opinion. But eventually, I had to learn that was illusory, really. In those contexts, I didn't have a personal self, so to speak, whom I could separate. In the eyes of others, it's an irreducible barrier. . . . I could not—in the eyes of others—rid myself of the authoritative role. So, eventually, I just gave up.

Accepting the notion of a barrier brings a sense of resignation and realization that others will not assume one's good intentions. Where before there was reward for a new thought, now there is suspicion. It strikes the new powerholder as unfair and unhelpful, causing problems where they need not have existed. Some feel it more keenly than others. The wife of a governor described the difference between her own and her husband's sense of the problem of the barrier this way:

> I was terribly uncomfortable with the distance and so I did everything I could to break it down. I think my husband was so problem-oriented and so "lets-get-on-with-the-agenda," he wasn't as obsessed with the problem as I was.

It is not irrelevant that both of these comments came from women who seemed to be more ill at ease with the barrier than men.

The barrier does not exist entirely because the powerless are fearful of power or suspicious of those who wield it. It also serves the function of elevating leaders, reinforcing the notion that our leaders hold their positions because they are different and better than everyone else. The barrier legitimates leadership. It owes its origins to the unlit world of psychology and how we deal with authority—how we have dealt with authority from infancy. It is linked to our earliest and strongest relationships with the world around us. The authority of the parent, is the beginning from which all else stems. Whether we want to be like the parent, control the parent, or submit to the parent, the pattern of relationships with authority is usually traceable in repeated situations over and over again in an individual's life.

Still, from the perspective of the powerholder, the existence of a barrier makes communication difficult. It is difficult for everyone directly and indirectly involved, and it is a major factor in the weakness of our understanding of how our institutions function. A weak understanding of a powerholder's actions leads to misinterpretation, false expectations, and frustration all the way around.

A Different Standing

Eventually, the barrier notwithstanding, the fact remains that those who stand on the top expect those beneath them to recognize their position. To many, the recognition of status is more important than the exercise of power, and it is that end to which they aspire because it gives both standing and meaning to their lives. Status is not a trivial matter for any of us, but it can be vitally important to those who lack a sense of security and assurance of their own value.

Recognition comes in varying degrees and at different levels of interaction: the total stranger who makes way; underlings, who themselves may run the gamut from obsequiousness to a bare acknowledgement of common interests; and recognition by peers. It can set the powerholder apart from the normal rules. "You can commit faux pas and engage in acts the normal person would be held up for having engaged in," said one former powerholder, "Because you have power, they won't directly confront you. It changes people's way of behaving in the world because the limits that other people operate within don't apply to you." Someone who works intimately with the laws that define others is guaranteed individuality and, perhaps, a meaning to life. Although we do not believe that anyone is ever really above the law, we often behave and encourage behavior in powerholders that would suggest to them that they are somehow above the laws of daily social intercourse.

The most dramatic expression of special identity I ever saw occurred in the mid-1960s, when I (as a minor cog in the Kennedy "machine") would occasionally accompany Senator Robert F. Kennedy on a trip around New York City, or to upstate New York. At the time, he was the "heir apparent." If power lies in the eyes of the beholder, a large part of the citizenry believed he would some day succeed his slain brother to the White House. He could walk through a hotel lobby and people would stand up and applaud. In fact, there were few places he could go without eliciting a strong, emotional outpouring. In his 1964 campaign for the Senate from New York—almost the first time he began to appear in public after the 1963 assassination of President Kennedy—huge crowds gathered around him, grabbing at his hands, wanting to touch him. Only the Beatles had been subject to that kind of mob reaction in the recent past. It certainly was not a common thing for politicians, and his strategists were not entirely sure this extraordinary outpouring would translate into votes in the November election.

I used to watch from the sidelines and wonder what it meant to him, what it would be like to be so public a figure. Kennedy distanced himself from it by believing the crowds were responding to his brother, not to him.[4] I had the impression, when I saw him toward the beginning of the campaign, that the intense emotion the crowds directed his way was like a light shining at him, a light from which he protected himself by a deflecting wall he had erected for that purpose. Toward the end of the campaign, and in the years that followed, I had the sense when I saw him that he had lowered his defenses and the light had become part of him. He was enlarged, ennobled, by the emotions of others. He had grown into that strange role of hero past and future.

There is no question that in the years after President Kennedy's assassination, years that were turbulent for the nation as well as the man, there was tremendous growth and change for the younger brother. The reporter Jack Newfield recalled Kennedy reading him a poem by Ralph Waldo Emerson, at the end of a day they spent together in New York in 1966. According to Newfield,

> Kennedy stood in the center of his own living room, silhouetted against a neon Pepsi-Cola sign in Queens, and began to read, in an unmusical monotone that was at the same time very intense in its buried feelings, a poem he must have associated with his brother:

> He pays too high a price
> For knowledge and for fame
> Who sells his sinews to be wise,
> His teeth and bones to buy a name,
> And crawls through life a paralytic
> To earn the praise of bard and critic. . . .

> But Fate will not permit
> The seed of gods to die,
> Nor suffer sense to win from wit
> Its guerdon in the sky,
> Nor let us hide, whate'er our pleasure,
> The world's light underneath a measure

> Go then, sad youth, and shine,
> Go, sacrifice to Fame;
> Put youth, joy, health upon the shrine,
> And life to fan the flame;
> Being for Seeming bravely barter,
> And die to fame a happy martyr.[5]

I think the poem meant as much to him of his own experience as it did of his view of John F. Kennedy, particularly the last stanza which Newfield thought he knew by heart. If one can read another's meaning from the symbols to which they respond, whether Robert Kennedy interpreted Emerson to express the experience for his brother or himself, the step they took toward the flame—the light—was a martyrdom of the self. I want to think that after a while, the light from outside merged with his inner self rather than destroying it, but the danger certainly exists for the domination of the flame.

The price of fame is exacted of all leaders to one degree or another. Such homage has an immense impact on one's sense of identity, an impact greater than the actual exercise of power. It expresses respect and a sense of specialness, of a difference from others that separates the individual from the commonality of humanity. As a sense of power can be lost in the day-to-day need to get the job done, deference remains apart as a ritual recognition of superiority. To some, the need for separation is critical. One powerholder stated unequivocally that he was more likely to respond more readily to requests couched in a deferential tone than to those that were not:

> I can recognize it in myself—and try to compensate for it—but I still have a tendency to go along with the desires, or advice, or demands of people who accompany their requests with deference. I don't think I am unique in that, but I . . . certainly respond unreasonably—more than objectivity would suggest—to proposals, requests, demands—not put as demands—which are accompanied with a show of deference.

While recognizing his need, he also recognized the cost: "We are trading deference for autonomy, because if you give in to the desire for deference, you give up autonomy." If others are aware of a person's need for deference, they have power over him because knowledge of how an individual will respond makes him predictable, and predictability is, by some definitions of power, at least, a measure of powerlessness.[6]

The "need" notwithstanding, deference signifies power, perhaps most dramatically in the higher reaches of the White House and the Pentagon, where, it is assumed, powerholders are inevitably preparing for, or going through, a life and death crisis. The seriousness of the struggle in the Pentagon, especially, is marked by the rank of the aide: colonels and majors abound who carry coats and make arrangements for someone's well being. In lesser worlds, these tasks are handled by bright young men and women who serve as aides and secretaries.

If others hang on to your every word, it is hard not to take yourself seriously, not to begin to think there is a reason. Being courted, after all, is the process by which specialness is always expressed, from a king to a beloved. Someone else devotes energy to satisfying your needs. The confidant is, as a former company president put it, "making himself likable . . . making himself a follower. Subverting his own individuality so you will share a little more of your power with him, or so he can be included in the glow of your power."

The role of deference in the experience of power may be different for men than it is for women. Most powerholders are male, however, and all of the examples I have used to describe it came from men. It was not something the women I interviewed talked about very much.

Realizing that you have power means accepting the specialness, the deference, the subversion of the will of others. A former assistant to the Secretary of Defense recalled his first sense of power this way:

I found myself one midnight, sitting at the head of a table, around which were gathered members of the impromptu task force that I set up to produce the budget and the program, and I brought in a general officer who ... was then on vacation.... They said "Well, he's on a pack trip in the Rockies." And I said "Find him." So they sent a helicopter out and brought him back.

But that was sort of incidental. So, here I was sitting at the head of the table, making decisions on a budget that maybe added up to $200 or $300 million. Substantial by those standards. And—oh, there was some kind of alarm system and I said, "All right, I've heard the arguments on both sides, I think we better cut that out. It's a $30 million item." And somebody said, "Well, gee." And I said, "Well, all right, let's reopen it." It should be more or less a consensus decision.... and we re-argued it, and I said, "All right, you've persuaded me. We'll leave the $30 million in." And, at that point, I thought to myself I know less about all these subjects than anybody else sitting around the table, but I'm making the decisions. Why am I making the decisions? Well, I thought—perhaps a little disinguously—because I am willing to take responsibility.

A less dramatic story, but one that was perhaps more meaningful to the individual involved because it places him with regard to his family, happened to John Eller who became an aide to the speaker of a state legislature. Not too long after his appointment, he was told to find scholarships for some youngsters who lived in the districts of the speaker and majority leader:

Very poor families. Very bright kids. I met each of the kids and had them come down and had all their applications filed, and in about a week had a scholarship for each one of them....

I was riding the train home and suddenly something hit me right between the eyes when I remembered a conversation I had with my grandfather, who was a county recorder out in Northeastern Ohio—where the counties are pretty important—so the county recorder had a lot of clout. I used to pass out his poll cards all the time when I was a kid.

My grandfather called me one day, when I was a senior in high school, and said "I want you to go over to the next couple of towns," still in the same county, "and meet with So and So." He said, "Put together a little resume, take the bills that you're going to have from school where you've been accepted, and give him those and he's going to have you fill out some other forms." And I went over and made my application—good grades in school, did fairly well. Lost the election for president of my class by one vote—little things like that. But I always thought I got the scholarship on the fact that I had good grades and this kind of stuff.

It was that night when I realized how I got the scholarship. Somewhere in the past my grandfather had helped somebody. And there was no way I could have gone to college without that help. . . . I suddenly realized that I had exercised power, and had called in some of the IOUs for these kids to help somebody else.

A less exciting exercise of power than dragging someone out of the mountains or distributing millions of dollars, but undoubtedly a more meaningful experience because he recognized his grandfather's behavior in himself, drawing from the inner world of identity and the earliest memories of family and the associations of power within the family. His realization that he was behaving as his grandfather had, made the position more valuable, more important, and more recognizable as power.

STANDING ALONE

Whether or not a new powerholder can find comfort in models from his or her past, the ultimate reality is that having power separates one from others. The new peer group or other powerholders offers some comfort, but it never exactly fills in for the lost camaraderie that comes from being one among others. No one else sits exactly in your seat, facing your pressures. The lessons the new powerholder learns come a little slower because no one else stands by and says "Hey, that's something else we didn't expect." First, you cope, and then, later—always later—you try to put things into perspective.

Realizing the Need for Restraint

John Ehrlichman came to Washington without really planning to do so. Although he was a college friend of H. R. Haldeman's, he was never close to Nixon, and had little experience in presidential politics. Before the 1968 campaign, he was the managing partner of a relatively small law firm in Seattle. His motivation for involvement in the campaign was, as he put it, "an itch to get involved in a larger picture," something done more out of boredom than ambition. He intended to return home after the election and had to be convinced to stay—initially as White House Counsel (a position created for him)—with the expectation that he would return to Seattle after a year and, in time, be appointed to the federal bench. It was a logical and reasonable career path. That he found himself mediating between Nixon's domestic policy advisors and later acceded to the position of Chief Policy Advisor is getting a little ahead of the story.

The first "inkling" of the power of the White House came when he was sent down from the President-elect's New York offices to work out the details of the inauguration. It turned out to be a "bigger deal" than he thought, coming as he did from the supplicant's role as a campaigner, and not having thought of himself in terms of the President's administration. His own perceptions notwithstanding, he began being speculated about in the press as one of the new Nixon people. Ehrlichman's lack of focus was probably not the norm in a White House staff that carried Richard Neustadt's *Presidential Power* around in its collective back pocket during the transition, but neither did he come from any of the power centers in New York, Washington, or California, from which the new President drew a number of his men, and where power is a more familiar objective.

Not thinking about power does not mean he was powerless, however. Shortly after they took office he wanted to do something about the street signs in Washington because he, like many newcomers to the city, frequently got lost, more often than not finding himself crossing a bridge to Virginia when he had intended to stay in the District. His secretary, wise in the ways of the Washington bureaucracy, found the individual in the Interior Department who had responsibility for street signs, and Ehrlichman called him up. Finding such interest from the new White House Advisor, the man at the other end expressed enthusiasm for the task, and, one thing leading to another, very shortly there was a major diversion of effort by the Department's personnel because "the President wanted better street signs."

Shortly after that, the Secretary of the Interior placed his own call to Ehrlichman, suggesting that it would be best if the White House lawyer worked through channels and called the Secretary, rather than disrupting his staff. After a similar incident in the Commerce Department, when wandering idly through the building led to the rumor that the White House was checking up on them, Ehrlichman learned to step carefully, limiting his movements and relationships to the more hierarchical representations of the governmental power structure. As he put it, he began to see the

> need to channel the President's power.... I didn't have any power. I had the President's power and it has to be carefully channeled, otherwise, you over-control, so to speak. Like driving a Volkswagen, you have to be kind of careful how you turn the wheel, and so I began to get a little sense of that.

The tendency for overkill cannot legitimately be called part of the exercise of power, because it is both unconscious and unintended. But the importance of learning the effect of these unintended consequences is that it helps the individual realize the gulf that now exists between himself and others. It helps him become aware of the irreducible barrier, and, of himself as a powerholder who must act deliberately, in carefully measured ways, aware of himself and the impact he has on others.

Recognizing the Limitations

If using power wisely means using it intentionally, one of the most conscious experiences of power is not its reach, but the opposite: its limits. The limitations of power seems almost a contradiction in terms, but it was one of the most important lessons learned by those I interviewed—the thing that they carried with them the most. Elliot Richardson, as experienced a cabinet officer as any in the nation, noted that "for almost anyone in Washington, the things that you have power over are the easiest to deal with." The difficult things—persuading and exercising influence over peers, superiors, and even subordinates—those are things that occupy one's time and energy. There are very few issues over which a public powerholder agonizes if the resolution is within their grasp. Most of the problems whose solutions lie entirely in one's hands are moral questions, such as whether or not a governor should commute a death penalty or let a convicted felon be put to death by the state. It is his choice and his alone, and the only thing he must satisfy, in the end, is his conscience. Most of the time, however, the morality of public issues is something seen in terms of the large rather than the small acts and decisions of daily life.

What forces powerholders to stretch to the limits of their resources are the things they cannot control. Victories that extend the sphere of influence are remembered most clearly, and are cherished all the more because they were hard-won. The experience of powerlessness is something with which we are familiar and it is not likely to startle someone new to the role of power.

Another element in the recognition of limits is that the horizons are ever-expanding for those who are on an upward track. "Well, it seems to me," said one observer, "that most people want to do more, so that means in a sense you are always reaching because as you become more able at a stage where you can have a greater influence, your horizons are broader. And you want to help in Indo-China also, not just Europe. It is never-ending."

As the need to believe that things will get bigger and better is part of life, so, too, is the need to believe that our leaders have power and can do what they—and we—want them to do. We tend to believe that those in power who talk of their limitations are just not good leaders, not good at the job of wielding power. They may not be, but the point is that power is a relative thing. One can have more power than others, but very few, if any, have enough power to do exactly what they want to do.

One former powerholder put it quite succinctly: "My feeling is that power is wonderful, as long as you don't have to use it. Once you have to use it, you realize you don't have as much as you thought."

Re-Ordering the Universe

One of the first priorities that presents itself upon achieving power is the sense that the organization needs to be looked at with a fresh eye. That is, after all, why people seek power in the first place—or, at least, the reason they give: that the organization needs the leadership they, and only they, can provide. This sense of reordering is especially true of political organizations, but it is also true of voluntary associations and just about every other kind of organization, with the possible exception of a corporation, where the need to show continuity often exists, even if only out of a sense of politeness.

The need to establish one's power comes first, even if nothing else is clear in terms of goals or objectives. As Kevin Harrington put it upon his accession,

All I knew that was instinctive was I felt the need to consolidate the power. Sort of promote the opposition out to judgeships and one thing or another, and get my own people around me, and you know, set the anchor deeper. And so I spent the first year doing that. . . . I gravitated towards the first law of the universe: order. Discipline.

C. P. Snow noted another side of securing the base in *Corridors of Power*: "As rule," the narrator of this novel of the British political Establishment noted, "you couldn't win over your enemies, but you could lose your friends."[7] Clearly, your friends are the ones with the greater expectations and, therefore, the ones most likely to be disappointed. Both sides need a certain amount of looking after.

Only after Harrington felt secure with the power—and others acknowledged that he had it, and were beginning to wonder what he was going to do with it—only then did he begin to ask that question of himself: "Now that I have it, and I'm not going to be knocked out of it, what do I do with it?"

It can be compared, I think, to neatening up the lines on a sailboat, putting everything away, as preparation for setting out to sea. If there has been competition for the position, clearly there will be some mess left about that needs to be secured or tossed overboard.

If there was no competition, it still takes time to learn the system and how to bring about change. It also takes time to get your people in place so that your tenure will be remembered. No matter how extensive the apprenticeship for the top position, being Numero Uno is a new experience and it takes time to learn the job and be comfortable with it.

The coming to power of a new president is a clear turning point, and something with which executive branches of government have experience. New men or women at the top frequently means new opportunities for those in the trenches of the organization to press their interests and their views (to say nothing of the interest groups which helped them get elected in the first place). It is a characteristic to be found in all new political administrations: from the presidency to the state and city levels. Each election brings an assumption that the new leader will make a clean sweep.

A slightly different perspective on the realization of power came from a woman who was a television network vice president.

I never sensed it was a powerful position. First of all, I'd done many other things in my life. I was counted the first woman to be a television director. I didn't have a sense that I had power to wield. People kept telling me—men kept telling me that this is a powerful position—while I was in it. But I was very pragmatic. It was the chair. It wasn't me. It was the position, it wasn't who I was that was important. And I was interchangeable with whoever was before me and whoever would follow me. That's clearly what that is. And the minute you stop forgetting that, you're screwed. Because, when you leave that position, you have nothing. If you've got into the fact that they like you, and they flatter you, and take you to dinners.

The sense of power can come from hostility as much as it can from flattery. Adam Yarmolinsky had been in the Kennedy and Johnson administrations from the beginning, but he moved from the Pentagon to the Poverty Program, and there found himself hostage for the passage of the Civil Rights Program in Congress. The North Carolina House delegation agreed to support the bill on the condition that Yarmolinsky be ousted, and sacrificed he was, albeit back to an office in the White House. He stayed there, with a nice office and a secretary for about a year, gaining wide experience with crossword puzzles. But, as he put it,

> my case was special, because . . . I was under attack and suspicion from the radical right. And there were several occasions when there was a real confrontation. . . . Therefore, I had a feeling that obviously I did have power, or otherwise they wouldn't be after me the way they were. Not that MacNamara didn't back me up—he did—but still I knew that J. Edgar Hoover, Strom Thurmond, Leandro Perez—you name them—were really out to get me. So my sense of having power was very much tempered by my vulnerability.

In the end, of course, Yarmolinsky's dominant feeling was his powerlessness in the situation, and it was a painful time for him.

There Is No Going Back

Having gotten there, looked around, and sorted out the terrain, what comes next is the recognition that you are the station at which the train stops. There is no looking back. There is no going back. Jack Flannery became chief secretary to Governor Francis Sargent in Massachusetts in 1970. He had been with Sargent as press secretary for several years (Sargent was the Lieutenant Governor before he acceded to the top job), but Flannery was replacing someone else in the position of Chief Secretary:

I just got overwhelmed. The first two or three months in that were awful. I didn't know what had hit me. And, as a result, I wasn't very good at it. I clung to the role I was most familiar with—his writer—but in terms of things that ———— did, for example going to talk to the Senate President, going to talk to the Speaker—and play that kind of shuttle role—I didn't want to know how to do it. . . .

I just coped. So whether I was easy with it after three months, or was just gritting my teeth and enduring it by that point, I really can't say. . . . I can remember someone saying, "Hey, you made a big mistake." Well, I didn't want to hear that because there was no going back . . . so I was going to learn to do it, or be replaced in it, and where would that leave me?

The higher one goes, the more public the position, the fewer the options. Having risen to captain, positions of first mate become foreclosed. Another related phenomenon, however, is that new leaders rarely look for help, particularly from the few who could offer experience in the position. No one says to their predecessor, as Flannery put it, "Hey, let's forget the last election and whatever I called you. What the hell did you do about X and Y and Z?"

A new leader cannot afford to show uncertainty or insecurity, and, certainly, cannot look to someone he beat in an election. Even if the transition did not come about because the incumbent was forced out by his or her successor, the position demands that the new incumbent demonstrate autonomy in the role. One former legislative executive said he noticed the independence of one leader from another when he was still working his way up. His predecessor never called the one before him for advice and, in fact, he resented any efforts at communication from that quarter. His successor also maintained silence with his predecessor, at least until he had firmly established himself in the role.

Whatever uncertainty there is in the beginning, whether it is insecurity in the role or not, it is handled by standing tall, perhaps in the hopes of convincing everyone—including the powerholder—that there really is a new leader, that power has indeed been passed to a new generation.

CHAPTER

3

———■———

Exercising Power—the Unexpected Experience

The world of the powerful, like all worlds, is insulated in some ways and vulnerable in others. The powerful live within the confines of kingdoms, always trying to push out their borders, enlarging their space, always conscious of others trying to breach their defenses and steal their territory. The battles for turf, however, are disguised in many different ways, and those who are least able to unmask them rarely survive in their positions for very long. Those who can sort them out have the best chance of surviving both the battles and the war.

Having power is exciting. It is a great intellectual and psychological game. It is play and pleasure, and rewarding. It is challenging and stretching beyond one's self to fit the public role and go beyond what was imagined before. It is being the grown-up among grown-ups. There is satisfaction in achievement and especially in competence. For those in the public world, there is the added reward of significance and the sense of being a part of history, of being remembered, of being touched by immortality.

THE VIEW FROM
THE BATTLEMENTS, LOOKING DOWN

Assuming that one's power stems from a leadership position within an organization, the powerholder is responsible for—and (sometimes) to—everyone in the organization. Relationships differ among those who are lower on the organizational chart. The nearest are staff aides, whose primary loyalty is—or should be—to their leader. Then there are those with line authority, whose loyalty may be divided between the leader and their own underlings. And there is the great body below who never, or rarely ever, come in physical proximity to the head.

There is a gulf between the head and the body, and communications are carried on across a tremendous chasm. I recall a cabinet secretary telling me years ago that, once he signed a memo to the staff, he had a sure and terrible feeling that it sank into an abyss as soon as it crossed the threshold of his office. It works the other way around as well. Complaints and suggestions rarely pass the other way. Even when there is face-to-face communication, the Great Gulf still exists. The boss says "X" and the worker says, "What do you think he meant by that?" Communication is probably *the* most difficult problem in complex organizations.

Trust

With such bad communications, it is not surprising that trust is a problem, but it exists even among those who see and talk to each other on a daily basis. It is not just a matter of balancing the give-and-take inherent in any relationship. It has to do with the quality of the relationships, and, in many ways, the quality of the individuals. It has to do with the difficulty of deciding whom to trust, and how to trust them. As one powerholder put it:

> The biggest single problem is that when you have real power, you
> are always sorting out the people who work with you: who will
> tell you what they think, and those who will tell you what they
> think you want to hear. And the second biggest problem is making
> sure you want to hear it.

There are three obvious problems of trust that a powerholder faces: sycophants who will actually lie to you; those who do not or cannot know the facts of a situation; and the biases of those who are telling you the facts.

Sycophants are the most obvious problem: the "yes men" who support you right or wrong, believing that the message is connected to the messenger. Wanting to be on the positive or winning side, they never disagree or express an unwelcome thought. The sycophant is all but a cartoon figure in our mythology of power. The only people among those I interviewed who bothered to consider the issue at any length (and with some bitterness) were those in the entertainment business, where success is even more difficult to predict than it is in political life. Because of the uncertainty—and the tremendous amount of fame and fortune at stake—the entertainment world relies heavily on supportive relation-ships. This is not an uncommon solution to the problem of uncertainty, as Rosabeth Moss Kanter and others have pointed out. The greater the degree of uncertainty at the top of an organization, the greater the dependence there is on homogeneity and personal loyalty.[1] It is a way of making "known" as much as possible, i.e., making the participants as much alike as possible; hence the focus on conformity in social charac-teristics: background, schools, clubs, religious affiliation, and so on. If everyone is alike, the odds are they will also see things alike.

In any world where the value of a project can be measured easily (although perhaps not before it comes to fruition millions of dollars later), there can be no stability at the top once the measures are in. In the entertainment world, with a hit, you rise—rapidly—and often at quite a young age. With failure, you are just as easily deposed. Studio heads and network vice presidents rarely last beyond a few years. Of course, if the business end of the entertainment world operates more like a yo-yo than a ladder, the uncertainty and instability mean a wider opportunity for those hoping to strike it big than is the case in more stable environments. Anyone can become a star overnight, so everyone courts the star-makers. "A lot of people smiled at me when I walked through the company," said a former music mogul:

> They held doors open. And I watch it all the time—when other people are doing it. And I know how distasteful it is to the man who has power—to have all this ass-kissing around him. Unless he is a real sicko. It's nice, but you know why they are doing it, unless you've lost all reason.

They court you with Christmas presents, and smiles, and when they work for you directly, they court you with their support.

The relationship between a powerholder and a sycophant is a two-way thing. It helps the powerholder believe in himself, which is a necessary condition for success—assuming, of course, that the powerholder does not recognize the sycophants for what he or she is, and assuming that the chorus of support is not helping the powerholder down a path that he would be better off not taking.

The second category of trust at the higher reaches of the power structure, is not with those who tell you what they think you want to hear, but with those who tell you what they believe to be true—and they are wrong about the facts. To at least one White House advisor,

> just the problem of getting the facts on which you could base a decision was terribly difficult. It's a huge marketplace in

contention, and everybody disputes everybody else's facts. Trying
to be the fact-finder and find something you can rest on is awfully
hard ... apart from the rest of it. And so you cling to people that
you think are disinterested or loyal, and sometimes they turn out
not to be reliable, and that's too bad, but you do your best to find
them.

Whole schools of public policy have grown up around the question of
making decisions in uncertainty, recognizing that in almost every complex decision some things are known and some are not. Some solutions
turn out to have effects and costs other than those that were anticipated.
Decision models abound in these graduate academic circles, all trying
one way or another to alleviate the problem of uncertainty and, thereby,
the question of trust.[2] To the individual at the top, however, the first step
comes back again to that leap of faith in one's self rather than in others.

A third problem of trust is more subtle. The views of others may be
based not so much on the outcome of their intentions and abilities, as
on the consequence of their position in the organization. No matter how
willing they are to be honest, or how accurate in gathering facts, there is
always a bias. The organizational term is "suboptimization," meaning
that each department in an organization measures success by the promotion of its ends, and is unable to discern success from the perspective
of the organization as a whole.

A classic example of suboptimization is one in which those who
produce submarines gauge the success of the navy on the number of
submarines it produces, and are not able to comprehend a more complex
fleet including destroyers, battleships, etc.[3] The application of the term
to individuals includes the perspectives of departments, and adds to it
the skewed outlook of special assistants. As one former powerholder put
it:

> You discover that everybody has a partial point of view. Everybody
> has a bias. A follower relies on a leader, and a true follower
> doesn't discount the leader's biases. A true follower always
> suboptimizes. ... Whereas the leader is constantly occupied as the
> position, the person who uses the power, who rules as well as
> reigns, uses his power to counteract suboptimization a levels
> below the one at which he is operating. And that requires
> discounting the biases of all the people who work for you. It is very
> tempting to think that one or more of the people who work for you
> really has "The Word," that you can really rely on that person. If
> you've got sense, you realize that you can't ever—that there isn't

anybody who works for you whose advice you don't have to discount. Oh, I'm sure about that. There aren't many things that I'm sure about, but I'm sure about that.

I can say that on some issues they see things that I don't see, and I've got to factor in what they tell me. . . . it's one of the great advantages of having them there. But I can't just take their solution. I have to calibrate it. And that's not what you do when you are the follower rather than the leader.

Assistants tend to be advocates, however much they may strive to review a subject and present an objective set of alternatives to the boss. It is a natural phenomenon to draw a conclusion and prefer one solution over others, advancing it, however unconsciously. The final authority will do the same thing, but it will be based on everyone else's views, knowing that everyone beneath him draws a conclusion and presents a case that will be skewed.

Structuring Self-Reliance

While the job at the top in any organization cannot be performed effectively without help from others, at some point, in some way, the powerholder must learn to stand alone, to trust himself. Such self-reliance depends upon some internalization of the role, and on overcoming even the desire to keep some separation between one's self and the role. Although there are benefits in maintaining the separation, the longer one stays in office the less the separation works, because sooner or later the behavior of others affects one's sense of self.

One solution to the problem of needing both separation from and union with the role is to structure the circumstances in such a way as to create a discrete environment at the top, which makes it easier to isolate the leader from the rest of the organization. One way to do this is to draw one's immediate aides from a different pool than the rest of the executive staff. The ever-present "Bright Young Man," and increasingly present "Bright Young Woman," are usually in marked contrast to others in the executive world. A mayor or governor may draw his inner staff from outside his political constituency. A former aide to Mayor White, for example, thought he always brought in "total outsiders. . . . Nobody with a constituency around him. It couldn't have been that consistent and not have it be conscious so that you didn't have a competing constituency that you were representing. ——— did have a constituency, but she was never allowed to play a central role." Certainly that is one way to guarantee that the battlements are not breached.

A third solution to the problem of trust we occasionally see is the apparent marriage between the powerholder and his or her number-one aide. The lesser partner may be a supplemental player who compensates for the senior's weaknesses, or he may be a carbon copy who extends the capacity. Woodrow Wilson and Colonel House, perhaps Richard Nixon and H. R. Haldeman, come immediately to mind. Another, less well known example—but one which includes individuals I have talked to in the course of research over the years—was Francis Sargent, a former governor of Massachusetts, and Jack Flannery, his chief secretary. Flannery started as press secretary and speech writer when Sargent was Lieutenant Governor. Speech writers may be peculiarly well-suited to the role of alter ego because of the intimacy of the process of verbalizing another's thoughts or intentions.

According to Flannery, Sargent was a father/brother/pal—all the more important because, as he put it, his own personality was undefined and insecure when they were in power. "My ego became so entwined with his," Flannery said, "an attack on him made me bleed." They were dependent, but not peers. Sargent relied upon Flannery for more than speeches and more than the "traffic cop" role of chief secretary. The Governor trusted Flannery to present him to the outside world, and the outside world to him. They came from very different backgrounds and, with the added input of a third individual—Albert Kramer—Sargent relied upon the differences to create a better mix, a better interchange of values, than any one of them could have achieved alone. It requires a good measure of internal security to tolerate such differences in one's aides, because conflict is guaranteed to exist between them on a daily basis.

A similar cross-cultural pairing appears to have been the object of Kevin White while mayor of Boston. Throughout his sixteen-year tenure, his top aides were as different as they could be from him. Two were Jewish, one of them well-to-do, the other from a working-class, out-of-state background. A third was a woman, originally from Cuba. In Massachusetts, ethnicity is a significant factor in identity and in political life. It is the mystical core of its culture. Drawing close aides from another world can be like adding another blanket for warmth, especially when it works.

A similarly dependent relationship existed for many years between Elliot Richardson and Jonathan Moore, both of whom came out of dominant Yankee tradition of the Bay State. Moore, as alter ego, was more of an extension of Richardson, with the elder partner trusting the younger to exercise similar judgments and values. John and Robert Kennedy were an even better example of such a supplementary relationship, with the younger brother playing the additional role of hatchet man: the one who said no, who fired people, who handled the negatives. Richard Nixon and H. R. Haldeman had a relationship that combined these characteristics in a slightly different way. They both came from California, but in contrast to any of the preceding examples, Haldeman came from the more secure upper-class world and it was Nixon, the senior partner, who had worked his way up the social scale. The Nixon/Haldeman relationship was, like the others, complementary, with Haldeman adding a knowledge of the outside world and of advertising to his organizational ability and capacity to manage a staff. Nixon appears to have handled emotional relationships awkwardly throughout his life, whether they were of a positive or negative sort. Haldeman was at least something of a buffer between his boss and the world.

It is likely that certain kinds of weaknesses in a senior partner are more easily supplemented than others. Insecurity, for example, is harder to overcome, but powerholders occasionally come to power because there are two of them who merge their personalities and their work patterns so well that they succeed better than either would have done alone. These relationships come about because of the problem of trust (in one's self or others), and it is a problem for all powerholders, whether or not they have an alter ego waiting in the wings.

Not all powerholders feel comfortable relying on another. Many feel a need to look as good in front of their closest aides as they do in front of the public, knowing that weaknesses that are known intimately can be exploited by the disloyalty of a former assistant. Some fear it is an abridgment of their responsibility to the office. Our first president, George Washington, was particularly conscious of creating the model of the relationship of the man to the office, and very sensitive to the accusation that he desired a father/son relationship with Alexander Hamilton (an accusation presumed accurate by Hamiltonian historians particularly). Whenever the question of his dependence on Hamilton became public in his lifetime, Washington went out of his way to disavow the fact. I think the President consciously balanced Hamilton against Jefferson (believing both men to be his intellectual superiors), and unconsciously fell into a dependence on Edmund Randolph to effect the compromise between them (Randolph was the first Attorney General, who succeeded Jefferson as Secretary of State in the second administration).

In the second administration, when Hamilton and Jefferson were both gone from the cabinet, Washington continued to rely upon Randolph. Several years into the second four-year term, Washington was brought a letter from the French minister to his government, that had been intercepted by the British. The confidential report suggested that Randolph might be involved in an inappropriate wheat deal, but also hinted that the decisions in the administration were really controlled by the Attorney General rather than by the President. Washington demanded the keys to Randolph's office and forced him out the next day. This from a man who, as commander of the revolutionary forces, stopped everything for several days in order to investigate the treason charges against Benedict Arnold before declaring him a traitor, despite the danger that the British might attack West Point at any moment!

Many powerholders—probably most—stand alone, perhaps because they do not need the ego support, or are too insecure to let another get that close. I would not conclude that the security or insecurity in itself predicts the likelihood of success or failure in office, but rather that when these marriages of two individuals do occur, and the leader is successful, it can be a happy compensation for the individuals and organizations involved. How long the minor partner remains in the role, submerging whatever need he may have to stand apart, is perhaps the more interesting question. Sometimes we think of it as mentoring or apprenticing, but the most successful partnerships are those which last well beyond the few years presumably needed to learn what there is to learn.

Trust comes in smaller doses than long-term alliances with an alter ego. The powerholder always needs to rely on others, and to delegate at least some responsibility, and the capacity to do that "rests singularly," as one former White House aide put it, "on the element of confidence." Chemistry plays a stronger role than credentials. There is no graduate school for the role of confidante. Business schools and schools of public policy frequently feed bodies into the role, but the roles of special assistant, assistant secretary, etc., are perceived as way-stations, not the end of the line for those who step into them with a graduate degree in hand. As Ehrlichman put it, "You cannot tell your tenth-grade teacher you want to grow up to be an advisor to the President." He went on to describe the relationship this way:

> The President needs—thinks he needs—people whom he can rely on: their loyalty to him personally. His intimate staff. It is very hard to graft on to a president. We brought in the chancellor of —————— University ... because he came from a university where apparently they had solved a lot of the unrest problems and so on. He had, I think, two meetings with the president, and Nixon said he didn't care for him, He sat over in the Executive Office Building for months, moss growing on his north side, and he had zero

"power" because the President just didn't care for him, didn't confide in him, didn't rely on him. On the other hand, we had guys working around there with no background at all: no training, no experience, but they had Nixon's confidence. They had "power." They had derivative power.

If the experience of the power is dependent to a very large degree on how secure each of the players is in the equation, insecurity at the top can be devastating to the organization, although bureaucracies have an extraordinary capacity to hide and compensate for the weaknesses of the individuals who hold power within them.[4] Insecurity in the near but nether reaches of power can be especially destructive because neither the individual nor the organization directs defenses that way. We protect ourselves from too much power in others; we rarely protect ourselves from too little. As one director of a Washington-based association noted, he particularly looked for self-confident individuals, not because they do a good job,

> but because they are going to cause less trouble. . . . I know who does a good job, because when they do a good job I don't have to do it, and that makes me more powerful. Inevitably, the people who need less handling—everybody needs to be stroked, and everybody needs for me to flash a nice smile—I just know it after a while. But those—often the ones that enjoy the most, whether they are 20 years old, or 30 years old, or 40 years old—are the ones who are really content with themselves. Most people are not.

Insecurity does more than make the job of the powerholder difficult because of the time and energy it takes to compensate for a poor job. It can be far more insidious, costing a number of people—including the powerholder—their jobs. A common scenario is the man who heads (often because he creates) an organization, but fears to have anyone around him who might be better able to run it. He surrounds himself with incompetents and inferiors to make sure he looks good. One example comes to mind of the president of a minor national sports organization who survived for years because everyone always said, "Well, if it weren't for X, we wouldn't be playing this game." Since most people who participated did so because of the pleasure it gave them, X's temper sufficed to drive away everyone who might have challenged him, because the cost of his anger outweighed the reward of their participation. Eventually, the activities associated with the sport splintered, and individual entrepreneurs emerged throughout the country.

Anyone who has participated at all in organizational life is familiar with the problem of insecurity in others. As seen from the perspective of the insecure powerholder, the world is fraught with challenges. Assassins lurk everywhere, ready to destroy the king and take away his realm. The larger the organization, the greater the need of the insecure powerholder to control it, to centralize authority, and hold tightly to the reins of power. The strain of holding on can wreck the organization, and is just as likely to hurt the individuals within it. For such a person there is no life after power, and he or she usually knows it. Identity gets wrapped ever more tightly into the role, and all thoughts of other lives, other pleasures, cease to exist. If the organization wins out and the powerholder is ousted, he or she will have a very difficult time surviving, may never let go emotionally, and find it especially difficult to start over. If the individual wins, the organization will be, at best, stunted—and at worst, it will not survive.

THE VIEW FROM THE BATTLEMENTS, LOOKING IN

The Good Stuff

Power is the expression of maturity, the goal that draws its sources from the most basic of human drives. The freedom of choice and autonomy associated with power may be the end of human achievement. It gives those who possess it a stronger sense of themselves, sometimes enlarged beyond reality, but certainly providing importance. Adam Yarmolinsky described the significance of power as a feeling of having grown up in the most human sense of all: being a parent.

> There is a satisfaction in having people treat you as a father figure, which is one of the things people do when you are in power. They look to you for support, advice, to make things happen, make things work out, solve problems, whatever. . . .
> If you are male, it is being a father figure. If you are a woman, you are a mother figure. And you asked me why isn't it more satisfactory to be a child than a parent; well, I think the response is that . . . the impulse that leaders cope with is that you want to relax and be a child and you can't. And what is it that makes up for fact that you can't? It is that parents really have more of what the world has to offer than children do. If you relax into being a child, you give up choice. . . .
> One of the things about being a leader and having power is that work is play. It is enjoyable, and challenging, and offers the

pleasure of being able to make significant choices. Now, making choices is painful, and I don't know how that relates to a child, but you are free to make choices. You are not bound to a routine.

Sigmund Freud argued that the creativity that comes from repression is the basis of society, and the highest achievement to which man can aspire. Others have challenged that notion on the ground that the kind of extraordinary creativity that concerned Freud was possible for perhaps 2 percent of the population. Instead, they suggest, play is the ultimate end because it is the adult expression of pleasure, stemming from desire rather than need, and is the closest we can come to the pleasures of the womb and earliest infancy.[5] Having autonomy and power over others can be akin to play, as Yarmolinsky describes it, because it is adult and it is pleasurable.

There is another element to the relationship between power and parent that has to do with the nature of authority. The parent/child association is the primary authority relationship, the one to which we relate all other similar experiences. Jeane Kirkpatrick spoke of the training in the uses of power she had acquired through being a parent:

> You have a lot of power and you don't deal with kids as equals because they are not equals. They're babies first of all, and very little, and there is an irreducible barrier, there is an irreducible responsibility. . . . Exercising authority without feeling overbearing or abusive in any way . . . is all a very normal family role for an active parent.

She used the analogy of parenting with caution because of the potential charge that she might have treated her employees at the United Nations as children. In her defense, and in the interests of exploring the experience of power, I would note that almost all of those I interviewed identified strongly with the comparison she drew.

The connection between parenting and play as a major gratification of the exercise of power is perhaps more interesting. In the philosophical context of seeking an understanding of human potential, the linkage suggests both need and the absence of need. There is the biological imperative to continue the species, and the drive for pleasure that may be its method. There is also a link to immortality and the fear of death, because of the impact of one's life on the surrounding world that, in a political/social context at least, is akin to children who will live on afterwards, remembering and honoring their parents.

A Sense of Competence

If having power is growing up—being the parent instead of the child—there are both costs and important gratifications. There is, for instance, the opportunity to get something done, to help someone when no one else could. The sense of competence that comes with the exercise of power is one of its most important values in promoting a feeling of being in control, a feeling of empowering maturity. It gives purpose, and in the public sphere, when tied to relevance, it promotes a feeling that gives many a meaning to life. Actually, it does not matter in what field one attains power, because success in one area leads people to assume competence in every area. David Braun, a former music executive, put it this way:

> There is an assumption that if you made it to the top in your field, you are very bright in a lot of other fields. You don't have to wait in line anymore. The perks are very nice. You have an inside track on information. People who have real power always seem to know everything that's important: they know the good doctors, the good lawyers, the good accountants. . . . You can't tell a story they haven't heard. They are in the gossip of our times. [They are] at the core—connected to everything that matters in our lives. Everything that seems to matter in our lives. That's the reward of being powerful.

One reason others assume that the powerful are "more equal" in many areas is because of the sense of competence, of self-confidence that comes with the territory. You come to believe in yourself and in your own abilities. One man's self-confidence is often interpreted by others as arrogance, but very little in life surpasses the sense of personal efficacy that enables a person to feel he or she can do anything and do it better than others. It gives place, assures opportunity, and, in the end, is a major component of identity.

Obviously, some skills are more desirable and easier to come by than others, and another advantage of power is the capacity to employ others to compensate for your weaknesses. Bureaucracies, in fact, are particularly good at such supplementary behavior, protecting their leaders from failure in their role as much as they limit their capacity to change the institution. A peculiar strength, admittedly, but not an insignificant one.

For most, the sense of success associated with having held power remains afterwards, even while they may tend to repress the weaknesses or remain fixated on the specifics of a failure. There is often a separation,

in retrospect, between the things that did not work out—the failures—
and the sense of competence that put one in the position of trying in the
first place. Failing at a task (often a subjective measure at the best of
times) does not necessarily mean one failed in the role, or was not suited
to the role in the first place. Glaring measures of failures, such as being
thrown out of office via impeachment or widespread disgrace, may stretch
the limits of what one can tell one's self, but self-deception is usually
easier to come by than acceptance of innate inability. There are always
others to blame. There are always the "assassins" who seek the powerholder's demise because he was too powerful or too good at his job.

Picking Your Own Team

Whether selecting assistants to complement weaknesses is a minor or
a major benefit of office, the opportunity to pick the team is consistently
spoken of as an important reward of power. It is the most direct way to
assure that organizations will remember, and that the changes you have
wrought will work their way into the institution in a lasting way. More than
one person, in fact, would have agreed with the proposition offered by
Robert Finch, former Secretary of Health, Education and Welfare:

> You exercise power through the appointments you can make, and
> that gives you a certain amount of satisfaction. Going out to get
> someone, bring them in, and work with them—that's very
> enjoyable. It provides a lot of satisfaction.

It can also be the source of a lot of frustration, especially if the
appointive process must pass through White House approval and a
Senate confirmation. Although Finch failed to hire John Knowles, the man
he wanted for Assistant Secretary for Health, he mused about the "per-
verse pleasure" he got in "coming back to California and bringing Roger
Egeberg in, simply because I was sort of responding to my old ties to the
University of Southern California. . . . A modest triumph that gives pleasure and a certain amount of satisfaction—particularly when it turns out
to be an able appointment."

The powerholder rarely gets ten out of ten in picking his team, but, as
in Finch's example, the ball always stays in his court. If the opposition is
public—as in a Senate confirmation hearing—the opposition must eventually accept some nominee, if for no other reason than to avoid appearing petty and obstructionist. If the process is less public, as in the
case of White House opposition to a cabinet department's nominee, the
superior power of the Office of the Presidency has a better chance of

winning out. Assembling the team, however, no matter how difficult a task this might be, remains a definite plus for powerholders, and is a major step in any hope of having an impact on the institution beyond one's own tenure in office.

An alternative to picking your own team, of course, is creating a new one out of the old. Those who succeed in winning the hearts and minds of the old guard often need to change the culture of the organization, making it more amenable to the person and the goals of the new leader, overcoming the hostility that is likely to be there toward themselves and possibly toward the organization. Ira Jackson, the former Massachusetts Commissioner of Revenue, was unusually successful in creating a new sense of value and commitment in the bureaucracy he led. The environment he inherited was typical of the dumping grounds we associate with government bureaucracies. Within his staff, however, he created a group that he called SERVE (Speedy, Efficient Refunds Very Early). According to Jackson:

> The group was representative of data entry operators, form designers, mailroom managers, analysts, tax law changers, legal procurement—every function that had deep walls and moats built around their baronial fiefdoms. . . . We had to change the law to make it simple enough so that people could rewrite the forms in English, early enough so that they could be distributed widely enough, so that people could have their tax returns in time to file early, so that we could meld it out over time, and we needed—people needed water coolers, and they needed green type instead of blue, and we worked it out.
>
> When it was done, and when there was victory, and when there was purpose—650 people who had never been told why they do what they do, 400 of whom are women sitting at vdt screens all day—loyal, career governmental employees, sitting and entering data into a computer all day long. No one had ever told them they do that so the computer can tell them whether they cheated themselves or the state, and to get refunds out to their friends and neighbors in record time. But they never knew how long that took, or why they were doing it.
>
> Now, we're showing them charts, showing we're doing a month better than last year, I'm in the press handing out the first refunds on January 13th to a single mother with two children in her arms, and we're getting editorial support and reinforcement in the paper.
>
> And when it is all over, the Governor gives SERVE—not me—or

the Department of Revenue—SERVE—the first Manny Carbalo Award for Excellence in Public Service. We took a representative group of 65 of the 650 to the Copley Plaza Hotel for dinner with the Governor and Mrs. Dukakis, and a week later, because 600 people who were other unsung heroes hadn't been to dinner, I bought a cake at tax payers expense. It weighed 650 pounds and was in the form of the Commonwealth of Massachusetts with a large refund check in the middle, made out to John and Sally Taxpayer for $500 million. I served a slice of that cake to 650 members of SERVE and it was almost like a religious experience, turning the tables, saying thanks, the feeling of satisfaction and community.

Winning—and knowing you have won—are rare and special pleasures in the complex world of organizations. Victory is all the sweeter if it is accompanied by an acknowledging ritual that says we did well to everyone.

THE DAILY GRIND

Dick Thornburgh described an experience common to many power-holders in our age of the case book approach to academic training for public policy. He was a guest in a class that had prepared a case study on welfare in Pennsylvania. They were "eager and ready to go," he said, but he began by saying "Let me tell you what I did before I came in here—if you want this to be realistic." He went on to enumerate the daily experience of being governor: he got a phone call from the state police about a protest at Three Mile Island; a prison official called about a hunger strike for religious freedom at his facility; a state rep told him he would not vote for any more of the Governor's programs until a three-mile section of road was paved through his district; etc. "It took the wind out of their sails," said Thornburgh, "because they thought I hadn't anything on my mind but welfare."

Focus on Process

The focus on process is one of the occupations of power least likely to be perceived from the outside, particularly in relation to substance. However one comes to power, whether riding the crest of an issue, or following in the footsteps of a mentor, the preparatory apprentice roles tend to be those of advocacy. Being the final authority, however, requires a different posture. Powerholders, whether mayors, governors, cabinet secretaries, or CEOs, focus most of their attention on the process rather than on the substance of issues, because they are concerned with meeting the demands of competing constituencies, with enabling their underlings to perform their jobs, and assuring the "i's" are dotted and the "t's" are crossed in projects that are going to sail publicly beyond the organization. The powerholder often feels more like a receptacle than a projector, but managing the institution is an essential part of leadership, even if it is considerably delegated away.

Organizational maintenance—always the first concern of any organization (at least one that is intent on surviving)—requires personnel training as well as selection, and grooming for succession as well as for the performance of the tasks at hand, even in public agencies where succession is premised on a quadrennial decapitation. Because no one can do everything, power is delegated, and those who use it in the name of the powerholder need to be supported and defended. It is the parenting role writ large.

Favors

Power can bring lots of things to those who hold it (money, fame, influence, satisfaction, etc.), but, other than the formality of the office, and the capacity to change what formally resides within that office, it is often measured by what can be done for others. This is a game at which those who merely hold influence can also play, but, for the individuals charged with organizational responsibility, it is one of the ways they support their internal and external constituents. Asking and doing favors for others are ways of establishing alliances and demonstrating worth to one's self as well as to them. As one person put it, "The greatest pleasure in the world is to hear of someone in need and you know how to solve it. That's power, or maybe it isn't power, maybe it is the effective use of your life. . . . The pleasure is putting the pieces of your knowledge together in a productive union, and it is one of the great ups of the day."

At the other end of the trade, if I ask you to get a job for a friend or relative, I am acknowledging that I think you have the power to do it. In getting the job, you prove the point and put me in your debt. It is an informal coinage system in the realm of the powerful, reaching well beyond the particular office. Favors can consist of something as minor as a phone call or a letter to a third party, or as great as a positive decision on a contract.

Many of those I interviewed spoke of returning phone calls—even from strangers—as falling into the same category: it demonstrates a basic respect and sustains the image of civility in the realm of the powerful. Not everyone feels the need to be so respectful and one of the most common adverse consequences of the loss of power is that the phone calls do not get returned.

I knew a man who served for many years as the alter ego to a cabinet secretary, and then became the head of a small program at a university. He carefully measured the respect he would accord others by how many times they had to telephone to get the call returned, and how long those coming to see him had to wait before being admitted to his office. The measure of civility he meted out was finely tuned. We agreed, for instance, that I, an old but inconsequential friend, could be kept waiting for fifteen minutes. More than that, I left. To get him to respond to a phone call from me, however, could take at least half a dozen tries on my part. From my perspective, it was institutionalized rudeness; from his it was a question of priorities and a way of setting the stage for future interactions, keeping me aware of my place in his world.

Ritual and the Public Role

Another demonstration of power is the amount of ceremony surrounding the individual. Ritual clarifies positions for everyone involved: the judge who dons his robes when sentencing a defendant; the ribbon-cutting and presentation of awards; and even the physical surroundings of one's office—flags, the quality and color of leather couches, bathrooms off the office, the size, shape, and history of the desk, even down to whether or not the office is supplied with a round or a square waste paper basket. All of these accoutrements declare the position of the power-holder to those who behold him or her, and are designed to assure a sufficient amount of deference.

Beyond deference, ritual also insulates the powerholder from the hoi polloi. It reinforces the position to everyone, not least of all the power-holder himself. Someone said, "You cannot be touched if you are perceived to have power," and nothing so much aids that defense as ceremony and ritual.

While ritual serves the functions of separating and legitimizing power, powerholders often complain of the emptiness of much of it associated with office, because they are brought in solely for the occasion and have had little to do with the event or the people. While the experience may be empty for the powerholder, it frequently has significance for others. And when it has meaning for the powerholder—as was the case with Ira

Jackson and the cake he served to his staff—it is a potent instrument for binding communities together, and can be exceptionally rewarding to all concerned.

The most obvious benefit of ritual is that it legitimates the circumstances. Both sides must acknowledge that power belongs rightly to the powerholder, and each side must perform its appropriate function. Ritual is that formal acknowledgement. It also helps keep the powerholder in focus, reinforces the sense of office, and bolsters the sense of identity, or at least the public identity. Many of those I interviewed, however, felt ill at ease with public displays of ritual, particularly when it was performed over and over again among strangers in places with which they had little direct connection. Their explanation for the discomfort was not based on the circumstances, however, but rather on their description of themselves as private people. They usually began by saying "I was not a typical politician:

> I never liked the politics of politics, which is to say I hated the banquets. I hated the parades. . . . I didn't like what a lot of people apparently like in politics: the big crowd, the applause, and so forth. I'd just as soon work in a small, quiet, dark corner.

Or another:

> I would go out and recharge power when I was in trouble. I would go out there because my conscience told me I belonged out there, but I never went out there for the love of being out there. Not for five minutes.

Bolstering one's identity as a powerholder can also threaten that individual as a private person, and therein lies much of the dilemma. If it is easy to believe your own press, imagine how much easier it is to believe your own image in the mirror of others' eyes as they prepare your path for the various rites of office. "You get locked in. Alone. And that's where you start getting into trouble," noted one former powerholder. There are many paths to isolation, but the ritual of office can certainly be one of them.

Other aspects of resistance to public show are less complex: when you go out in public, strangers are not always deferential. There is always the danger of running into "the barroom drunk who tells you you are doing everything wrong and then throws up on your suit." There is the boredom that comes with the repetition of ceremony, and the role-playing when you have had nothing to do with the project or the people, or even when you have heard the same remarks thousands of times. Some of those who are uncomfortable seek power rather than fame because what they are challenged by is the problem-solving of government or business. Some could be said to be shy, but shyness in a powerholder probably reflects a more complex set of factors.

Some, of course, find tremendous psychic rewards in these roles. They may go into politics, or seek the role of CEO, because they want to "give speeches and get clapped at," as one young boy explained his run for class president to his father. Or they may derive real pleasure from the contact with others the role affords. Ginny Thornburgh, wife of Dick Thornburgh (the former governor of Pennsylvania and current United States Attorney General), put it this way:

> There is nothing like campaigning—touching people and meeting the range of people. It is an invigorating process intellectually, physically, spiritually, psychologically. Every bit of your ability is in play.
>
> I think there's a difference between people who are good speakers and people who really like being with people. You only understand how people feel if you're among them and with them and you're in their homes. That's how you come to represent them.
>
> We both love that. And that, in a way, is more fun than governing. Once you are elected, people want to put a distance between you and them, and Dick and I worked very hard to break that down.

Having a public role certainly provides a point for contact and opens up the possibility for communication with a stranger beyond remarks on the state of the weather. Many genuinely enjoy the opportunity for such communication. A surprising number—if my sample is any indication—find it uncomfortable.

THE FRUSTRATIONS OF POWER

Limitations

One of the singularly American characteristics of our culture is our belief in our ability to do things: create programs, change institutions, solve problems. This belief is associated particularly with the American creed of individualism: anyone can be whatever he or she wants to be, can do whatever he or she wants to do. Although we think that we can solve any problem we put our mind to—even, and perhaps, especially, our collective mind—the belief is based on a conception of individual liberty, and in order to assure that liberty, we constrain our collective acts. The net effect is that however much those I interviewed loved having power, they were unanimous in concern for its limitations.

That power is constrained is not a startling observation, but it is something the empowered are far more conscious of than the powerless. It is something they learn upon accession to power, and relearn again and again throughout its use. Most of the working day—90 percent is the usual estimate—is spent securing their base, supporting their staff, extending the limits of their boundaries—all things over which they have little control. Those things that are within their capacity are easily dealt with and take little time, whether or not they have a great impact on others.

The most common problem, particularly in the public sphere, is the fact that the powerholder rarely has the resources to do what he or she is charged to do. Responsibilities frequently outstrip authority, but the expectations of others remain. Kevin White noted that the longer he was in office, the greater the expectations of his power:

> People thought I could do anything. Therefore, anything that wasn't
> done, I didn't want. And anything that was done, I wanted—even
> to the minute level of re-assigning a policeman on a beat. It was
> not the reality, but it was the perception. It was blown out of
> proportion: the who and what I was with power.

If power exists in the eyes of the beholder, it is an impression, an image that must be maintained, but in very many respects it is a false image. If the mayor could not do what his constituents wanted, who could? Did the capacity to change things rest with some lower-echelon city employee over whom he had no control? Was it divided among many agencies, or was it beyond anyone's control? How could his constituents imagine that he could not help them?

If the mayor lacked direct authority or knowledge of specific problems, he did have the capacity to make problems visible, and, to many, that is a significant and enduring characteristic of power: being a super sales- man, calling on the media, using his prestige to motivate his underlings. For those who need to solve problems, of course, only being able to point them out is less than satisfying.

In 1960, political scientist Richard Neustadt published a book entitled *Presidential Power*,[6] in which he described the power of the president in two ways: the president on horseback leading the troops, raising expectations, expanding the horizons; and the president in sneakers trying to convince those beneath him in the hierarchy that what he wanted them to do was really in their own interests. Most of the time, the solutions to most problems require sneakers.

From the mayor's perspective, his experience of power was more like being stationed on the borders of his realm, fighting to overcome his limitations. In the end, he said, despite his recognition of the requirements of democracy, he had become a convert to the idea of stronger central authority because "you never have enough power to deal with the problems with which you have to deal."

Looking up the organizational chart, the appointed powerholder is bound by the interests of the White House or the state house. There are the president's stated programs, and the coalition of public and private interests that elected him. A White House aide described it as part of his job to have a weekly lunch with cabinet secretaries to "keep them in line," lest they fall too much under the sway of lesser interests (the bureaucracies they oversee, the interests expressed at that level, or congressional committees).

Looking down, most large organizations are constrained by rules and standard operating procedures that make any change problematic. Bureaucracies, whatever their many failings, are institutions designed to rationalize the distribution of power and, therefore, to limit its abuses (and uses) by any single individual. Whether or not this cumbersome system has become too cumbersome is a little beyond my immediate inquiry, but how it affects those charged with running them is not.

One of my first lessons in seeking change in the government, when I worked in the Department of Health, Education and Welfare in the early 1970s, was the inevitability of hearing two responses. The first response came from everyone (except the Secretary who had appointed me to institute a women's program): "Well," my listener would say, "if the Secretary really wants to improve the status of women, why doesn't he just do it? He should write a memo." The second response came from everyone inside the government, including the Secretary: "But what can I do? Nobody listens to me." And this from those inside . . . imagine the frustrations of those outside the government!

The lack of belief in one's personal ability to change institutions may be a post-sixties phenomenon. Certainly the leaders of the Kennedy-Johnson years acted on the assumption that an individual could make a difference, and their programs were based on that assumption. Whether such boundless confidence in individual ability returns to the national psyche or not, the more recent past has been characterized by less confidence and a greater sense of our limitations.

Another problem with standard operating procedures—regardless of the beliefs of those who are bound by them—is that they make much of the activity routine, which, after all, is their objective. For those seeking change—and power really is only seen and felt in change—the routinization of so much of their activity becomes a burden. Albert Kramer, who went from being the chief policy aide to Governor Sargent in Massachusetts to chief judge of a district court in the state, noted that, at his level at least, most of the decisions on cases that came before him were worked out earlier by the district attorney, defense lawyer, and others:

> The power of a judge is a tremendous power, but it has been so routinized that the important principle that there is a *person* before me often gets lost. And there are many reasons for it: the caseload is so high, yet you've got to dispose of them. So, the prime directive is no longer justice. The prime directive has become to move cases. That has become the number one concern, and so more lenient dispositions get decided. I intervene to prevent that but you have to consider the pressure on the judges to accept prior decisions that are worked out in plea bargaining between the district attorney and defense lawyers. They are also under pressure to move cases and they can get really angry if a judge attempts to change an agreed upon disposition. "Judge, we have negotiated a plea here!"

The routinization is part of the bureaucratization, which in turn, is part of the effort to constrain power, since the rules of bureaucracy limit the wielders of power as much as they limit those who become its clients. The judge was left with ceremony, ritual, and the opportunity occasionally to break out of the routine, but not so much as to upset the staff:

> So I put a good deal of faith in the ceremony of sentencing . . . how I pronounce it, and what I can construct so that the sentence has meaning and gives direction for the course to follow. What you do is you put your energy into the expression of your decision, as well as the decision itself—except if you are really buried with cases. Then you go through nine cases like this: "Fiftydollarfinegoodby."

There can be great power, but if it is exercised without affect by the powerholder, it can be boring, particularly when those most subject to his power are not his peers—whose lives are like his—but rather those who come from the lower levels of the society. The powerholder must derive some measure of satisfaction in exercising it over another for it to be meaningful to him. Without emotional contact, power becomes routine, and the powerholder, at least, loses the sense of its importance.

On the other hand, the prestige of a judge does carry beyond the courtroom. As Judge Kramer noted, "The reason why everyone respects a judge is that they believe that, sooner or later, they are going to go to court." A little insecurity perhaps tucked away in us all! As a joke, he occasionally suggests to his friends that he will send them a "Get Out of Jail Free" card, which often leads to a pause in the conversation, and then, he says, "they say they will be glad to get the card."

Vulnerabilities

However civil the world of the powerful may be, bounded as it is by limitations and courtly manners, it is not placid. There are personal costs associated with it that vary with individuals and institutions. Among peers, rather than among those over whom one holds sway, inter-personal politics, the politics of personal preferment, or sometimes court politics are often the order of the day. The higher one is in the reaches of government, particularly, the greater are the ends, and the more intense the belief that your position is *the* solution. This may be more true in the field of foreign rather than domestic policy, but if so, it is only a marginal difference. The world of high governmental power is undoubt-edly made all the more difficult when the participants carry with them an ideological framework that is not shared by the majority of those in power, as was the case with many of the Reagan appointees. While the certainty of views of the ideological actor may help shield him or her from more dangerous thoughts of personal vulnerability, if the ideological framework is breached by realities that do not fit it, the repercussions might be felt throughout the personality structure.

A more common vulnerability stems from the envy of others. It is personal, insidious, and difficult to defend against, because it is usually hidden and clothed in other garb. It is the most virulent form of insecurity in all human relationships, but particularly in organizations. Envy is most typically a problem for those who stand out, apart from the norm, hence women and minorities who become token members of the power elite are peculiarly subject to envy from other members of their group.

The higher you go, the more vulnerable you are to the attacks of others and, in some ways, to your own limitations. You lose the capacity to start over as an anonymous individual. The world gets smaller. The number of options shrink and, possibly, the higher you go, the greater the fear of falling. "Your vulnerability can grow real or unreal within your mind," said one powerholder. If you fail, it may be front-page news. You are scrutinized more thoroughly, and "the enemies are there—with a lot more to lose or win. And those particular vulnerabilities, if you get up there, become bigger in your mind because the exposure at that level could be greater."

The higher you go, the greater the expectations about your power, the more difficult it is to control the frame of the debate, especially through the media. Every recent president has complained about the bias of the media and the inability to get his message across. The "bias" is inevitable if, for no other reason, because reporters, editors, and publishers have their own agenda. There are a large number of books and theories about why the media is both the problem and the solution, but the point I want to make here is that the expectations of what a powerholder can do are held as much by his or her constituents as they are by the media. Nor are they entirely misplaced, because the public powerholder, at least, has the ultimate responsibility for the behavior of his administration, regardless of the fact that he is blocked by insufficient funds, conflicting and separate authorities, civil service reforms, and the natural insulation of a bureaucracy. He accepted the responsibilities of the office when he ran for it or accepted his appointment to it, and the limitations come with the territory.

You do what you can, and usually what you can do requires compromise and sometimes a form of corruption of the best of all possible solutions. You give a job to the crony of someone who can give you a needed vote, so that you can enact a program that will help others. You appoint someone as ambassador because he contributed to your campaign, putting you in the position to do whatever.

With all of that, sometimes you lose. Coping with defeat is an inevitable part of success. Whether you lose on an isue or lose the office, there is a need to develop a capacity to go on. One experienced powerholder described the exercise of power as a combination of "dogged persistence and optimism." Changing institutions and opinions is never easy. Even maintaining the status quo can require effort. Defeat can come from all directions: from peers with their own independent power bases; from the inability to influence superiors, or the inability to affect the attitude and behavior of inferiors.

Someone described the behavior of a former powerholder who withdrew more and more from his staff as time went on and was thwarted in his efforts to change things.

I remember we used to try and organize and had scheduling meetings to try to figure out his schedule. His secretary would arrive and be under instructions from him not to tell any of us—his staff—what his schedule was! So, we'd say it would be great if he would do this or that, and she'd say, "Well, maybe he will and maybe he won't."

Backing away, insulating one's self from the pressures of others—even one's staff—is not an uncommon reaction. No one wants to face negative situations if they can be avoided, and with enough power—enough control over one's time and activities—almost anything can be avoided. We are well versed in stories of presidents who require their chiefs of staff to limit not only access but also the choices that are laid before them. It is a human reaction to stress, a way of limiting vulnerability.

There are many hurts to be suffered with power. Some are more personal than others. Some just eat away at the public role until they, too, become personal. Controversy is a normal part of the process. Rarely is any one person, or any one interest, completely satisfied, and winning is usually a relative thing. The retreat to privacy is sometimes a retreat to study and reflect, but far more often it is a retreat from the abrasions of public life. Total strangers who attack you on the street, former allies who support your opponents—there is a never-ending list of the way pow-erholders can be hurt. Retreat is one way of coping; another is to put the blame elsewhere. It takes a great deal of maturity to accept responsibility for failure, and sometimes the energy to be mature runs low.

Getting Tired

Exciting as it is, many contend that if you hold power too long, you wear out. Ten years seems to be the optimal time before an extraordinary sense of déjà vu develops. Said Kevin Harrington,

After a while it becomes boring because the problems don't ever really change. If you have taxes this year, you might not have them for 4 or 5 years, but they are going to come back. If there is an educational problem, it will come back again, or health, or environmental issues—the problems are cyclical. And the eternal political problems are . . . constant: the senator or representative who wants a larger office, or more help, or more this, more that. A constant, constant thing. In the beginning it is a bit of a challenge. After a while it's tiring, boring. The problems don't really change.

Harrington remembered talking with Kevin White about an article in the *Boston Globe* one morning concerning the retiring mayor of Baltimore:

> The reporter asked him why he was quitting, and he said, "Because every single morning my secretary comes in with a big silver tray, and it is piled high with"—and he used a particular vulgar expression—actually it was letters and so forth, but translated it was junk. "Every single day," he said. "I'm just tired of eating it."

The two Massachusetts pols laughed about it and agreed with the sentiment, and within a few years both voluntarily gave up their posts.

Some describe it as just running out of gas. Sometimes you just get tired of going to sleep at night thinking "the whole city may burn up tomorrow." Sometimes you know your capacity to exercise power is at an end, no matter what. Harry McPherson described a scene with Lyndon Johnson before he announced he was not going to run for re-election to the Presidency:

> Two weeks before—on a warm day in mid-March . . . Joe Califano and I had lunch with him, sitting in the Rose Garden. An unusual thing for us to do. And he said, "I'm not going to run again. I don't think I'm going to run." We didn't take him seriously at all. Kind of scowled. And he said, "Well, why should I run?" I said, "If I were you, I wouldn't run. That's me. If I were Harry McPherson in your position I wouldn't run, the situation is so awful. The unfairness level is so high, directed at you personally. I would find it hard to endure it and I wouldn't run. But I think you have to. And why? Well, for one thing, nobody else could get anything through the Congress. There won't be any continued momentum for the programs that we started."
>
> He said, "No, that's not so. Anybody can do better than I will be able to do in the next term. I've asked Congress for too much. They're tired of me." He said, "Congress and I are like an old man and woman who lived together forever, and all we really know about each other—we only remember each other's faults at this point. There's just no romance anymore. They'll give anybody—any new man a year—a honeymoon: Nixon—they'll give him one; Bobby, they'll give him one."
>
> Somebody walked in who had an appointment and Joe and I

walked back to his office and I said, "Phew, I couldn't think of another one." And he said, "Neither could I."

John Buckley described his decision to leave his office after ten years:

I think I realized—I never wanted to be sheriff to start with—and I never wanted to be the sheriff for the rest of my life. In fact, I had really gone two years beyond what I originally thought I was meant to be there for. So, it was only natural for me to realize there was no future for a liberal Republican in Massachusetts. There was nowhere for him to go. I had tried. I ran for the Republican nomination for Congress and for governor. . . . All these things, and I was just so liberal, I was way out of the mainstream and the conservatives were really coming in. I remember, I was campaigning up in Lowell—shaking hands with people leaving a store. And a lady came out. She was very agitated. Really agitated. So, I gave her a brochure—and she went "You liberal! You liberal!" screaming and yelling and she had bundles in her hand, and I said, "Let me help you," and I took a bundle and went down to her car, and she was furious. I mean, I had never been yelled at so much in my life. She blamed us for everything from the rain to the tax problems and everything else, and I realized that lady really drove home something that I should have seen a long time before that. That there was no future. I had to either change my beliefs, or I had to get out.

I remember going to a funeral of a court officer up in Lowell. He had been on the Lowell School Committee 33 years. He was a great friend of Tip O'Neill's. I'm up there with all these fellows: chesterfield coats and the gray fedoras. I'm in the backroom and they say, "You should have been one of us, Sheriff." I looked at them and I said, "You guys are too conservative for me." It was true! They were much too conservative. So, I don't think I would have been—maybe I would have been happier as a Democrat.

Well, I think also the fact that I had grown up in Malden where everybody was a Democrat, and everybody was corrupt. My mother—that famous line from my mother—"I don't care what you do when you grow up as long as you are good and you don't go into politics." Every day—she said that every day to one of her sons! I can remember her looking into the crib at my younger brother and saying it to him, and we all would finish it together. My mother would start and we would finish it. I didn't go into politics until she actually died, but I couldn't go in with those Democrats. But I sure did take the wrong party!

You get tired and sometimes you realize that this day is not your day. Whether or not you know what will happen to you next, you realize it is time to move on. Often, of course, powerholders get tired but stay in office because they have lost the capacity to take the risks they could when they sought power. They are older, or their families require more, or their reserves of energy and hope have worn thin. Exercising power takes tremendous commitments of time and energy, and even though the psychic rewards go a long way toward sustaining the activity and the drive, the time almost always comes when the pressures and problems outweigh the benefits. And if the decision is not made by the powerholder, it is frequently made by his or her constituents and the office is lost to another. It is a rare individual who can hold power beyond a decade in our society, particularly power that rests in the ultimate hands of constituents who may decide on their own that it is time for a change.

The capacity to exercise power can rise and fall, and rise again, even while the powerholder retains the authority of office. Presidents, for instance, are routinely measured by their power in relation to Congress and public opinion. They are able to achieve their objectives when they are high on the scale, and they are all but impotent when they are low. Clearly this is a calibration applied to all powerholders, almost all of the time. Maintaining power requires realistic assessments of where one rests on the scale at any given moment, and the capacity to perceive reality and measure one's standing in the eyes of others. It is not a constant thing. But making a realistic assessment is not a simple task, either. We should never underestimate the capacity of anyone— powerholder or not—to deceive himself, or to allow one's self to be deceived by the support of close allies. Wishful thinking aside, how does one ever know if the worst is at hand or is yet to come?

One wonders, for instance, about the understanding of those who are embattled in their positions to the point that observers believe them to be powerless: people such as Evan Mecham, the Arizona governor who was impeached in 1988; or House Speaker Jim Wright in 1989; a number of Reagan appointees such as Edwin Meese, James Watt, Richard Allen, Anne Burford, and Donald Regan; and, the most obvious example, Richard Nixon. "Stonewalling" joined the American vocabulary during Watergate, but what goes on in the minds and hearts of those on the other side of the wall?

It is human nature to believe you will be able to weather the storm, whether or not you are guilty. Certainly, the innocent—or at least the unindicted—must feel the attacks are particularly unwarranted and painful, but it would be naive to think only the innocent expect to be exonerated. For one thing, many of the guilty often say they did no worse than anyone else, genuinely believing in the essential corruption of the entire system. They often say everyone does it, and they were just unlucky enough to get caught. Whether "everyone" does it or not, what is unassailably true, however, is that the best (and perhaps last) chance an individual will get to defend himself exists only as long as that individual is in office and the object of attention. The media will hound one's every step while in office, but that same person will be hard pressed to get any media attention when out of office, even if he or she is exonerated.

What is at stake is one's reputation, honor, and everything that the public will know about you for the rest of your life. In addition to the individual and his or her family, the lives and well-being of close aides and associates are also at stake. They, too, will be putting their reputations at risk, often by staying, sometimes by going.

The moment of public crisis is a great test of character (or at least of timing). Those who pass it will be heroes; those who fail will be marked forever. Winning or losing is a judgment ultimately made by history, however, not by one's contemporaries, not one's enemies, not even by one's friends. The capacity to stand at the top of the mountain and look beyond the storm does not come with experience, because each crisis is unique. Power is often lost—when it is lost this way—over absurdities. Who could have imagined that the presidency of Richard Nixon would fall because of a failed break-in at Democratic Party headquarters? The fatal blow comes most often in the small, inconsequential acts because they are the least watched and the least guarded against. Such errors catch the power holder unaware of the dangers they will reveal, particularly if the powerholder needs to—or believes he or she needs to—focus on the larger issues. Bob Woodward quotes William Casey explaining why Richard Helms, one of his predecessors at the CIA, did not quit:

> "There were a lot of people leaving then," he explained, "and I asked Helms why he didn't leave. Helms said, 'When you sit here each day and you see all of this, and see all the Russians are doing, you feel' "—he paused—" 'you feel beleaguered and you just can't leave.' "[7]

It is easy to lose one's self in the immediacy of the work to be done and in the essential role the powerholder plays in that process, rather than face the challenge to one's authority. The scale in one's mind weighs the values of one's contribution against the costs to the organization if one stays. It is not difficult to imagine how much more each of us would value our own contribution. From the perspective of the individual, exercising power requires confidence and optimism. Doubt about whether or not to stay for yourself, or leave for the sake of the office—especially doubt that can be perceived by others—can become a mortal wound. As one observer noted, "If you don't exude confidence, who in the hell is going to follow you? You show me a self-doubter in politics, and I'll show you a dead man. Rapidly. Because the sharks will bite." There is every reason, therefore, to resist all suggestion of loss and defeat and to assume victory in the end.

Still, if power, like beauty, exists largely in the eyes of the beholder, scandal can destroy it. While there are constitutional rights that assure an individual due process, there is no right to power, particularly to public power. We generally hold those who rule us to a higher standard. Perhaps it would be more accurate to say that we hold them to the public standard that may, or may not, be breached in more private circumstances. It may not be fair, but neither is power.

The need to hold powerholders up as models of morality stems from the nature of power, and from the needs of the powerholder and the powerless alike to believe in the legitimacy of that individual to be in a position of power.

Another reason for the need to believe in the morality of powerholders, and why we so readily (and often so viciously) turn against our leaders when we think them vulnerable, is doubtless based in the need for a powerful parent: someone who will take care of us. While the anxiety associated with the loss of structure is particularly material to the powerholder, it also affects those within his or her fiefdom and those in the world beyond. It is quite a common thing for the people who remain in organizations to feel anger toward those who leave them, for whatever reason.

Although power essentially flows down a one-way street, there is a presumed relationship or contract. From the perspective of the powerless, holding power is an honor conferred upon someone that should not be treated lightly. A former public executive noted that his erstwhile constituents seemed to be offended when he said he did not miss the job—perhaps, he speculated, because they did not believe him, perhaps because he had voluntarily given it up. Angry as they may have been at him while in office, giving it up is like a father giving up his children, and they resented it, at least for a while.

CHAPTER

4

---■---

Structures of Power: The Context in Which It Exists

The experience of power is not abstract. It depends upon the relationship between the powerholder and those over whom he holds power. Even while it wraps itself into the character of the powerholder, it is something perceived and measured by others. How it is experienced depends on the context in which it occurs: the structure of the institution and the history of the times. Assuming that the historical context is generally beyond any individual or any organization's control, the focus of this chapter is on the structures. Although there are important commonalities, there are differences in the experience of power when it is held in a bureaucracy or a legislature, a government environment or a private corporation. Power is exercised more easily in some settings than others. It is more rewarding at some times than others. It matters whether someone is a cabinet secretary, elder statesman, mayor, agency head, or chief of staff of a congressional committee. We need to explore something of the differences before we can be sure of what is common.

A defining structural difference is based on how power is achieved. Elected powerholders are, in large measure, self-selected. Those who are appointed to their positions in the public sector have ties (and responsibilities) to their appointers, and they generally come in as outsiders to their agencies and those over whom they hold power. In the private sector, with the exception of those who create their own companies, the development and promotion of leaders is an important factor built into career paths by both the individual and the organization. Some CEOs may be brought in from the outside, but only after they have proven themselves especially adapted to corporate leadership. More commonly, leaders in the private sector are selected from within, after demonstrating strong conformity to the organization's culture.

A second structural characteristic is how much autonomy the power-holder has to enable him to accomplish his or her aims. It matters whether or not the powerholder can hire and fire others, and how much control he or she has over the environment—i.e., whether or not power must be shared with others to accomplish a goal.

A third issue is not so much an organization characteristic as an environmental one: the nature of power for those who exercise influence from the outside, as distinct from those holding direct responsibility for the organization or the task at hand. The term "rainmaker" is often applied to influence-wielders, presumably in reference to the American Indian who could call upon the gods to bring the rain.[1] He is an inter-mediary who is necessary in times of crisis. He does not plant the crop, nor does he make the rain, but he knows something of each and brings with him a special message that only he can relate. "Mandarin" is another term applied to the same sort of person, someone whose power comes by virtue of his training and past attainment which may, or may not, be specific to the task at hand.

The structural characteristic that has the greatest impact on the ex-perience of power is the size and scope of the organization or activity. Running or advising a mom-and-pop operation around the corner may provide the same degree of control over the structure as in many other organizations, but it bears little resemblance to heading or advising a major federal agency or the White House itself. As a rule, the larger the organization, the more formally it is structured, the stricter the adherence to rules, and the more finely measured the power within it. Smaller organizations tend to be more informal, and power is apt to be distributed in a collegial fashion, which means that you do not do to someone else what you would not want them to do unto you.

THE WAYS THAT POWER IS ACHIEVED

Those who hold power most securely are those who are elected to office and those who own their own firms, assuming they are at least moderately insulated from outsider takeovers. Almost everyone else serves at their pleasure and, while elected officials are accountable to the voters, a good proportion of them can stay in office as long as they want. There is an old political saying that mayors, governors, and presidents accrue grievances, while legislators accrue name-recognition. The extraordinarily high rate of incumbency in our legislatures (generally well over 90 percent) attests to the truth of the adage. It takes a strong opponent (or outrageous behavior on the part of the officeholder) to oust an incumbent member of the House of Representatives. Senators, although far more vulnerable because statewide races gain much more attention, are also usually assured re-election unless they came into office in unusual times, behave unusually recklessly while in office, or come from a state where the partisan distribution is even and highly competitive.

Legislative Power

Secure as they may be, the impact of being accountable to an electorate is not insignificant, even—and perhaps especially—for legislators. Yale political scientist David Mayhew published an interesting book in 1974, entitled *Congress: The Electoral Connection*,[2] making the point that the behavior of members of Congress is first and foremost explained by their concern for re-election. While I would not contest that conclusion for a moment, it nonetheless remains true that the daily experience of power for an elected representative is rather varied: he worries about the power of the electorate writ large, but more likely has at least as much, if not more, power than most of those with whom he comes in contact in his district; and when re-elected many times to the legislature, particularly, has significantly more than some, while significantly less than others. Burt Margolin, an astute state representative from Los Angeles, described the difference this way:

> When you are in the legislative branch, there are two forms, two dimensions of power. At the level of your constituency in your district ... from the first day, most members have a sense of influence and power, because among the citizens of your community, you are simply elevated—one in three hundred thousand, one of five hundred thousand—who casts his vote in Sacramento, or wherever the state capital happens to be. Community groups and citizens groups defer to you where they hadn't before. They seek your opinion. They lobby you. They want you to side with them in a particular battle or dispute.... Suddenly you are surrounded by people—all of whom want to talk to you—and all of whom consider you important.
>
> When you go into the legislature, in converse, among your peers there you don't have power when you first come in the obvious sense, because you are the newest entry into the body and although seniority is not rigidly enforced, it is always there in some form or fashion. And for a legislator, it takes a while to establish yourself in the context of your job in the capital.

Legislatures are more free-wheeling institutions than bureaucracies, largely because of the assumption that all members are equal. It is, of course, a fiction, but it is an important element of the organizational culture. Partisanship is the principal organizing tool, and the leaders of each session are elected through party caucuses, even though there is eventually a formal vote by the whole body. The distribution of power in these bodies is always finely balanced, and legislatures are structured and restructured as one reform leads to another abuse and the power gets out of balance. It is the ever-popular "law of unintended consequences." Typically, individuals rise to positions of authority because of seniority, which was originally a reform against the arbitrary exercise of appointive power by legislative leaders in the past (and the concept of legislative leaders was itself a reform against the undue influence of external interests). Seniority, as a mechanism for controlling abuses of power, has come increasingly under pressure in the past few years, although a consistent solution to the problem has not yet arisen. The attack on unpopular seniors has led to an increase in campaigning for leadership roles within the legislature through the use of campaign funds, among other things, but this moral reaction does not quite constitute a reform in the structure itself.

Among legislators, relationships are overtly courteous, and strong efforts are made to avoid personalizing conflict. Friendship "across the aisle" is valued as a measure of the professionalism of the legislator. For those who seek influence inside the body, an understanding of the motives and needs of one's colleagues is essential. Such perception only comes to those who are willing to listen and pay attention to their peers.

Power among legislative members is derived in one of two ways: it can be held broadly and diffusely within the body, focusing on the process and the established leadership; or it can be held narrowly and aggressively, by focusing attention on a specific issue (in which case, the legislator may become *the* authority in a given field). It can be pragmatic and consensual, or it can be specific and/or ideological. According to Representative Margolin:

> The legislature tends to respond to aggression, and people who are intent and focused upon a goal and are prepared to pay a price to pursue that goal . . . are people who are able to move through bills and accomplish limited goals. They aren't necessarily powerful within the institution on global issues that affect the state of California. To do that you have to develop a consensus and you are not a consensus-builder.

People who achieve power first in an executive setting—and then move on to the Senate—often see themselves as having lost power and gone down in stature, even if the scope of their decision-making responsibilities has been expanded. As one observer noted:

> Legislative power is a personality cult almost, and in a sense the visibility matters more than any actual authority, because it is a measure of where you are. In an uncertain world—and Congress is an uncertain world—every measure counts. But no one person has that kind of power that an executive leader has. . . .
> Take the Senate: take those who have been governor, and those who have never been governor. They all say—those who have been governor—this place is a mess. A Bismarkian mess. . . . I am not the focal point of attention, and there is real sibling rivalry around here. I had power once and now I only have influence. While a guy coming from the state legislature, or the House of Representatives—now the Senate—hell, he's on the ascent!

One difference between legislative and executive power that only occasionally arose in interviews, but which strikes me as relevant to the sense of power, is that a legislator who focuses on narrow constituency issues can be successful in getting the highway appropriation through for his or her district, or any number of other pork barrel issues, but for those who enter politics because they are attracted by the larger issues, satisfaction requires addressing larger problems. And the larger the problem, the less likely it is that victory will come easily, or when it does, the less likely it will be that any single participant will be given credit for it, beyond the not insignificant reward of being part of the process that makes the important decisions of the age. Many derive genuine satisfaction in being engaged in the fight, and it is quite likely that for these individuals, the reward of participation is undervalued as compensation to the psyche for never winning.

There are many ways power is achieved in a legislative body: knowing more about an issue than anyone else (sometimes, but not always, linked to seniority); knowing the preferences of other legislators (and, therefore, how they are apt to vote); being willing to do the homework and the housework (i.e., knowing the facts and staying in the room long enough to write them into the bill); or by creating fear in others because of one's temper or one's humor. Christopher Matthews makes the latter point about former Maine Senator Edmund Muskie, whom he described as winning "not because he was the smartest man in the room—although he may well have been—but because he was willing to be the last man in the room." But beyond that, according to Matthews,

> Muskie's celebrated temper added a barometric factor to his conferences with the House. A conferee's greatest asset is a reputation for being "difficult." Normally, Muskie wore a Mount Rushmore countenance. But when he wished to feel goaded, his temper would erupt and in stages: first, a minor tremor, then a greater burst, then progressing up the Richter scale to a full, shattering explosion. Few people wanted to see it run its course. Three centuries ago, La Rochefoucauld wrote an assessment that fits Muskie precisely. "Fortune sometimes uses our faults for our advancement," he wrote. "Some people are so tiresome that their merits would go unrewarded were it not that we did not want to get them out of the way."
> ... Some walked away happy that they had achieved roughly—*very* roughly—what they set out to achieve; others were simply happy that they walked away....When the crunch came on an issue, he possessed an unlimited vat of righteous indignation. "Why should I compromise?" he would yell. "I don't need a bill *that* bad.[3]

The power of legislative leaders varies from legislature to legislature, based on its history of abuse and reform, and with the individuals who hold those positions, depending on their view of the office, and how firmly they hold it in their grasp. All of these permutations aside, however, there remains one unalterable characteristic: *the power is held only as long as it is accepted as legitimate by a majority of their peers*. Kevin Harrington observed that the external perception of his constituents as sheep who would follow him anywhere was missing the mark:

> That really is not what's happening. The senate president wouldn't last one day. He could not force an idea that they don't want. But, see, the members don't want the press to think that they would vote against proposition X, or Y, or Z, because it is a controversial issue. They want to create the impression that they can't do it because of the terrible senate president. That's not the case! That's absurd! I could not force you to vote against some principle. I can't do it. As senate president, you find what the consensus is and fashion it.

Over an individual legislator, or a minority group of legislators, the leader's power may be unbeatable—at least on any given issue, but alliances shift and an extra vote on one issue may well be a necessary vote on another. From the perspective of the leader, according to Harrington, once he has taken a position and put himself behind an issue, he could not afford to lose.

> When you find that something you are for is going to be defeated—or something you are against is going to go through—you better act quickly, put a fresh coat of paint on it, and find some excuse to change your position, and then have them write, "Well, now that Harrington's changed his position—now it is going through, or now it is going to be defeated." In reality, all you have done is joined the opposition without letting the opposition know that. You can never afford defeat. You can't afford to lose . . . a legislative leader must carry the perception that if the chair wants it, the chair can get it. . . . You can't afford the weakness.

He went on to explain a lesson he learned early in his career when he had a minor political problem and was visited by an old friend:

> He came in to cheer me up and he said to me, "Swallow the blood." And I said, "Excuse me? Pardon me, Charlie?" He said, "Swallow the blood." And I said, "I don't know what you are talking about." He said, "I was a fighter and in one of my first fights a fellow hit me right in the mouth, and when I came back to the corner, my trainer said to me 'Swallow the blood, Charlie.' I said to him, 'If I swallow the blood, I'll get sick.' My trainer said to me, if he sees you bleeding, you'll be a lot sicker because he'll go right for the blood."
>
> I always remembered the expression. Don't ever let them see you are hurting. Don't ever show weakness. Don't ever let them whisper you are starting to slip, you are not on top.

A governor or a president cannot expect to win on every issue, according to Harrington, because he is dealing with an equal branch of government in the separation of powers. While there is something resembling an employer/employee relationship between a legislative leader and the members, the leader can never entirely forget that he or she holds power in a peer group which measures him in every session, on every vote. If he fails, they are there to see it and be hurt by it. Voters, who exercise the ultimate power, are not peers, nor do they spend their time and energy in the company of their representatives, as do legislators.

John Eller, the former top aide to a speaker of the Massachusetts state legislature, described the power as one derived from the will of the members ... never out of sight or mind. Symbolically, the Speaker's door might be closed to the staff and the general public, but when the House was in session, the door from his office to the House floor was always open. He knew where his power came from and had to satisfy it, and that is the way that office ran, right down to the fact that if a member comes in and there is a staff appointment, that member is seen first. That power resided in the membership.

Former Speaker of the House Tip O'Neil, who went to Congress from the Massachusetts legislature, notes that his approach differed considerably from that of his predecessor, Sam Rayburn—who ruled, in retrospect, at a simpler period in American history, when authority was respected in its own right. According to O'Neill:

> Sam didn't know twenty members of his own party. When he first became Speaker, he knew plenty of congressmen, but as the years went on, he became increasingly isolated in the party. By the time I came along, he was dealing almost exclusively with what the press called the College of Cardinals—the committee chairmen. . . .
>
> Rayburn went up to Eddie Boland and said, "New member, son?" At the time, Eddie had been in the House for seven years and had served on the Appropriations Committee for five, but Sam had no idea who he was. He didn't care, either. As for Republicans, he probably didn't know more than three or four. If you wanted to see Sam Rayburn, you made an appointment two or three weeks in advance.
>
> In 1977, when I became Speaker, I came into office with a very different approach. For one thing, I knew about 80 percent of the members. For another, if you wanted to see Tip O'Neill, all you had to do was show up in my office. I might have the biggest businessman in the world waiting for an appointment, but if a member of Congress wanted to talk, he always came first.[4]

Executive Power

From the perspective of the powerholder, a significant difference between executive power and legislative power (beyond the size of the electorate, if there is one) is that the accountability flows up rather than down. Appointees look to the elected official in the public world, or to a governing board in the private world. While legislators seek compromise to make things run, executive leaders need compliance from those beneath them to make things happen. H. R. Haldeman, at a conference of former White House chiefs of staff, recalled a time when he intentionally ignored a direct order from Richard Nixon:

> I was ordered by the president unequivocally and immediately to commence lie detector tests of every employee of the State Department because there had been a series of leaks which were seriously damaging our negotiations in Vietnam. The order to solve the problem was that every member of the State Department staff *worldwide* was to be submitted *immediately* to lie detector tests. That was an easy order not to carry out because it was physically impossible to do. But we didn't do it and the president said the next day, "Have you gotten a lie detector program started?" And I said no, and he said, "Aren't you going to?" And I said, "I don't intend to," and he ordered that it be done.
>
> I again didn't do it on the first round that time, then went back to him later that day, and after that time . . . I went back and said, "Mr. President, this really is a mistake. There are other ways of dealing with this problem at this point, and we will be back to you with a plan for doing that." We came back in a few days with a plan, and he said at that point, "I didn't think you would do it."[5]

In all probability, there are not too many times a staff aide, or an underling in the hierarchy, can get away with disobeying the direct orders of a powerful executive, although much depends on the relationship between the two. Covert disobedience (e.g., leaking information, etc.) may last longer, but unless the aide has another source of power at hand, he or she is as likely to be out of a job as the powerholder.

If the executive is appointed to office by a board, he needs their support or he will never be able to govern those beneath him. Someone used the example of a college president known to exercise enormous power within his university, "He scares the whole freaking place!" he said, "But he double checks with thirty-two people. They call and he drops everything," he said. "It's the board of trustees."

Having the support of one's superiors (whether an individual, a board, or an electorate) brings with it the capacity to set your own agenda and, barring crises, control over your own time. As Ira Jackson noted,

> Reality for most folks in public life is that, sure, they are driven by congressional testimony or a crisis, or X, Y, and Z, but mostly there is time. You have the luxury of doing what you want to do.
>
> The Mayor would wake up every morning and he would have a

clear blank agenda. It wasn't filled with eight meetings. Meetings with the Mayor only get called if the Mayor wants them. Nobody can meet with the Mayor unless he says it's ok. So, you can walk in the office and say, "What will I do today?" I got all this power . . . what will I do today?

Having such freedom assumes, of course, that the mayor is not facing any overriding crisis, but certainly he or she is more likely to be freer than anyone else.

On the plus side, a mayor, governor, or president presides over a sufficiently large institution in which almost any task that comes up— other than personal appearances—can be delegated to someone else. The capacity to delegate effectively, while still retaining responsibility and awareness, became something of an issue in the latter years of the Reagan administration, when it began to look as if too much was being delegated. But, as one former powerholder noted, "There is no job description for president, governor, or mayor. All the things get done by other people."

Appointees who head agencies get closer to job descriptions, although even they usually have the capacity to charge others with specific tasks. Their time, however, can be taken away just because they *must* respond to the interests of those above them (as well as to legislators), assuming those above them have an interest. Any group that is small enough to meet and make a decision can control the time and energy of those they place in office. Above cabinet secretaries, at all times, is the White House and its associate, the Office of Management and Budget. There will be assistants to the president who are specifically charged with overseeing the departments, generalists on the president's staff, and finally, of course, the president himself.

Then there is Congress, with its oversight responsibilities. Robert Finch, who was Secretary of the Department of Health, Education and Welfare in the early years of the Nixon administration, described the time he spent satisfying his accountability to members of Congress, noting that he was "always rushing to the Hill":

I had to work with 16 separate congressional committees and subcommittees—literally—where they wanted to see the Secretary first. We could eventually turn it over to an assistant secretary. . . . The Secretary of State has to report directly and periodically to only a couple of committees at best, and anyone who has gone through congressional hearings knows you don't just go down there and give your testimony because the members will just come through in sequence and ask their several questions, and they don't know what's been asked before so you just go over and over the same ground, and you chew up a couple of days every time you do a full-scale appearance.

To each congressional committee must be added the independent interest groups (both pro and con) only partially represented by the committees, their representative agency heads within the Department, and any other agency—in or out of government—with whom the executive of a complex domestic agency would trade. And then again, federalism adds another layer of fifty states and untold numbers of local authorities, each of which may require attention. It is easy to see how time-consuming the process can be.

This is not to say that a cabinet secretary's time is entirely consumed by meetings, but only to note that it differs with the complexity of the tasks under an organization's aegis, and has a tremendous impact on the autonomy of the powerholder. Whatever goes on in these gatherings, they take time, and they require some measure of role-playing by the powerholder, conveying the sensibility that he or she has power, a sympathetic interest in the issue (whatever it is), and a plan to do something about it.

Clearly, there is latitude in this. Elected executives need to be more-or-less responsive to legislatures and to public opinion. At the very least, they need to have one or the other of them on their side. Political analyst William Schneider frequently makes the point that presidents can act with Congress against public opinion—as in the Panama Canal Treaty, and tax reform—or with public opinion on their side against Congress, as in the case of Ronald Reagan's 1981 tax cut and budget. By the same token, Congress can act with public opinion against the president, as in Social Security legislation, aid to the Contras, and the Robert Bork nomination to the Supreme Court. The only overriding control the public has is an election—a certain, but not necessarily a timely, tool.

Another difference between executive leaders and legislative leaders is that the former must have a vision of what they want to accomplish. Sitting on top of an organization helps in developing a long perspective because, as one former elected executive put it,

When you have absolute power, your ideals are higher, and your purposes become—not more self-centered, really. It isn't being egotistical, it is being ego-centric because you don't have to go outside the source of your power.

Legislative leaders do not need—and often do not have—a higher ideal. What they need is a stronger sense than anyone else of how the process works, not what it does. Those who have strong ideological commitments, in fact, may be at a considerable disadvantage in attaining legislative leadership.

Staff Power

If we accept the notion that the elected official and heads of large organizations, whether elected or appointed, delegate much of their work to others, it follows that those who receive the work exercise significant influence over the issue involved, deriving at least some sense of satisfaction by defining it and carrying out the tasks necessary to achieve their ends. Harry McPherson, who worked for many years as an aide to Lyndon Johnson, noted that "Every leader bent on great enterprises consumes his staff as fuel. There is a reciprocal benefit in this, since the staff enjoys the prestige of contributing to events beyond its inherent reach."[6] The aide who works for an "amiable" boss gains "anecdotes for one's wife and friends that magnify the staffer's own position—making him seem at ease with power, and therefore powerful himself."[7] That sense of power, even in the midst of a carefully balanced and sustained power structure such as a legislature, is a heady reward that can work its way into the sense of identity of anyone.

It surprised me somewhat that everyone who spoke of the power of staff aides argued that those who worked in the executive branch tended to be more abusive than their counterparts in the legislative branch. There was an almost universal sense that executive branch staff were inclined to believe they would be there forever, and to behave in ways likely to get themselves into trouble more often. This is a rather broad generalization to make, but insofar as staff aides were recognized by themselves and others as having power or influence, those who spoke of it did agree on the slant of the abuse. As one legislator put it:

> the staff people that most governors bring in think that they are working for a royal governor. They really don't understand the separation of power, the checks and balances. . . . It creates the impression that I'm all powerful—me, Charlie Brown—I'm working for the Governor. I'm all powerful and I'll be here forever. And they don't think about the day they are going to be out. A legislator (and his staff), conversely, almost always thinks about the day he or she is going to be out.

Kevin Harrington described a telephone call he received from a newly-elected governor's staff aide. "Mr. Harrington?" she said, "The Governor will see you every Thursday morning at 11:00." The Senate President told her to put him on hold and to repeat exactly to someone else in her office what she had just said to him. "A few minutes later she came back on the phone and said, "Mr. President? The Governor would be happy to make himself available to legislators every Thursday morning at 11:00."

Colorado Senator Timothy Wirth, who has served in the executive and in both houses of Congress, also spoke of the tendency of executive aides to undervalue the legislative branch and why that offends him:

> They wouldn't be here if it were not a political process—an electoral process. And that is viewed with enormous disdain by a lot of people in the administration who do not understand electoral politics. . . . You, know, Lyndon Johnson was right in saying the person hadn't been elected dog catcher. He's been through the political cauldron, and been through the subtleties of what makes various interests get balanced out—in the true sense of politics.

Although both these views come from the legislative side, several of those I spoke to who served in the executive branch had the same perception: that most aides came to their jobs with a bloated sense of their position and power, and viewed legislators with a measure of contempt, thinking them vain and self-serving.

There is another perspective that is equally misleading about the nature of the staff job. H. R. Haldeman described his role as chief of staff to Richard Nixon as a powerless job. "I did not have power," he said, "I was concerned with process."[8] The belief that process is not power is more than modest or self-effacing, it is naive, particularly in that instance where he controlled communication to and from the president. Such views of powerful roles frequently lead to misuse and misinterpretations of intention and behavior.

Legislative aides live in an environment of carefully-balanced and formally-expressed respect by the elected members of the body for each other ("My Honorable Opponent,"etc), and are inculcated from the beginning with the illusory nature of their power. As one observer noted, "Especially Senate aides, who are de facto senators on many issues, can be there today and gone overnight." He recalled the very quick and sure burst of the illusory bubble, and the personal cost, associated with the electoral defeat of their bosses when the Republicans lost control of the Senate in 1984:

All the Republican aides who ran those committees for the past several years—they had enormous influence over national policy. They were workaholics, and they worked night and day, and they were the senator for all intents and purposes. And it's gone overnight.

Although legislative staff aides (and legislators themselves) may be gone overnight with the turn of an election, they usually have the capacity, if they wish, to hang on longer than their bosses. There are always other legislators and committees for whom they might work, while former legislators do not, as a rule, work for current legislators. Former executive branch aides, most of whom are political appointees (as opposed to civil servants), are out on the street along with their bosses once the term is ended, especially if they are succeeded by the other party.

Another factor in the difference between legislative and executive aides is just a product of the structure: aides in the executive branch are placed near the top of a pyramid. They do not necessarily have authority over those beneath them, but they do have that all important concomitant of influence—access to the top. It does not take a big leap in imagination to understand that an aide to a Cabinet secretary would perceive his boss as being singularly more powerful than almost any individual legislator, and, by extension, the aide also as more powerful than legislative aides, and, not infrequently, more powerful than most legislators. It is partly a product of a man-to-man measure, and partly a consequence of the environment, wherein those on top of a pyramid have more power than those who share power in a collegial setting. It is also quite likely that the aides reflect the sensibilities of their bosses, and that an executive feels more powerful than a legislator, at least for the shorter period of time that he or she is in charge.

Staff aides are not powerholders, in the sense that I have been using the term, because they clearly wield power on behalf of someone else. Although they are never accorded the measure of deference given their bosses, they do gain some of the high of power: the excitement of implementing ideas (frequently their own); respect from others seeking their influence; and a sense of belonging, of being part of the political game. Special assistants also have the advantage of sitting high up in the structure, which gives them the benefit of the broad view. They often consider themselves in training for leadership and have established mentor/protégé relationships with their bosses. Given the uncertainty of elections and the consequences of working for an individual rather than an institution, it is not surprising that most aides in all branches of government tend to be young, and consider their time on the job as a form of training.

Getting agreement on an idea, writing the speech or the press release, and pushing the legislation through, goes a long way toward a sense of accomplishment in both the executive and legislative branches, although there are limits to what that might mean in the large scheme of things. "But you see," a former aide to a governor said to me,

> all you have to do is a press release and its over. I'm not sure one of those [ideas] got forever into the system, but you had a sense of change. It was easier because you never had to face. . . . I mean, I've always had a feeling that you could never win through a bureaucracy. You cannot set a thing in motion over everybody at the bottom. You have to put out an idea that people from the bottom catch up with and say, "I like the mood that's up there," and you create that. In their own ways—and you'll never be able to predict exactly how that comes out—at least they're more positively going in that direction.

Insofar as power means being able to accomplish a goal, the aides to high government officials (executive and legislative) have power. Insofar as power means having others defer to you, important aides are deferred to by many. They are not usually, however, part of the peer group of powerholders, and must themselves defer to others (the chief assistant to the head of a major conglomerate could conceivably have status equal to the CEO of one of the subsidiary companies). They cannot afford to let themselves become deluded by their grandeur even if (perhaps especially if) they are smarter or work harder than their bosses.

AUTONOMY AND OBJECTIVES

In the long run, much of the sense of accomplishment in having power is dependent on being able to attain some goal. Although there are important rewards in knowing that you were part of the process and fought the good fight, it falls a little short if there is no legacy to point to when it is over. Having the responsibility for the problem—particularly in public life—however, is not quite the same thing as having the authority to accomplish the task, because power is so carefully and so extensively diffused. This separation of power is especially characteristic of the public sector, and it is a major factor in the failure of most political promises. There is a presumption that private institutions have more autonomy, and although the differences between the two are not quite so black and white, and one could argue that a corporation has even less control over the market than a government agency, it is a fair generalization to make. Putting aside for the moment the fact that the goals of a public agency are usually significantly greater than those of a private organization—and, therefore, that much more difficult to achieve—it does seem appropriate to consider the structural differences between them.

Public versus Private Structures

One significant difference between the public and private spheres comes in the way that new leadership establishes itself. In the public sector, a newly-elected or appointed official is expected to demonstrate a clean sweep of the old guard. The very fact that a retiring president takes all of his papers with him all but guarantees that there will be minimal institutional memory left in the White House for his successor. Even in the happiest of turnovers of office (e.g., when the newly-elected official is of the same party as his or her predecessor, who could not run for re-election because of constitutional limits: George Bush succeeding Ronald Reagan), the new leader must put his or her stamp on the office and sweep at least some of the old rascals out, however lovable they may have been. Although candidate Bush said throughout most of the 1988 presidential campaign that he was going to bring "wholesale change" to the government, he rarely gave the impression of being anything but a Reagan loyalist until the day he came to the Republican convention in Atlanta. Only then did he consciously begin standing alone, trying to shed the image of the loyal vice president, the image of a follower.

Independence in executives is an important virtue, a problem always faced by vice presidents and lieutenant governors seeking to succeed to the top job after having demonstrated loyalty for four or eight years. Should they succeed, the best evidence of independent thinking is replacing political appointees with their own people. Although a number of President-elect Bush's nominations for office were drawn from the Reagan administration, both he and the retiring president made a point of asserting his intention to put his own team together, requiring all the Reagan political appointees to submit letters of resignation.

The first series of appointments Bush made were renominations to recent Cabinet positions, that had been filled with his apparent approval during the waning months of the presidential campaign. And all of these appointees, in turn, sought to demonstrate their leadership by establishing change in their departments. Richard Thornburgh succeeded the beleagured Edwin Meese in August of 1988, and said, according to the *Washington Post*, that

> Bush stressed in their meeting—and he [Thornburgh] agreed—that he wants "new talent to infuse some new life" into government ranks. It would "be a mistake not to have substantial turnover," says Thornburgh.

Lauro Cavazos succeeded William J. Bennett in the Department of Education. According to the *Post*,

> Cavazos has made clear that he is very different from his predecessor. To education groups, Bennett was seen as an adversary, while Cavazos has gone out of his way to garner support from educators and their organizations. Bennett supported the Reagan administration's budget cuts in education; Cavazos has vowed to fight for additional funding. And many of the ideological, conservative appointees in the Education Department have left.[9]

In marked contrast to the passing of the torch in public affairs, when leadership changes hands in the private sector, the new CEO typically makes a very serious effort to demonstrate continuity with the past, lest customers, stockholders, employees, or business analysts become uneasy about forging ahead into the unknown. There is a need to show insiders and outsiders that the firm is in good hands and will remain profitable (assuming the change was not brought about because the firm was on the brink of bankruptcy). Although the argument can be made that some of the most significant decisions in business are those that seek to change direction before decline is even a prospect, most of the time most of the effort is designed to demonstrate stability and continuity.

The corporate world also often faces the problem of the predecessor still lurking about in the guise of chairman of the board making sure there are no unexpected departures from the past. Compared to an ex-mayor, governor, or president, the past CEO of a firm plays a major role in his immediate successor's affairs. The interest in succession, in fact, is given considerable attention in the business world, partly in the interests of stockholders, but also because it is strongly in the interests of those who run large companies or aspire to run them. As one traveler from the public to the private sector put it,

The thing that struck me most was this obsessive—quite appropriate—but rigidly-directed management succession planning. I mean, you are lucky in government to think beyond the next day. What they're doing [in the private sector] is thinking about someone who's been here fifteen years and where they should be going for the next twenty-five years. For every job there are three likely candidates if that person gets hit by a truck tomorrow.

And you know, they've got the time and the luxury and they should be doing it, but I've never participated in a conversation in government like—God, if the governor died, what would the lieutenant governor be like?

Business schools make much of the notion of "mentoring," pointing to the significance of bright young men and women attaching themselves to a rising star so that they, too, will learn and rise. The issue of succession merely follows the concept of mentor relationships to its logical conclusion. What is less obvious, however, is the interest of the mentor in seeing himself or herself perpetuated in the institution by the protégé. The need to believe that the new leader will behave exactly as the old leader would—a need felt most particularly by the old leader—promotes the accession to office of a protégé, but frequently causes his ouster from office within a year because such dreams of immortality are rarely satisfied and the old mentor will still have enough influence to complain about it. A typical scenario will see the successor pushed out within a year, followed by a second successor who is more successful because the expectations that he will follow the old ways are not as great, the issues are somewhat newer (and ones the old CEO will be less likely to have been involved with), and the old leader has lost some, if not all, of his early retirement clout. It is likely that the new leader in the private sector would prefer the same degree of autonomy as his public counterpart, but he does not usually have much choice in the matter because authority given to the new leader is not quite so absolute—there are no term guarantees (contracts notwithstanding), and while the reins may be passed, the old leader still has access to the whip.

In the public sector, an ex-president is out and he does not choose his successor, albeit he may have made known certain preferences. A former president does not hang about Washington, and he is not frequently consulted, at least not by his successor. It is, in fact, an interesting phenomenon that a successor rarely, if ever, asks his predecessor's advice about anything. As Jack Flannery noted about the experience of his governor, Francis Sargent:

> It was a horrendous waste for a guy to leave office after six years as governor and nobody ever called him up and asked him anything. Now Michael Dukakis (who succeeded Sargent in 1975) did not call and say, "Hey, let's forget the last election and whatever I called you. What the hell did you do about X and Y and Z? Nor did Sargent do the same thing when he became governor. It never occurred to him. He wouldn't have demeaned himself by calling his predecessor and saying, "We weren't all that friendly, John, but tell me how did you cope with the Department of ———— where you've got a commissioner who is a fool and . . . ." Never happens. So all this experience and expertise in the best of cases ends up at a class at the Institute of Politics. Other than that, it gets lost. You know, it is frittered away.

Even in the rare situation in which a public executive is able to select his successor, there is little to no communication. John Buckley recalled that the few times he was asked for advice by his handpicked successor it was about people, "something," he said, "I was never comfortable with. . . . I'd rather not get those calls." But even those few calls stopped when his immediate successor was followed by another one of "his people." The former public leader may be called upon in time, but only after the new leader has very firmly established himself, a process that is likely to take several years. For those who wait by the phone, it is a long, lonely watch.

BORROWED POWER: APPOINTEES AND RAINMAKERS

Influence from the Inside: the Appointees

Although I would argue that much of the experience of power is common to all powerholders, I will accept the proposition that those who run organizations (whether through appointment, ownership, or election) have a different experience from those who wield influence from the outside. The commonality between those who are appointed and those who are elected is the way others respond to them. Someone used the analogy of driving a borrowed car: it goes down the road just as quickly and comfortably, even if it can be taken away in a moment. The proverbial "buck" may slide by the appointed officeholder from time to time, but most of the people she deals with during her working day are those over whom she holds power, and everyone behaves accordingly.

A more significant difference in the experience of power than that between elected and appointed executives is likely to be the difference in the size of the arena in which power is exercised: a cabinet secretary is apt to be treated with more respect by more people than is a county sheriff, although few would want to push either one of them to the borders of their reach.

There are other important differences between the Final Authority and the appointee: loyalty and peer relationships. The appointee *must* be loyal to the Final Authority, but the latter is primarily loyal to himself, and secondarily to the office—which may include loyalty to a particular constituency, or to the electorate in general. Loyalty to those whom he appoints—if it exists—is a distant third. There is, in fact, such a thing as being "too loyal." Many would argue that Jimmy Carter was too loyal to his young aides who had been with him for a long time in Georgia, and that it hurt his ability to understand the Washington world. The same charge has been leveled with equal validity against Ronald Reagan. Keeping faith with someone who serves you may make you a better human being, but it bears no relationship to the exercise of power or your responsibility to office.

Loyalty does not flow entirely down a one-way street in political life, but it certainly follows the current most of the time. Individuals, like organizations, want to maintain themselves. If the subordinate is not loyal, the president may not be reelected and the subordinate will be out of office. This may not always hold true, but an act of disloyalty (for whatever reason) usually has the negative consequence of lessening one's credibility in general. In the political world, which is fraught with uncertainty, loyalty is one of the few measures of a person's worth. Staying loyal is a little bit like doing a favor: it is a chip used to get in the game, or to stay in it. It can also be deposited in the bank against a rainy day when support would be helpful coming the other way. In both the public and the private spheres, loyalty is usually a prerequisite for promotion.

Being loyal and getting on with everyone is not quite the same thing. Battles are always fought on the inside. Jeane Kirkpatrick differentiated between what she referred to as "court politics" and "outside politics:"

There is in the administration what might be called the "politics of personal preferment," if you will. Interpersonal politics. I came to distinguish in my mind between what I think of now as court politics and outside politics ... or, as I thought of it to myself at one stage, as Shakespearean politics and Machiavellian politics [Machiavellian being public and Shakespearean being private, court politics].

Interpersonal politics exist in all organizations, public and private. Issues may be used by one side to attack another, but such abstractions are never what the battle is about. The battle is about power: my right to it versus your attempts to thwart me; my autonomy versus your efforts to control me. In the best of times, these struggles are carried out in the context of opposing positions on issues—forcing each side to improve its positions by making a better case or a better plan of action. In the worst of times, they are revealed in personal attacks which do little but create more enmity.

The second significant difference between powerholders who are final authorities and those who hold power at someone else's pleasure is that the final authorities are less likely to be subject to interpersonal politics, if only because they have no peers inside, and everyone within a government organization is in danger if their leaders fall. No one is ever entirely free of the dangers of envy and personal animosity, but attacks on an office holder are more easily depersonalized as being attacks on the office, and they are more likely to come from outside the organization, enabling the powerholder to mobilize his or her troops as a support group.

In contrast, appointees are like the wagons drawn around the circle to fight the outside battles, but inside—in the inner court—they are constantly jockeying for position among the wagons, a never-ending morality play in progress. Robert Finch described the cabinet officer's lot in relation to would-be or actual powerwielders in the White House this way:

> You can't cut off the heat you get from the White House ... even if they are doing it with slight nibbles and a grimace here or indication there. They can cut you to death in the White House. And every time some unhappy senator or congressman comes in to complain about what you are doing, nobody was defending you over there. That's what really hurts, does more to make you concerned and curtails your effectiveness ... if you don't like to have to run in and reassert your authority on every major issue when you cover so many different areas as it does domestically in my case.
>
> I felt I had to carry.... I was trying to keep the mandate that I thought we had.... trying to hold the country together.

They were tumultuous years, then, the years of Richard Nixon's presidency. We were at war at home and abroad, so it is not surprising, really, to imagine how the Secretary of the largest domestic agency—the one most populated by Democratic liberals who thought of Nixon as an alien president—would be viewed with suspicion in the inner court, even by their own, even when the Secretary was a personal friend of the president's. But Finch made another point about the differences between the Cabinet and the White House that suggests the problem is built into the structure, and not just bound to the times:

> There is a campaign mentality that is never totally erased when you take over the White House. And that's when you get in real trouble, because you can't even deal effectively with your own people. In whichever party you are, you are still trying to keep track of who was with you when you were fighting for the nomination. And some House member, who was maybe supporting your opponent, comes in and—if the old campaign staffers have their way—they're going to cut him off.

The fear of knives coming at you from the rear comes with being the appointed head of an executive agency, although not all presidents have been successful at controlling members of their cabinet, who may jab at them as well. Exercising power, after all, is a skill based on talent, experience, and a desire to wield it. But Finch's point is well taken, and with the right to run your own agency also comes the danger of being cut off by those closer to the throne: the special assistants who are there, in part, to keep you in line, and all those groups and individuals on the outside who have the capacity to go around you to the Final Authority, or, worse yet, to the public—that most final of authorities.

Influence from the Outside: the Rainmakers

There are costs and benefits associated with each side in this equation of powerholder (borrowed or not) and influence broker. We can distinguish the characteristics of each role, but we cannot predict who will be better at one or the other, or whether one role is more satisfying than the other. It is not uncommon for one individual to play both roles several times over the course of a career.

If it is true that most of the people who fall into the category of rainmaker are those who once played the game from the inside as legislators, special assistants, or highly-ranked appointees, it should be noted that rarely will this role be taken by a former elected public executive, although he may be trotted out from time to time to lend legitimacy to an issue. He or she may also occasionally volunteer a view privately, but the principal difference is that the former powerholder will not wield influence as a way of life, a way of making a living. Those who have held the reins tightly are all but incapable of holding them loosely. As Kevin White put it, "there is no afterlife" for those who really hold power. There is for those who wield influence. He described it this way:

> Power is something that you have to learn to handle (and something that becomes part of you, although you may not be conscious of it). And the sign of it is that sometimes they [the powerholders] do the damnedest things because there is no delineation for them in the exercise of it. They can do the most menial things in the exercise of it, like sleeping out on the ground—as a congressman did recently in support of the homeless—or suffer the most ignominious insults like getting spit on in a public demonstration. When you have power . . . it can be demeaning . . . and you can do things that other men, even men of influence would not do in the public arena.

Rainmakers, in contrast to powerholders, rely upon their status, their dignity, their image of established Wise Men. For the most part, they are not "men of the people," who share in the pain and suffering of the downtrodden, nor do they easily take abuse for their troubles. The capacity to be hurt, or even to lose and still survive, rests more with the powerful than with the influence wielders. Rainmakers cannot afford to be seen without the access that defines their power. Harry McPherson described Clark Clifford as the quintessential representative of the breed:

> Clark Clifford has made a great and deserved reputation as a rainmaker and a great counselor, as someone who can bring about a good result in Washington for businessmen clients. He had a particular reputation as someone who was so wired into the Kennedy and Johnson administrations that all things fell before Clifford. I am reasonably sure that Clifford did not ever use his access, or if he did, it was rare—to speak to either president about matters in which one of his clients was involved. . . . I think he gave counsel. I think he carried water for the presidents, as in going to see the steel industry, or going to see automobile manufacturers,

or going all over Asia as Clifford did before he was Secretary of Defense. . . . I am almost certain he would not have risked his access talking about cases.

However, A) his clients didn't know that he would not discuss their case, and B) it didn't really matter because everybody else in the government, and the Justice Department, and so on—knowing that Mr. Clifford was there—just assumed that. . . . By God, if the Secretary of State called them and Clark Clifford called them—you picked up Clifford's |call| first, because he was, after all the President's friend and adviser and helper. And that's power—in the eyes of the beholder. Not really the exercise by Clifford of direct power to go to the president. It is power covered by an aura of intimacy with the great.

The aura of power may be missing in any given situation for the powerholder in a confrontation with another powerholder or a voter, but, according to Kevin White, it is never lost. Those who really hold power continue to hold it until it is gone, and then they "don't look back." They do not seek the role of rainmaker.

The truly powerful, according to the mayor, want it, need it, and use it on the inside, for themselves alone. The rainmaker depends on the outside. If the rainmaker's power rests in the eyes of the beholder, so, too, do his rewards. Influence supports the rainmaker's sense of self-esteem, said one man who often plays the role. Having that opportunity promotes "the approval of the people I want to have approval of—my friends. That is very important. We set our own value system—people whom we consider peers, that is, different from an elected politician who has to consider the voters."

Although more dependent on external values, the rainmaker's audience is a relatively small and carefully measured peer group. The powerholder seeks glory in a wider, far more impersonal world. He has, after all, no peers other than other powerholders.

At times, rainmakers may well have more influence over the course of events than powerholders, but once the image slips, it goes, and the rainmaker may not get the opportunity to "borrow the car" again. One rainmaker described another one this way: "On the day he found out that I had more votes, not only did it not rain, but the sun shone brighter |for me|. Well, from that day on he was no longer considered a rainmaker." Conversely, if the influence wielder is thought of as a "comer," the sun can shine very brightly. Either way, it is a measure of a climate that exists beyond the rainmaker's direct control.

CONCLUSION

There are other differences in the experience of power that move beyond the structural context of the world in which it is exercised. One is the difference between being a representative of either the dominant or the minority cultures of powerholders—i.e., a white male versus either a female or a minority male—and it is the subject of the next chapter. Another, which is not so conveniently catalogued, is the difference in the personality make-up of individuals. Many social scientists who write about power and the individual approach the subject in terms of personality characteristics, such as James David Barber's models of presidential categories—positive, negative, active, passive—with the suggestion that an active/negative president is the most likely to get in trouble.[10] My focus has been on the commonalities of the experience that is found among a variety of individuals, with the assumption that the experience of power has an impact on the sense of identity of the powerholder, regardless of the nature of the individual. The psychological make-up of powerholders is clearly significant, but the external variables which surround them—such as the structures of power—are easier to comprehend and more likely to be shared.

CHAPTER

5

---■---

Men and Women

Despite the fact that power is distributed more widely than it has ever been before, there is still a dominant culture in the land of the powerful that reflects its major population: white males. If power has an impact on the character of those who wield it, and character is at least in part molded by culture, there must be differences in how it affects those who come to it from minority cultures. There are several possibilities: first, that those who accede to power do so because they are like the majority population (or can adopt a similar mien), and therefore power will affect them in a comparable way; or second, that the women and minority males who achieve power retain their sense of difference and are changed in a somewhat different fashion. In all probability, both these propositions are true in some measure for everyone, although it is likely there is a shift in emphasis from individual to individual. A third possibility is that men and women have a different experience of power, and, therefore, wield it differently. One woman I interviewed, for instance, felt uncomfortable with the word "power" and preferred the term "opportunity," because, she said, "it is softer, and the same thing, but power always implies a we/they, kind of up/down, hierarchical status." Opportunity implies both change and intention, but does not presume an emotional relationship with anyone, particularly a relationship that is potentially coercive. Although her view may not be typical of most women who hold power, it is grounded in both recent feminist theory and popular prejudice about the differences between men and women. Some scholars have noted, for instance, that women in power think of it in terms of increased responsibility, rather than something that comes at the top of a pyramid.[1]

EXPECTATIONS

The latter half of the 20th century has been dramatically marked by a focus on equality, and the civil rights and feminist movements have made great strides in bringing acceptance to the notion that these segments of the population ought to have a place in its leadership. Accepting the idea and living the experience, however, are not quite the same thing. Every woman I interviewed said she attained success because she was lucky: "I just happened to be in the right place at the right time." Did they plan careers? No. Very few people do—including men—but the women were even more vague in terms of their expectations. Younger women are more apt to think of themselves as having both a successful career and a family, but those who fall into that category are still too young to have attained much power. I would define the turning point in attitudes as that period— coming after the first round of the feminist movement in the late 1960s and early 1970s—when co-ed dormitories in colleges began to emerge because they fostered more diverse relationships between the young men and women who found themselves in complex companion or sibling relationships, rather than just in sexual relationships. It seems to be a small thing, but most of the women I have interviewed in the past several years spoke of the 1970s and the emergence of co-ed dorms as the period of demarkation between the attitudes of the recent generations of professional women and men.

The possibility of alternative roles and relationships notwithstanding, sex-role expectations come exceedingly early. Changing them later is the result of a conscious decision. At some point, most women who attain power say to themselves, "I will seek a career, an identity in my own right that is not bound to the success of a husband." It is still the case that most of the women in America who have power inherited it. Although I interviewed women who made it on their own, I suspect the differences between them are not very great. No matter how high you start, most women still expect to "marry up," to find a mate who is older, richer, smarter, and just generally more powerful. The actual patterns change, of course, but the expectations we start out with as children remain potent.

Expectations of power are tied to expectations of identity. Although women expect less in terms of personal success in the world, we have a much wider choice than do men. A man's identity in American society is defined by his title and the amount of money he makes. A woman's identity is more complex and she is far more likely than he to have a separate life to which she wants to return outside of the office. Women, according to Shirley Williams, "are less dependent on institutions for the human element in their lives:

It is quite evident to me that very many men—even those who are reasonably happy men—actually get their emotional satisfactions out of their relationships with their colleagues in their place of work—whether it is Congress, the office, or the corporate boardroom. Their network is, you know, who I golf with on the corporate board. Who do I have a drink with after the board meeting is over. Many men have that [at] the center of their existence and are destroyed by their retirement from their employment. . . . I look at corporate culture as one in which it is men who almost don't want to go home; and women, who, generally speaking, have many reasons for wanting to go home, really do live two interspersed lives. Marriage is an attachment like a kind of caboose at the end of the train for the traditional corporate male.

Since the expectations of a woman's achieving power are so low, whatever power she may attain is considered a plus. Although this measure is changing in some circles more than others, a woman still has the option to be successful without a career. On my thirty-third birthday I announced to my mother that at my age, Mozart, Alexander the Great, and Christ were dead, and I had yet to conquer the world. "Yes, dear," my mother said, "and you aren't married and don't have any children either."

There are changes. Single women are not automatically counted as failures. Married women, and women with children, are not automatically sure they have done all that they could. Women can make choices about careers and families, although I think "choice" is not the precisely correct description since the options rarely appear clearly marked, or even occur at the same time. Still, while almost all of the possibilities are acceptable—with varying degrees of comfort for everyone involved—the reality for women is that we do not absolutely need to succeed in the professional world, we do not need to make a great deal of money. Men do.

A 1986 study of women in the corporate world, by Nehama Jacobs and Sarah Hardesty, suggested that many women who seek success in the world find it less rewarding than they thought it would be. "Women make the mistake of thinking they can find identity and self-esteem by attaching themselves to prestigious corporations," said Nehana Jacobs in an interview. "Myths about the work world have created a romanticized view of the corporation and the possibilities it offers. . . . When the corporate mystique fails to live up to its billing, there is a subsequent sense of loss and betrayal."[2] Those who "make it to the top" are asked to give up almost everything to the corporation, including outside interests, relationships, and children.[3] Such sacrifice is anything but empowering.

It would be naive to think the costs of success to women do not lead to a certain amount of resentment, but it is not something that can necessarily be resolved by choice. Shifts in the expectations of women have been well documented by sociologists and by the popular magazines: the generation of women who came of age at the height of the women's movement believed they could "have it all." In a few years, being "superwomen" began to be recognized as an extraordinary undertaking, and many opted out by leaving the market to raise children, or by dropping out of corporate competition to start their own businesses. What these women are opting for is power over their own lives—the power to be boss that is denied them in larger firms.

Anne Wexler, in fact, defined power as having control over her own life, and when she measured herself against her male colleagues in the business, she did not think they held the same aspirations:

> I look around me and see the men who are my age . . . and I see them with a lot of pressure on them, and how much time they spend away from their families, and how intensely motivated they are—running all the time—appraising, competitive—all this other stuff. And I think to myself, I never want to be like that. Maybe there is something wrong with me. I don't care if my business is the biggest business in town. I made a decision about what I want to do in terms of lifestyle, and for me, I am able to do it. . . . Not everybody is.

If there is a major difference in the expectations of power between men and women—and if there is a choice—it is that women seek control over their lives more than they seek money. Men start out with marginally more control over their lives, so their sense of self is often measured in relation to other things: success over others, and income—which is also to say more money than others, since wealth, too, is a relative thing. It is also possible that women with power expect to be associated with men who have money. In any case—for women—money may be easier to attain than power, although everything is relative, and obviously a base line of economic security comes first.

This focus on money and power in identity is a peculiarly American characteristic. Other societies are more inclined to include class and family in the formula that determines one's place in the world. The size, complexity, and mobility of life in the United States combine with our egalitarian ethic to lessen the impact of these two traditional determinants. In more religious times, Protestant America would have said that these outward signs of success were a measure of inward grace. Class and family still count, of course, but we are less finicky about holding to it in the face of either great wealth or power. We are almost as snobbish as anyone else, abut retain a genuine respect for success. It may be that money is valued partly because it is such a measurable assessment of worth—as are titles—and in that respect it may not be irrelevant that most of the achievements traditionally associated with women are neither measurable nor unambiguous

THE EXPERIENCE OF POWER

Because there are differences in expectations of life's chances, there are different reactions to the experience of power between men and women. There are different fears and rewards, different relationships and needs, and different styles of behavior.

Different Fears

Having power makes men "manly," and although there is something of the aphrodisiac effect of power no matter who holds it, it does not make women "womanly." "Manly," for instance, is a synonym for brave according to Roget's Thesaurus, as is "strong" and "noble."[4] In the early days of the women's movement, the image of power was somewhat in conflict with the image of femininity, and was an issue of concern to the women who were moving up in organizations. "Will I be lovable?" was a typical question. It is still a question to the extent that a professional woman must maintain a feminine identity (exclusive of being a sex object), and there are still relatively few models of women with power. Power, as a factor in identity, was—and is—measured unfavorably with regard to women as women, and favorably with regard to men. One still hears the complimentary, "You think just like a man." Clearly, thinking like a woman is still presumed to be less estimable.

If having power is a threat to a woman's sense of femininity, not having power is threatening to a man's sense of masculinity. His sexuality does not get called into question automatically, however, unless he has a woman boss (or is afraid of having a woman boss). Remembering that we are concerned only with those who have power (and recognizing that most people do not have it), it has remained generally true that having power reinforces a masculine image and threatens a feminine image.

The image might be different for women were we not so clearly aliens in the land of the powerful. The women who do hold power are so few in number in any given organization that they tend to be tokens, and as such they fall prey to stereotyped expectations about their behavior. The same is true of any minority in a dominant culture. The tendency to view women and minority participants in power as stereotypes has the added dimension of encouraging the individual woman or minority person to play the role. It is an easy way to find a niche in a group, and it works for everybody involved.[5] It is a familiar way to interact with others, sometimes even to think of one's self, but it is hardly the path to take to reach one's best potential. Since most stereotypical characteristics tend to be negative, stereotyping has an insidious impact on the individuals involved: men are described as being competitive, women as being aggressive; men are forceful, women are bossy.

Mindful of the interpretations, women with power are careful. Everyone in power needs to protect their position, but women also have to protect themselves against a variety of charges regarding their gender, ranging from a fear of losing their sense of femininity to the fear of alienating others, particularly other women. As one woman noted after a long career:

I've always felt that if I talked issues in a mixed group I would be talking to the husbands and ignoring the wives. I have always been conscious that women could consider me a threat and I have been careful to eschew husbands. I tried hard to be safe.

Sheila Widnall, an aeronautics engineer at the Massachusetts Institute of Technology, told a newspaper reporter that she "considers it dicey for a professional woman to expose too much of her personal life to view," and acknowledges that in her dealings with others she uses humor to "get them into a good mood."[6] Such guarded behavior may not be required of all women in power all of the time, but neither is it uncommon.

It appears to be a peculiarity of human nature to accept that those who are not like us are either better or worse. If the dominant culture is white and male, any non-white and non-male (with whom women can identify and feel equal) who moves into the elite world is subject to resentment from other women because "she is no better than me." Any differences in talent, education, energy, commitment, and experience are minimized in explaining why the less fortunate member of the group has not also risen. The late Esther Westerfelt, a sociologist who studied the early influence of the feminist movement in the late 1960s, noted that when housewives were interviewed, they typically hoped their daughters would have a better life than they had, but not too much better—because too much of an improvement would reflect on themselves and on their inability to affect their own lives.

A corollary of this evaluation of women in power is that if the powerful woman is perceived to have failed—or to be in danger of failing—there is an additional fear that the consequences will fall upon all women. It is for that reason, some scholars have argued, that women are harsher than men in their criticism of women in positions of power.[7]

The sense of sisterhood and brotherhood specifically promoted by the feminist and civil rights movements has gone a long way toward alleviating some of the resentment. But while token leaders may be conscious of being role models, they know they may also be subject to the envy of those who would emulate them. Most of the women I spoke to say they make a point of promoting other women and of encouraging them to raise their career expectations. I suspect, however, that such altruism is an image easier to hold about one's self than to project to others, at least to those inclined to be envious. The powerful speak to the powerless across a chasm in the best of circumstances. If it is difficult to communicate commands, it is almost impossible to communicate intentions, especially those that offer an unexpected good.

Envy is a problem I have seen occur over and over again: younger women who mistake an egalitarian demeanor for equality; who see the similarities, and not the differences between themselves and those above them. Part of it is the disillusionment that comes with familiarity in any power-laden relationship, and is something to which men as well as women are subject. A male attorney spoke of his idol in the law firm in which he first started out:

> I was totally captivated by the senior partner in the firm. I could attribute to him absolutely no flaws or faults. And he used to say to me, "Stop pedestalizing me." He said, "I have feet of clay," and I wondered why he was telling me all this. He said, "When you find out, you are going to be equally harsh in your judgment of me as you are now in your idolatry of me." And that's exactly what happened.

It is easier to analyze envy than it is to contend with it. It comes from insecurity, from fears that go back to earliest experience. It is a "nasty human emotion and there is nothing you can do about it," Betty Friedan once said to me. For those who achieve power and who become subject to the envy of others, it is a difficult thing with which to cope, because it is clothed in disguise and hides in the shade out of the limelight. It attacks men as well as women, but because women in power are so few and so visible, they are obvious targets. It is difficult because the powerholder trains her guns on the borders of her realm, pushing out the boundaries in the interest of getting the job done, fighting for turf among peers. Protecting against envy requires posting guards in the rear and keeping your eye on the dissatisfactions of your subordinates. It is difficult because it is unexpected and reflects anger where you thought there was none. Envious persons rarely exhibit hostility directly to the object of their concern. They pretend friendship, and hide their attacks behind rules and in the behavior of others.

At least one scholar who has studied these relationships has found that women are far more likely to feel that they have been unethically dealt with by other women than men are to feel they have been unethically dealt with by other men. The statistical difference is an astounding margin of 52 percent. While 48 percent of the men studied viewed the unethical treatment they received from women to be intentional, 62 percent of the women thought the unethical treatment they received from other women was intentional. This data, however, should be tempered with the next conclusion, that while only 15 percent of the men thought the unethical treatment they received from other men was intentional, 80 percent of the women thought the unethical treatment they received from men was intended.[8] It would be improbable to assume that such large proportions of working women misread the intentions of their colleagues, both male and female.

Having suffered from attacks of envy by other women, I find it hard to accept Friedan's view that it is beyond control, or at least beyond containment. I know, for instance, that confronting it helps, although one may not always know whom to confront, or have the opportunity to do the confronting. One woman who has had the opportunity said it has happened to her a number of times in her professional life:

> I've always confronted it and I don't know if it's ever been
> satisfying to the other people. . . . There have been lots of
> situations when somebody has said to me, "Well, you're getting
> this and I'm getting that." It always has been an unequal world . . .
> and my answer is that I'm twenty years older. It just doesn't come
> automatically. You just can't be me if you haven't done what I've
> done . . . if you think you are getting a raw deal. If I want to go
> away for a month and you can't—that's because I'm me and you
> are not.

The key, of course, is understanding and recognizing insecurity in others. A longtime Washington observer explained why he thought women were likely to be more vulnerable to attacks motivated by the insecurity of other women:

My wife and I have had this discussion many times. For males—I can't really talk about females—for males, it begins in the sandlots. If you have the shit beaten out of you by a gang, or a couple of guys, and come up and stand up again—somehow or other—there is respect. In those locker-rooms when you are in junior high school and high school—and it can get vile and crude, and certainly rough—"Hey, your penis isn't very big," to "Why did you make an error in the ballgame today?"—All of it can be devastating to the ego, but if you can handle that, then later on what happens in a meeting, what happens in a law firm—nothing. And women don't treat each other that way. They do it behind their backs. . . .

Learning to handle the envy of others is part of the experience of power common to everyone. That women in power are particularly at risk may be because women are not raised in sandlots and do not participate in the same locker-room banter boys do, but are instead raised to be nice and not to confront others, clothing hostility in other garb. Feminist psychologists have pointed to the "massive" cultural prohibition against women's anger. In a symposium sponsored by the *Boston Globe Magazine* in 1985, Jean Baker Miller noted that anger is "always declared pathological for women. . . . It's been intolerable. Nobody wants oppressed groups to be angry."[9]

Differences in Attitudes About Deference

Those who seek power because they want to distinguish themselves from others, want and need a different experience from those who seek power for the opportunity to change something or make others happy. Although the former motive does not describe all men, nor the latter all women, there are indications of differing gender preferences. The difference is manifested in attitudes about deference. While deference is part of the recognition of power for men, many women view it with a measure of distrust. If we can accept the notion that deference is a concomitant of power—perhaps its most visible attribute—the difference in reactions to it reflects a very deep difference in attitudes about power. The nature of the difference has some bearing on how men and women experience power, and what it means to them in terms of their own identities in the long run.

The uneasiness many women feel about deference is based on two things: at the most obvious and superficial level, it is a rejection of something that women achieve only slowly and with great difficulty; and secondly, the behavior that is characteristic of a deferential relationship runs deeply against the grain of a woman's sense of morality because it is divisive.

Deference is a formal recognition of status, but women are usually treated informally. Even when we are let into the room, we are addressed by our first names while men are referred to by their last names. We are expected to "get the coffee" (and all that entails), while men expect to be served. It usually takes a woman longer to achieve power than her male colleagues, during which time she is very well aware of the greater obstacles she faces compared to men. Power is not hers by birthright. It must be taken, and, usually, the rewards are harder to come by: we are likely to be paid less; promoted more slowly; and find it significantly more difficult to be recognized. Study after study shows that women have a harder time being heard: a woman's ideas are often attributed to others; we are interrupted more often when speaking; etc., etc. The patterns represented in the statistics of these studies have an intellectual abstraction to them that does not come close to the recognition of their reality when one is obviously slighted, or overtly ignored in a setting that matters.

Women in power are also less likely to be married. A recent survey of college presidents, for instance, reveals that 93 percent of men, but only 49 percent of women presidents, were married (excluding nuns, priests, and other members of religious orders).[10] A similar *Wall Street Journal/* Gallup Survey finds that 42 percent more women executives are likely to be single or divorced than the national average. Of those under forty, 72 percent are single or divorced, and almost a third of these do not plan to have children:

> The most senior women are the least likely to be married, and the divorce rate is highest among the age group with the highest status: one-fourth of the women aged 40–44 are now divorced or separated. Less than half (48 percent) of female corporate executives have had children, and fewer than 3 in 10 now have a child at home.[11]

Society, in every sense of the term, is structured around the notion of couples and families. Unmarried women, more than unmarried men, do not fit the norm, and even though many successful women say they have had to choose between a career and a family, there is still an air of expectation, of instability and unfulfillment in their status, that is reflected in a subtle but real diminution of status. The unmarried woman who is not performing the traditional (to say nothing of genetic) role of nurturant is not deemed virtuous, in the Aristotelian meaning of the term: she is not behaving according to her nature. I am not suggesting that women resent the role of nurturant, but rather that we are aware that it is something expected of women in almost every circumstance, and not expected of men, unless there is a power relationship involved where one is clearly superior to another. In the artificial nature of modern complex societies, however, assumptions about one's nature can be misplaced.

There is a third drawback to the unmarried status, which is that when the marriage is successful, the spouse of either sex provides support for the powerholder in a number of ways: emotional; physical in terms of the chores of daily living; and, often, an enhancement of economic strength and standing.

The negative feelings of exclusion aside, it is quite probable that there is a much deeper ethic at work that leads to different attitudes about deference. It seems likely that if women value inclusiveness and relationships, deference represents separation and isolation. Deference, in other words, embodies just the opposite of the feminine sense of morality.

The compelling argument in favor of this view of an alternate morality was made by Carol Gilligan, a professor at the Harvard Graduate School of Education, who published an important book in 1982, entitled In a Different Voice, dealing with differences in moral development between men and women.[12] It is based on a psychoanalytic proposition that identity is formed in males by a separation from the mother, and in females in relationship to and continuity with the mother. The consequence for later development is that women value relationships and happiness as the highest good, and men value the equitable distribution of power. Male justice is based on the "vision that self and other will be treated as of equal worth, that despite differences in power, things will be fair;" while the vision of female justice is that "everyone will be responded to and included, that no one will be left alone or hurt."[13]

By extrapolating from Gilligan's theory, it is possible to understand the world of power in bureaucratic organizations as a male culture. They are designed to distribute power, if not equitably to the extent that everyone has an equal amount, at least fairly, to the extent that everyone recognizes its boundaries, they are limited by rules of behavior (standard operating procedures) and a linear incremental possession: those above have more, and those below have less. If women hold a conflicting value dear, it seems likely that differences in behavior are inevitable. According to Gilligan, "women not only define themselves in a context of human relationships but also judge themselves in terms of their ability to care."[14] It is not just opposition, but an alternative value of inclusiveness that suggests we consider exclusiveness immoral.

It is that sense of immorality, combined with the detrimental impact of its uses against us, that leads most women I interviewed to say that the deference they were accorded was a false thing: "It is not me, it is the position," or "I don't really like people to defer. I never did. It's not natural to me. I think that maybe one could get corrupted by this if one stayed long enough."

Resistance by women to deference becomes a complex defense whose object is to retain one's identity, one's sense of dignity in the face of breaking with tradition, and perhaps, in the long run, a step toward imposing or at least validating another kind of morality, another code of ethics that values inclusive relationships instead of ordered affiliations. I suspect that whether the uneasiness with deference is due to the problems of attainment, or the valuing of other kinds of relationships, it breeds hostility (however covert or unconscious) toward the dominant culture that does the excluding. It is likely that any group would denigrate that which is used to keep it out, and deference is the most visible expression of that exclusion for women. This unacknowledged guerrilla war may be part of the unspoken cause of the hostility by men toward the notion of women in positions of power. Carla Singer, a former television network vice president, described the culture of her world and the male attitude toward women this way:

> My theory is they are never going to invite us in. The only way you are going to get in is through legislation. And if it's legislated, and if there is enough interest, they'll get used to it. I mean the guys at ——— got used to it. If they wanted to go and huddle, they did it in the men's room. They didn't in front of me. But there was no reason for them to invite me in. I understand that. . . .
>
> Sure, in middle management it's great because everyone is working their way up. Everything is less threatening because he knows *she's* not going to get to the top.

A woman from the world of government spoke of the fact that she was frequently the only woman in the room:

> I never saw another woman at very high levels. I do believe that there is *enormous* resistance to women at top levels. The trouble is I can't prove it. And I mean "resistance." I don't necessarily mean dislike, much less hate. Just resistance. That's mainly what I

encountered. Including amongst the people with whom I have very good relationships—good working relationships.

These complex attitudes about deference form a mutually reinforcing phenomenon. A consequence of the resistance is that women downplay the values of the culture that excludes us. Jeane Kirkpatrick, who, besides her experience as a member of the Reagan foreign policy establishment, is a political scientist who has studied the issues of women and power, speculated about the issue this way:

> I think it goes with the fact that we don't quite fit. The roles don't quite fit us, and we don't quite fit the roles. And because we are never wholly defined or contained by established role structures, we are thought of as "loose guns." And this is probably one of the reasons that women in positions of authority are not entirely welcome in any bureaucracy.

It is not a specific "role" that we do not fit—a job description of the Secretary of State, for instance—but rather the complex of roles within a job: the interactions of roles defined by power relationships.

There is a tendency today, in both men and women, to say that it is a healthy thing to recognize that deference fosters an artificial environment. Perhaps it is a subversive tendency, reflecting the true impact of feminine morality in the real world; whatever the source, the assumption is that adopting an attitude of disdain makes it easier to stay in touch with your own identity, and it certainly eases the transition out of power back to the world of private identity.

There are times in our history when we appear to be especially sensitive to the dangers of power, such as in the mid-1970s after Watergate. In contrast to the "imperial presidency" of Nixon, we took heart in the homeyness of Gerald Ford making his own breakfast, and Jimmy Carter carrying his own luggage. A story in a similar vein was told by Thomas Dine, a longtime Washington observer who used to work for Senator Frank Church. He said that the Senator went to Israel in 1972, when Golda Meir was Prime Minister, and was scheduled to have tea at her home:

> She welcomed him to her apartment. Once inside, the Prime Minister asked the Senator and his party, "How many teas, coffees, and juice? You must have orange juice." At that point, she took everyone's order. Church was somewhat mystified. He had expected her to reach for a button on or under the table to ring for servants. Instead, she went into the kitchen. He began hearing the clinking of cups and the hissing of a boiling water kettle. So, he

went into the kitchen. He couldn't believe it: the Prime Minister was making him and the others tea and coffee! She looked up at him half quizzically, "What can I do for you, Senator?" He said, "Madam Prime Minister, let me help you." She said, "I've got it all ready. But, Senator, there are other ways you can help."

The story is charming and significant, reflecting both the egalitarian behavior of the Prime Minister and the greater emphasis on egalitarianism in general in Israel, especially within the Labor Party, which always made a point, for instance, of having its leaders go about without ties. The disarming intimacy and informality of the tea-making cuts through the layers of formal difference and status, without giving away any of her power—and it was probably intentional. The Jewish grandmotherly role, Golda Meir chose to play was certainly more characteristic of the way women in power behave. It was not unlike, for instance, Jeane Kirkpatrick's response to the personal danger of the Arab U.N. ambassador. While ignoring the traditional lines that separate persons engaged in a power relationship, it actually brings more power to the individuals involved because it is based, ultimately, on a humanity that transcends cultural differences, enabling them to reach an understanding on one level that opens the way for action on the problems before them.

While the differences in attitude between men and women about deference are a reflection of differing attitudes about power, it is clear that many individual women and minority group members who succeed to power do so by behaving more like the dominant white male culture, even while retaining reservations about that culture if they are going to be true to themselves. We are also familiar with the opposite case, of course, when the successful individual identifies so strongly with the dominant culture that he or she rejects the minority background and values. It is the zealotry of the convert, found in responses like: There are no barriers; we are our own worst enemies, and so on. These attitudes are also defenses, but I suspect they are not as healthy as the more directed anger of the alternative approach of maintaining a distance from the culture. Distance, at the very least, provides perspective.

Regardless of the causes and the nature of the defense, there are consequences to the different attitudes toward deference held by men and women. Women are more inclined to measure power by the ability to "get the job done," whether or not we hold a title. We are more apt to accept lower status positions at the entry level, believing that it will be easier to move up once we have a foot in the door. We are, in other words, more flexible with regard to the perks of office, from salary and title to all of the other accoutrements associated with deference, from office furniture to inclusion in the fun and games of life at the top. Not without some resentment, I might add, but women are certainly more apt to accept power under these limited conditions than to risk being excluded altogether. And they are certainly more likely than men to acquiesce to this second-class treatment and, perhaps ultimately, second-class power.

The question remains as to whether power under reduced circumstances is still power, or still as much power? Is it getting the job done? Or is it being acknowledged as the person who gets the job done? Clearly, it is a bit of both, but the more you distance yourself from the embodiment of the role the less likely it is that you will have an impact on it, or that the power will have an impact on you. This has both positive and negative consequences, depending on the individual, the situation, and the objectives.

Different Organizational Styles

Carol Gilligan describes two markedly different interpretations of hierarchies. The male perspective sees it as a web wherein "each image marks as dangerous the place which the other defines as safe. . . . the wish to be alone at the top and the consequent fear that others will get too close." In contrast, from the female perspective it is "the wish to be at the center of connection and the consequent fear of being too far out on the edge." She argues that these "disparate fears of being stranded and being caught give rise to different portrayals of achievement and affiliation, leading to different modes of action and different ways of assessing the consequences of choice."[15]

Women in power are apt to ignore the linear paths of power, and to behave in a more collegial manner with those above and below, as well as horizontally. One woman described her behavior this way:

> If I wasn't satisfied that it was really going right—that I was getting all the data I need—I would pick up the phone and call the people that I knew were actually doing the research and writing the memoranda on the issue, and put the questions to them that I knew—that I thought we didn't quite have the right answers to. Which is to say to cut into eight or ten levels of bureaucracy, instead of asking the deputy, who asks the counsel, you know, who asks the division chief, who asks the ———— by which time, you've probably lost the question entirely. Like the game of gossip. And I would go directly—as a person—to the person who is doing the

research, and put my question and get an answer and have a response. That's a terrible violation of the bureaucratic role.

Sociologist Jean Lipman-Blumen describes the difference between the way women and men use power as that between "macromanipulation" and "micromanipulation," suggesting that the former comes about because women are excluded from the dominant male power culture and are left no alternative but to seek our ends through "the use of interpersonal behaviors and practices to influence, if not control the balance of power." Restricted to informal relationships, women "'become well versed in interpreting the unspoken intentions, even the body language of the powerful. . . . By various interpersonal strategies of micromanipulation, women have learned to sway and change, circumvent, and subvert the decisions of the powerful to which they have seemingly acquiesced."[16]

I am not suggesting this behavior is entirely sex-linked and never associated with men, but rather that it is more typical of women. The argument can be made, for instance, that the surreptitious behavior of Oliver North revealed in the Iran/Contra scandal was exactly thus: avoiding normal bureaucratic channels in the interests of getting things done. The charge against him was that, by ignoring normal channels of communication, he voided the safeguards built into the structures (i.e, the rules of behavior that protect both individuals and organizations). Bypassing the standard distribution of power can be a potent strategy for success, but it is akin to guerrilla warfare. It also comes more naturally to women, focusing as it does on achieving an end by including all of the necessary players and excluding the formal distribution of power.

Another woman described the pattern of maintaining relationships, without expectations of using them for political ends:

> I was very friendly with—not my immediate boss—but his boss. . . .
> It had nothing to do with politics, but my boss perceived it as
> politics. Women I don't think do. He'd [my boss's boss] stop by my
> office and we'd chat, and we'd talk about his kids. The other guy
> thought it was a political thing. . . . Men are very devious though,
> and very into games.

The charge of deviousness could be leveled by both sides, because she *might* have used the relationship for political ends, but the point is that what was a "natural" thing for her to do, was "unnatural" to him.

These are individual examples drawn from thousands of interactions a powerholder is apt to have every day. Most of the time, I think, most powerholders conform to the norm, but when there is deviation, women are more likely to behave in ways that run counter to the formal structures of power in bureaucratic hierarchies. The question is, what are the consequences of these different styles for the individual women and for the organizations, assuming that men are more apt to follow the patterns of what can be thought of as male structures?

There are often tremendous benefits that accrue to those individuals who do not follow the traditional lines of authority because they can bring more resources to bear on their goals. In the short run, at least, they can create a sense of excitement and involvement, particularly in those lower down in the organizational pyramid who do not normally get an opportunity to participate with their superiors. They can usually "get the job done," if it is specific enough, and time-bound. I am not sure, however, that these short cuts through the power structure can be sustained over a long period of time in a strict bureaucracy, partly because those who are overlooked will eventually move to get back in, and partly because those lower down will seek to move up (using their participation as a reason), or at least become an accepted part of the power progression.

I had some experience with the approach on a short-term basis when in the early 1970s, I created the women's programs in what was then the Department of Health, Education and Welfare. My position was even lower than that of usual special assistant: I was an intern in the office of the Assistant Secretary for Planning and Evaluation, although I was later hired as a consultant and held the title of Director of the Women's Action Program. I was perceived to be a protégé of the then Secretary of the Department, Elliot Richardson, which gave me much more clout than any legal title to the job, but I was constantly coming up against the prerogatives of those above me in the hierarchy, which could have been critical—and perhaps was in the long run; but for the year or so I ran the program, it worked well. Knowing that I was something of an anomaly in the Nixon administration (being a Kennedy Democrat and a student activist), I had much more leeway because everyone knew that I was temporary. Once I was gone, the program was emasculated (an appropriate, if somewhat ironic choice of words under the circumstances), and eventually put to death. While it lived, and while there was some institutional memory in the government of how it worked, I was often hired as a consultant by other agencies to explain how to bring about change in the government.

It is likely that the success I had with it was, at least in part, due to the fact of its being an experiment, and in part to the imagery of power linkages. My successor went down in flames by trying to demonstrate a similar association with the Secretary. Whereas I relied on news stories of Secretary Richardson's interests and saw him only occasionally (and after all, who would come to write about a women's program in those days but supportive women who were chained to the women's sections of newspapers), my successor followed him everywhere. There were other problems as well, but the conclusion I draw now—long after the tempers have died down—is that the loose gun strategy worked quite well in the short term, but had inherent dangers for the long run. The system, after all, finally managed to get Oliver North.

One of the most critical factors, in terms of organizational response to women and minorities, is how many individuals in the out-group are in positions of power in the organization. Tokenism is insufficient to change the dominant culture. One-third membership of a minority in a dominant culture appears to be the necessary minimum for that minority to have influence, and there are very few significant institutions in American life that come close to or exceed that ratio.[17] Anything less than a one-third/two-thirds ratio seems to encourage the sense of tokenism, stereotypical attitudes and behavior, and a sense of alienation or not-belonging. Anything surpassing the ratio decreases other reactions, and, common sense would suggest, leads to adjustments in organizational style.

Different Relationships/Different Needs

Given the statistics on the marital status of women in power, it is not surprising that all of the women I interviewed were either not married, or they had unusually supportive husbands. In some instances, they were "commuter marriages," and came together only on weekends. Anne Wexler, who lives and works in Washington, for example, described her marriage to Joseph Duffy, the Chancellor of the University of Massachusetts in Amherst, this way:

> One of the reasons I have such a satisfying life is because I have a supportive husband. There's never been a time since Joe and I have been together that he hasn't been the biggest booster I have and vice versa....
> I have the perfect life with my husband in Massachusetts. I don't have any pressures. If I want to work until 10:00 at night, I don't have to worry about cooking dinner or going out to dinner. If I'm tired I don't have any pressures, I don't have to talk to anyone. And if he's out at night, he doesn't have any pressures about worrying about me waiting for him....

I think most women don't have those kinds of structures, so you have to think about what you are going to do if you're married and you want a career. You have to make choices. You have to choose to be able to be sure your kids are going to be all right, and you have to choose not to climb into bed with a book if that's what you like.

In contrast, she mentioned a friend of hers who is the chief of staff to a governor:

She's essentially more of a policy person herself, and a politician, and she's running the whole show and doing a fabulous job. . . . But she goes home and says to her husband "How was your day?" And his answer is "Screw you, you were in the news again!" He's the Last Angry Man. . . . Here is a guy who is challenged in terms of his own success, and he can't stand his wife.

He may be the last angry man, but he is not alone. Handling the stress of a powerful job and having to face stress at home is difficult for either gender, but if the very fact of success for a woman is going to cause stress for her spouse—and thereby herself—it requires a serious reordering of her priorities and values as well as his, especially if his sense of masculinity is at all tied to his standing in the world relative to his wife's.

Micho Spring was Deputy Mayor of Boston in Kevin White's last term in the late 1970s. Her husband, William, worked in the Carter White House in Washington. Unlike the Duffeys, whose children by earlier marriages were grown, the Springs had a small child. It was not an easy arrangement, but having arranged for live-in child-care, it permitted both parents the luxury of working late during the week.

As for the women who were not married, their prospects for relationships were seriously constrained. As one television executive noted, she had a list of escorts, but no man in the industry wanted to get involved with her lest he need to do business with her later on. "I used to have a list," she said, "in that kind of a book—of all the single guys to take with me to functions." There are, of course, other restraints: enough time to meet someone; the danger of overpowering a man by her accomplishments; the time to maintain a relationship should one, by chance, ever develop.

The biggest problem is not logistical, it is the power. It is part of our cultural heritage to expect the man in the relationship to be the stronger. Perhaps it is more than culture and reaches to biology, but I am not about to speculate on the physical evidence. Power is not the same thing as brute strength, even if there is a correlation.

Everyone who works feels the need of a wife: someone to clean the house; prepare the meals; take care of the social obligations, including the raising of children, and be supportive when all the world seems hostile. Most women who are very successful can at least find domestic help; if not, they tend not to be very successful for very long.

The feminists have held to choice as their primary objective. Women should not have to head firms, *or* stop being housewives: *women do have to have the opportunity to decide which role they want to play, and the same opportunity as a man to play both.* Clearly, however, having the goal and being able to attain it are two different things.

Women who attain power are conscious of the routes they took and very aware of the pitfalls. They typically worked harder than their male colleagues to be recognized in the first place. They are wary of sexual innuendo in relationships above and below them. They are wary of arousing the envy of other women (both in the workplace and outside). They are consciously caught in the conflict of appearing to be just like the boys, and one of the girls. It is the catch between "thinking like a man" and still being "feminine." A sexual identity is required of women, but it is not required of men.

An interesting question we might ask ourselves concerns the consequences of being so aware of the land mines lurking along the way. I have seen resentment in those who fail to succeed—women who have trained younger men to rise above them again and again, who become so frustrated and angry at the system that they lose the flexibility to raise themselves above the emotion, the sense of unfairness. But what of those who succeed? How do they handle themselves in a world in which they have had to submerge their identities, to put on a costume and play a part?

It is a reasonable question, but the answer is hard to find. Those who become too angry do not rise. Those who can put on the clothes of the dominant culture may bear it less malice. Many believe there is no discrimination, and all it takes is hard work and dedication. They need to believe that, because the alternative is too difficult to accept: that the world is unfair and threatening; that their success is itself aberrational; that they are different from everyone else.

Although almost everyone (especially women) says they succeeded because they were lucky—they just happened to be in the right place at the right time—it is usually true, but it is not something anyone wants to put too much stock in because it destroys the notion of self-determination. On the one hand, we are caught in our desire to control our lives, and on the other, we need to believe that we are both alike and different from everyone else.

Another element in the capacity of women to rise in the male world of power is the more insidious nature of the sex-role segregation of tasks. It has come to us partly as the issue of "comparable worth," i.e., that the jobs women are likely to perform are equal in value to better-paying jobs held by men: teachers earning less than garbage collectors, for example. Another facet of the same issue is the tendency to devalue the volunteer work of women while valuing the "civic" activity of men. Before her appointment to the United Nations, Jeane Kirkpatrick studied women in state legislatures. In comparing the research to her own experience she had this to say:

> I had not really thought specifically of the uses of power as one more example of how relevant the experience in traditional roles even is to the performance of a variety of public tasks and public roles. I became very much aware in writing *Political Women* in looking at the background of those legislators. . . .[18]
>
> In thinking about those days and those women, I was struck by how relevant that community activist and volunteer route is to public life. How many of the tasks, including administration and organization of people, and mobilization, and follow-through are required there. But I never really thought—until I went to the U.N. myself—about how much and how many of the learned skills of family—including and especially handling of power—are to the role.

It is easy to see how much our expectations influence our perceptions. It is much more difficult to alter either expectations or perceptions.

Responding to Pressure

The need to cope with pressure exists in many lives and lifestyles, but almost always comes with the territory of power. At the risk of generalization—and with only a touch of facetiousness—I think that when the pressure gets too great, some men (those who are inclined to handle it badly) are apt to respond in an aberrational sexual manner, while women are apt to shop. Both responses are related to identity: assuring yourself that you exist, that you are powerful—or, in a woman's case—that you can look good, that you are feminine. Both behaviors are akin to feeding one's self, taking care of yourself when others have failed to take care of you.

The sexual scandals that emerge from time to time at the top are shocking, not just because less powerful men never do the kinds of things men of power are caught doing, but because they seem so risky. Why does a powerful congressional committee chairman risk everything by chasing after a strip tease artist, or a prostitute? Why do some men in power behave like public utilities, available to any woman who comes near them? These encounters are not romantic relationships, they are sexual. More than that, they are about anger and aggression. In the deepest sense, they are about power: conquest, possession, dominance. Whether the women respond because they are paid to, or because they are attracted to the power, does not lessen or alter the motivation of the male.

As for women, we laugh at the shoes in Imelda Marcos' closet, or the clothes and other objects bought by Tammy Faye Baker. Clearly, these women could have gotten by with less; why did they need to go quite so far? Forty years ago, Hollywood films promoted the notion that female characters would go out shopping for a hat when things got rough. It may well have been a true portrayal of the upper-class woman's behavior. It certainly meets my objective of coming face to face with one's self in the mirror and working on improving the image!

The scandals reveal something of the underlying nature of things. We do not hear very often of powerful women seducing every male they can, or powerful men spending fortunes on clothes. Both behaviors are excessive and aberrational. Both are derived from more basic needs, simpler responses to pressures that are specifically characteristic of sexual identity in our culture.

SEX ROLES AND POWER

There is a relationship between sexuality and power. Several years ago, in an obscure Harvard journal, I published an article based on observations of patterns of behavior in three campaign organizations.[19] At the time, I had been working on my dissertation on campaign organizations, and would not have noticed the pattern had it not been so clearly prevalent in the three campaigns I was using as case studies.

The research was done in 1974, at a time when the gains of the women's movement were just beginning to be felt. Women were holding positions of power within these temporary organizations for the first time. It was also the immediate post-Vietnam, post-Watergate era, and a new generation of participants was emerging in politics. They were relatively young, mostly single, and well-educated. They were the generation of the political movements of the 1960s, but they were not of the movements themselves. They were moderates rather than radicals. They believed in seeking change within the system rather than outside it. Even though they had not stood on the barricades, they had adopted some of the values of their generation: they were wary of power, believing in an inclusive decision-making style. They offered an idea and immediately negated it, unless it was picked up by someone else. They stuttered because they did not want to sway others by virtue of a charismatic style. These characteristics of the time might also be described as feminine characteristics that emerged to balance the more typical male behavior that had brought us so low in the years just past.

The people who worked in these campaigns were not seeking power *per se*. They were exploring the possibility of a career in government, believing full well that their capacity to attain a position would not be due to their contribution to the campaign, but rather to their education and other qualifications. They were not "paying their dues," as had their predecessors in previous generations.

The men viewed the women as professionals who had something to offer to the campaign beyond their sexual identity, which was something of a change from the previous decade wherein a leader of the Student Non-violent Coordinating Committee was widely quoted to have said the only position for a woman in his organization was prone. The women who held power, however, worried about what it meant to their femininity, and talked among themselves about wanting relationships with the men. Because people in politics are relatively socially conservative (when not pressed to extremes), the women did not act on their interests by approaching the men. There were, consequently, far fewer relationships among the staffs of these campaigns than would have been expected a few years earlier.

The same pattern existed in all three organizations, with one additional factor: in each case, there was an older man—someone in his forties— who was a friend of the candidate's, who was putting in his time in the campaign in the hopes of finding a job. He was the kind of person found most typically in campaigns in the 1950s and 1960s. And in each instance, the older man roamed the halls chasing every skirt he saw. Also, in each case, he was something of a laughing stock to everyone else.

The question I asked myself about these obvious patterns in 1974 was, what had changed? Clearly, there was a de-emphasis on the relationship of power and sexuality, except as it related to the uncertainty of the women. I concluded that the drives for sex and power were related. They are connected to aggression and the fear of death to the extent that they are expressions of individuality, concrete assurances of significance, and especially of existence.

Other factors come into play in the campaign organizations (such as their temporary nature, the logistics of never having to account for one's time because almost all of it was taken up with the campaign, etc.), but what may have been exaggerated behavior in these organizations was not unknown elsewhere. Campaigns put a lot of pressure on those who participate in them, but by the same token, they give us the opportunity to examine behavior in the equivalent of a hot-house setting.

We have images of associations of power and sexuality that range from power moguls, who sleep with every woman they can, to the celibate revolutionary caught up entirely in the pursuit of power. Whether sex is a sublimation for power, or power a sublimation for sex, the relationship exists. With the exception of femme fatales, who use their sexuality to gain power over their conquests, these images are about male behavior. One of the women I interviewed had been on a battlefield in wartime. She noted that the urge for a sexual relationship when the danger of death was ever-present went both ways, and that is clearly the most extreme form of pressure. I can only wonder, however, whether the motivation in that instance was based on power or powerlessness, and whether it is not just another variant of the connection between sexuality and power.

The point is that there appears to be a connection. The most I was willing to conclude in the article was that if something changed in the status of one, something changed in the other: more power might lead to a greater or lesser libidinous energy. I did not go so far as to suggest that more sex might lead to a greater or lesser interest in power, but it could be true.

The drive for sex is thought to be a basic drive because it is essential for the survival of the species, while power is considered to be more derivative, although it is clearly essential for the survival of societies to which the species must belong in order to survive. Either way, however, it seems clear that some men who are under pressure in the search for, or the exercise of power, seek sexual relationships that do not ordinarily conform to our expectations of romantic liaisons and mature relationships; and that women in the same situation are less apt to behave the same way.

WOMEN AND POWER

If we can accept the notion that power in our culture is a white male province that has been breached somewhat by women and minorities, our belief still holds true that those who cross its borders are different from those of their kind who got left behind. This sense of specialness holds true for everyone, including white males, but while it may be confirming for them, it sometimes has a different impact on others.

Of all of the women I interviewed, only one had to face the question of ultimate authority within her world. She described herself as a traditional woman who had always played non-traditional roles. The key to her inability to acceptance of the notion of the ultimate power role was her sense that she is inherently traditional:

Growing up as I did . . . I learned some things about what little girls do and what girls and women do, and also what they don't do. And then, I suppose, I learned that girls don't become contractors—my father was a contractor. And I think I have actually—out of my life of role-busting in terms of lots of contexts—encountered a kind of absolute prohibition, which like any good inhibition, prohibits me from even thinking about it [the top position].

She suggested that one of the reasons women failed to seek really top level offices was because "they had internalized inhibitions and notions of appropriateness that constitute that inhibition." A man described the experience of power as making him feel grown up and being the "father," and it is quite likely that many people—men as well as women—have an inhibition when it comes to actually filling that role and replacing the father.

An interesting part of the inhibition was that she could not bring herself to think about, to reason with herself and say the world has changed, things are different now. It was an absolute inhibition to the extent that she blocked herself from thinking about it:

If I were to kid myself just a little, I would say I don't want to pay the price. There are elements of the price that I really wouldn't want to pay, but the fact is that I know that I can't think about it. I think a lot of women might not realize when they couldn't think about it. That's because they couldn't feel their way into a role, even to think about it.

She went on laughing to note that "Since I can't think about it, I can't find out. But it is simply, you know, an inhibition." As a person, she is thoughtful and quite bright, and was bemused at the block the question raised for her. She said, as did many others, that the bottom line for her in the performance of every job she has ever held was, "Why not?" If others can do it, she has the self confidence to know that she has as much ability as many, and more than most. She knows from experience that she is as capable as anyone else—male or female—and believes that she could perform any job with that single exception of the one at the top.

I suspect she would believe in her ability to be the final authority if she could think about it, but that step in imagination, which must precede the act, is the very one she cannot take. The inability to imagine yourself in a role other than the one you have is what characterizes traditional societies. For all our changes, our displacement of tradition in favor of modernity, there yet remains a hard core of accepted roles that we do not quite comprehend.

I am not quite sure what to make of this inhibition. I believe it is there for her, and certainly for many others. I am not sure that it is there for everyone, or that it is exclusively a sex-role inhibition. Extrapolating from Carol Gilligan's work again, it is plausible to argue that *the* most prohibitive factor is the isolation of power at the top. If women value relationships and continuity, there is no question that we would devalue activities that are isolating. By the same token, since almost everyone I interviewed spoke of the problem of trust as an immediate and constant part of the experience of power, it does not require a big leap of imagination to conclude that power is isolating, and that women find such isolation questionable, perhaps something to fear, perhaps even wrong. The fear of success by women described by Matina Horner is probably a related phenomenon: a fear of loneliness; a wish for relationships; a connection with others.

I do not believe I am arguing biological determinism here. Gilligan makes the point in her path breaking work that she is describing a "different voice," that happens to be found more in women than men, although not exclusively. Not all of the women I interviewed would have agreed with the traditional woman I quoted, although most of them did not have the prospect of achieving such high degrees of power.

If we can accept the notion that fear of isolation is a factor in keeping some people away from positions of power, it might be appropriate to question whether isolation is a necessary condition of power. Our culture is built on constraining power, imbued with the sense that every citizen retains enough autonomy—enough power—to do whatever he or she wants to do. We recognize this is something of a fiction, but it is nonetheless part of the aspiration. It is the "American dream." Part of the isolation comes from the constraints we impose. The presidency is the best example, separated as it is from the legislative and judicial powers. Another part of the isolation comes from stepping out of the norm, above the rest, above the demos. It is an inherent conflict in the wish to be human, and part of humanity on the one hand, and human—special, memorable, significant—on the other hand. It is the difference between male and female perspectives.

One cultural explanation may be found in the peculiarly macho quality of American society. It strikes sensitive foreign observers like Shirley Williams as more male in its philosophy and approach than other advanced economic societies: "America sees itself as a pioneer/gunslinging/cowboy society, where men are the center of everything," she said, and went on to suggest that this leads women to react in a way "which is confused" when it comes to power:

> They don't any longer want to be the role that is traditionally ascribed to them—the pioneer wife and mother, or the supportive wife and mother, or the beautifully coiffed wife and mother—which are the roles that they have been given: the First Lady role, if I can put it that way. Or the pioneer wife role. They are unhappy with that, but they haven't yet really decided quite what they want to be. And it is a great deal easier in a European country, specifically in a European monarchy; there's a woman prime minister of Norway, a woman prime minister of the U.K., both of them monarchies. And that seems to me to be associated with the fact that the idea of women in power dates back to Boadicea, Queen Elizabeth the First, Victoria, Queen Anne, Swedish monarchs, Norwegian leaders, French queens . . .
>
> A European woman might say I'm not up to it . . . but she would not have the sense that I am up to it, but I still can't do it. I find it is a strange undermining process for women in this country. I think it is because they have for so long, really, had a very strong stereotype of what women ought to be like, which is again reinforced by the films of the 1940's and musicals—the whole popular culture—and they don't really know where they are at.

If Ms. Williams is right, as I believe she is, the prospect for American women, at least, may be a little less gloomy—if the changes we see reflected about us in the popular culture themselves are either the cause or the effect of changes in the rest of the culture.

CHAPTER
6
■
Private Relationships

There are several assumptions we make about the private lives of our public people. At one level, we want to believe that our leaders are cultural ideals and have somehow merged their private needs with their public role, enabling them to put the public good above personal satisfactions. At another level, we suspect their motives and think of political leaders, particularly, as being in it for their own good: lining their pockets and feeding their uncontrolled egos. We hold the powerful up as models as individuals and as families, but there is also a strain of thought that argues they are incapable of sustaining a private life, and are acting out an unresolved inner conflict; that they put their best foot forward in public, reserving the warts for those at home (hence that inevitable question "What is he or she *really* like?). Another expectation is that at least some of the private need for emotional support is satisfied in the public arena by the close aides and associates with whom one spends most of one's waking hours. Family life loses out because the power-holder has neither the need, nor the energy for its give and take.

The pathological view is the more common one held by those who consider the subject at all. It is, in fact, the basis of the field of political psychology. The argument was developed in the 1940s by Yale political scientist Harold Lasswell, who suggested that it is an unresolved oedipal conflict that leads private men to seek public lives in the first place. Hedrick Smith's 1988 book on power in the Washington community cites local psychiatrist Steven Pieczenik, suggesting that "the quest for power and the relentless pace derive from a deep, inner feeling of inadequacy and dissatisfaction that breeds loneliness."[1] Another view offered by political commentator Richard Reeves describes the quest for power as closing the politician "off from other men until, day by day, he reaches the point where he instinctively calculates each new situation and each other man with the simplest question: What can this do for me?"[2]

In all probability, all of these views—conflicting as they may be—are validated in the experience of the powerful. There are costs and there are rewards, and how much one is willing to pay may depend on how much of a reward one seeks. As one observant politician noted,

> Part of it has to do with how many steps up the ladder you want to climb. If you want to climb up the ladder, the competition can be intense. . . . The people who want to go up, and who have it on their agenda, are the ones who tend to be constantly consumed by their public life and who neglect their private life.

On the other hand, if you are satisfied staying where you are, the tasks—and the time it takes to do them—become much easier to handle.

Just as there are different degrees of intensity, different temperatures of power in the centers of power, so too, is it likely that there are different degrees of need on the part of powerholders and power-seekers. Some people require more intimacy than others in order to function and believe themselves content; some require less. It would seem, for instance, that women are less likely to be so driven for power as to exclude important relationships, which may be the principal reason for the scant numbers of "qualified" women at the highest levels.

Perhaps the most important factor is that—in the Washington milieu at least—the quest becomes focused: the ambition of most of us is to move up, climbing the ladder to the next rung. In politics, particularly in national politics, the ultimate prize is visible and potentially available to all. You do not have to go through steps 4 through 9 in order to reach 10. You can run for the presidency from almost anywhere (in theory, at least. Winning may be another problem). When the end is visible and almost within one's grasp, the appetite increases and narrows, deflecting all potential interferences, not the least of which can be meaningful relationships with others.

The Washington political culture is a world unto itself, and one of its most common elements is the time it consumes in the public's business. When the work day is finished, there is a never-ending stream of cocktail parties and dinners where the powerful are expected to meet and drink. The closer one gets to the various sources of power, the longer the hours and the greater the number of days. A five-day week is all but unknown at the upper reaches of the government. If something can be done, if someone can be seen, no stone is left unturned, and no early departure for hearth and home can compete.

It is not inherently venal, but it is idiosyncratically Washington. The never-ending consumption of time does not happen in state government, or at least, not nearly as intensely. People do go home at night. A governor, like a president, is not expected to be involved in evening affairs every evening of the week. The pace is slower because most state capitals, although like Washington in the sense that government is usually the biggest business in town, are unlike Washington in the sense that the world need not be watched for round-the-clock crises. City government, on the other hand, is closer to the people, and mayors and their staffs are expected to be available to be in attendance at meetings and other significant events. For them, public life may often be in crisis, at least to the extent that it requires their presence. But Washington is a stately city filled with important people involved in significant events—perhaps too many important people. As the wife of a former Washington V.I.P. put it:

> As far as we were concerned, my husband was the most important person on earth; well, certainly in the United States. We got to Washington and there were 500 people—counting spouses—at our level in government. And we were just nothing. And yet his responsibility was very, very important.

Whether we think the quest for power is pathological or not, or whether it is driven by other more altruistic motives, we assume that private values and private behavior have an impact on public concerns. Myra MacPherson wrote an interesting book called *The Power Lovers* in 1975, based on interviews with Washington politicians, their families, and aides. She concluded that there are serious problems, not only for the individuals involved, but also for the system they serve:

> A need to alter present-day political priorities seems crucial to many public people if the quality of their personal lives is to be improved. Not only is it injurious and destructive to those individuals who felt the need to conform to mythical models of political wives, children, and politicians, but it is also injurious to the political system that such hypocrisy was long the accepted, unquestioned, and "proper" behavior.[3]

It is not really clear how much of the problem of sustaining relationships is cause and how much is effect. If MacPherson is right, part of the problem comes with "the system." It is built in by the Constitution, the distance of Washington from home, the nature of transportation and communication, the proliferation of interests, and the nature of democracy, as well as it is by the ego strength (or lack thereof) and ambition of those who participate in it. If the pathological view is correct, the inability to sustain relationships is a necessary and sufficient condition to serve the system.

All sorts of combinations of causes and effects combine in Washington, and there are times when it gets out of hand, drawing the attention of even the least observant to the peculiarities of power and to the occasional individual powerholders who bring greater psychological needs to their roles than can be met or complemented by external factors.

The notion of a disqualifying imbalance between public and private morality reached a kind of feeding frenzy in the 1988 presidential election with the ill-fated candidacies of Gary Hart, Joseph Biden, and Pat Robertson. Hart's behavior is the most interesting for my purposes because so much time and energy went into probing the question: Was it appropriate for the media to pursue his private affairs (in every meaning of the term)? After all, as was frequently pointed out, applying the same standard to past leaders would have disqualified John Kennedy and every other president who is known now to have lived a less than monogamous life. I never saw any larger comparisons, but the same standard could also have been applied to some of the greatest leaders in history.

The standards of what is acceptable behavior have clearly changed, or so it seems. At an obvious level, it is no longer appropriate to engage in indiscriminate affairs, because it will be reported by a press that used to turn a blind eye to such activity, and, more seriously, because it implies that women are seen primarily as sex objects, and the inference can be drawn that a male power seeker is only comfortable with a woman who is not his intellectual or professional peer. From the feminist perspective, aside from the lack of loyalty to his wife, this is extraordinarily demeaning to the notion of women's equality. It signals bad news to women who aspire to being taken seriously as professionals, because it suggests that the men whom they might consider appropriate mates do not feel the same about them. Although I believe these points are valid, I think the most significant error made by Hart was his recklessness and lack of judgment in daring the press to follow him, and then pursuing the affair; the scandal only served to emphasize the changing values in behavior and in the media.

What proved fatal for Hart was the lack of control he had over his private needs (whatever they were, however we view them). That the race for the presidency is exceptionally arduous, stretching everyone engaged in it to the ends of their reserve, is in some vague inchoate way felt to be appropriate given the demands of the presidency itself. At least it is a justification that is offered when questions of its singular arduousness are raised. The question we theoretically pose ourselves is how will this individual really behave under pressure? What is he or she like underneath the coiffed campaign image? What we are looking for is the private character. Character and judgment are always issues in the selection of a leader; being a good human being, on the other hand, used to be required only of saints. It may be that, in our more secular world, we require our leaders to fulfill both the laws of man and the laws of God. We want them to be great leaders and great human beings. The two objectives are not necessarily as related as we would like them to be.

The first time I participated actively in a campaign was Robert F. Kennedy's race for the Senate in New York in 1964. It was a difficult campaign, despite the crowds that followed him, because he was seeking to oust a popular Republican who had paid a great deal of attention to his re-election needs. A few days before the election I stopped in at Schrafft's to have lunch at 4:00 in the afternoon (campaigns run on their own time schedules). There were two ladies at the next table and one of them asked her friend what she thought about the election. The companion said that she and her husband had decided just the night before "to vote for Bobby because of the way he treated Jackie at the funeral."

The whole campaign never needed to take place for this couple (and I could have had lunch several hours earlier)! For those of us old enough to remember President Kennedy's funeral, the image to which she referred comes easily to mind: when they prepared to leave the gravesite, Robert Kennedy reached over and took Mrs. Kennedy's hand and they walked away together. It was a private act in a public setting. It was an impulsive act of compassion that revealed the man beyond the image.

There is something of an irony in our construction of a system that stretches a man or a woman to the ends of their endurance, forcing them to abdicate their private relationships, and then judging them on how well they sustain them, or how much they are sustained by them. The system may or may not have gotten out of hand, but the point remains that the quality of private relationships enters heavily into the evaluation of one's success as a person, and of one's potential as a leader in our world at this time.

There is an alternative view to the dominant belief that those who enter politics, or seek power, are inherently unbalanced. Another Yale political scientist, Robert Lane, noted that political life—more than any other—requires more energy than a truly conflicted individual could ever give.[4] I think his point is well taken and applies to many of those in public life today.

The pathological perspective assumes, for instance, that men seek power in public life as compensation. Many of those interviewed in this study, on the other hand, entered politics because their families were in the business, and it was the easier path to follow. Many of those I have interviewed over the past decade and a half say they entered because they were motivated by an issue or an individual (John and Robert Kennedy are often cited by Democrats, and Barry Goldwater by Republicans). They moved up because they found themselves on a ladder with an arrow pointed clearly to the next step. Still others were motivated by significant events in their lives that drew their attention to issues, or just simply to the fragility of life and the need to make a contribution now before it is too late.

It would be naive to ignore the pathological view entirely, and particularly to ignore the personal histories so often and compellingly reported in popular books and journals. The attractions of a particular time—including its heroes and its problems—can coexist with less benign needs. These are not mutually exclusive phenomena: a powerseeker can be driven by unresolved inner conflicts *and* attracted to public causes. The end result may, in fact, work quite well, with one need compensating for another. Another perspective was expressed by Harry McPherson, who drew a distinction between the public and private worlds that is based, not on the question of pathology, but rather on the differences in substance between them:

> Political issues were distinct and verbal, if complex; the business
> of dealing with one's parents, wife, children, boss, colleagues, and
> friends was far more threatening, as it involved dark tides of
> emotion into which one might be swept at any moment. One could
> always "have a view" about a political issue, and even in angry
> debate there were tacitly accepted ground rules. In an encounter
> with one's private demons, there was no assurance that one would
> survive with ego intact.[5]

I am not proposing to resolve the debate. I want only to point out that the popular prejudice runs in favor of accepting the notion that there is an important danger lurking here for the system and for those who would lead it. At the very least, there is a conflict between the values we subscribe to, of individuals grounded in family life on the one hand, and the demands of a democracy that requires those who hold power to exercise their responsibilities and be accessible to their constituents day and night.

FAMILY LIFE

The single largest obstacle to sustaining a private life is the lack of time, resulting, as one former powerholder noted, "in distorted relationships." According to some, the press for time even impedes the private side of professional relations, leaving most interactions as "short-takes." The higher up one is, or aspires to be, the more others account for your time, and the more likely they are to fill it up. The few hours one is able to get at home do not necessarily mean time spent in private. As one former White House advisor put it, "When you come home you are not through. You have a few hours, and what you have is always subject to call. The quality of life,' so to speak, was entirely at the White House. It was not at home." Energy, as well as time, gets eaten up this way, and as one long-time political observer put it:

> People who seek power, whether or not they achieve it, but who spend most of their time and energy seeking it, may easily lose the ability to enjoy the aspects of the quiet life that include quiet relationships. . . . When you lose power you can spend more time with your wife and it's boring—not because your wife is boring, but because you don't have the capacity—an inner capacity—that you have destroyed, or failed to develop the inner capacity to enjoy that kind of relationship. If it [a relationship] is not enjoyed on the run, it isn't enjoyed.

The eating away of private time is not something that happens all at once. Getting to the top usually requires the same commitment of time and energy it takes to stay there. Does this mean most powerholders prove the pathological presumption? Perhaps. It certainly makes a case for it, if we also assume that the interest in and capacity to support private relationships is a measure of health.

The same political observer considered the possibility, and said he was trying to think of someone who was the exception that proved the rule. "I would think of Harry Truman," he said after a few moments, "who always maintained a lively private life and his public role never got in the way of it." Although we do not think of Bess Truman as a woman who shared the problems of the office with her husband, we do have several examples in recent years of couples who seem unusually dependent on each other in both public and private affairs: Jimmy and Rosalind Carter, Nancy and Ronald Reagan, and that one team that seems to merge two public lives to make a private one: Elizabeth and Robert Dole.

Another couple who fit the model are Dick and Ginny Thornburgh. He served in the Justice Department under President Ford, was governor of Pennsylvania in the 1980s, Director of the Institute of Politics at Harvard when I interviewed the two of them in 1988, and shortly thereafter succeeded Edwin Meese as Attorney General. He is, as they say, a man with prospects for future Republican administrations. She, while very much involved in his career, also pursues interests of her own in care for people with disabilities. Her interest in this grows in part out of her experience of raising a handicapped child of Dick Thornburgh's first marriage, which was ended by an automobile accident that killed his first wife and seriously injured one of his three small children. Early on in his political career, which was given impetus by the accident and the real-ization that life was short, the Thornburghs decided that they had to do it together. According to Ms. Thornburgh:

> In the beginning Dick would go out campaigning alone because we had three children and I was pregnant. We discovered that he couldn't tell me what happened to him. He was too tired, or it was too hard to describe these things that were so varied and so new to us. To come home and say "The room was this size . . . , or the crowd was this big. . . ." You just can't do it night after night.
>   So, we started spending money for sitters so that I could campaign with him and share the experience. Then he didn't need to explain.

There are other ways the Thornburghs share their worlds with each other. While she points out that he encouraged her from the beginning to develop interests of her own, they rely upon each other for the criticism they might not get from others. "If I am not writing as sharp a letter as I might," she said, "or speaking with the authority that I should," he will make a note of it.

> He and I do that for each other. We have high expectations for each other, and even though one never likes to be criticized, we do that in a very trusting way. And that's just wonderful, because generally what happens is that when you become more prominent or more successful, fewer people want to criticize you to your face. They want to say, "Oh, Boss, that was terrific!" But are reluctant to say that "it is too long, or that's a repetitive section, or you've got to tighten that." Most of the stuff that we've been able to say to each other has been omitted by others.

The Thornburghs may be in the minority of public figures who believe their careers have enriched their private lives, but they are not alone.

There are benefits to families that are almost always, if not ignored by those who would chronicle their woes, at least passed over lightly. One former public official, who left state government to become a banker, felt that his children (who are almost invariably described as being the victims of public lives) regretted the move:

My kids have mourned this transition. They really have. I mean, kids are exuberant, and my kids are no exception, but they certainly have. They loved the people, they loved the visits, they loved my freedom, seeing me on the evening news, and in the paper, they loved me—they loved the me that was being fulfilled as a public servant. And they knew instinctively, in a scary kind of way, when I said I'm leaving, that this was a powerful—and from their perspective—almost tragic circumstance. I mean, they reacted much more strongly than my wife or I did. And you know, they still have not reconciled themselves to me as a banker and they miss the Department. I've been here 9 months and they haven't been by yet. I'd bring them by the agency all the time. And they sensed a freedom of expression, and fulfillment, and anxiety—I certainly don't carry the anxiety that I used to home, you know. I don't pick up the morning newspaper with trepidation the way you do in the public sector, but they just ... the power and the fame, and the reinforcement at the playground was just a small part of it. They sensed this community, family, wisdom, teacher thing—parenting analogy. I just think kids are real discerning about these things. . . .

I think a formative experience for my daughter [occurred] when she was 6, I took her to a speech on a Saturday morning. I didn't have to be Commissioner of ———— to do that, but I can't imagine doing it at the bank. She sat on the podium with me, and my boy, who is now 7½—he was then 2½—and he remembers the swearing in. My family remembers when I was Commissioner I used to go by the Governor's house on Sunday morning and bring some bagels and he'd make breakfast and you know, whatever. And the kids loved that.

I'd bring a lot of work home and engage my wife: here's a letter that I want to put right; here's a speech would you help me with it; with this article. Phone calls late at night, personnel decisions. She was very, very deeply engaged—and I don't think I've bored her with the name of one person I work with at the bank. It's just a job.

These stories suggest at least the possibility of a balance, a reward, or an alternative experience for public figures and their private relationships. It is a little simplistic to suggest that the opportunity to hold power, particularly public power, can be an enriching experience for everyone involved, but—if one goes by the literature on the subject—the thought that it might be positive is all but new and startling.

Clearly, the dominant wisdom is based on considerable experience and many troubled, if not ruined, lives. We all know stories of the children of famous individuals who suffer from trying to live up to (or live down) the parental image. Undoubtedly, it can be a difficult and trying experience for everyone concerned. Powerholders have just so much time and energy, and not infrequently will put the public good above private needs, or at least the needs of their families. John Ehrlichman, who has been tried in every sense of the word, described the breakup of his marriage in his memoir of the Nixon years, *Witness to Power*. His circumstances were extreme. Watergate was not the only problem he faced in his life or his marriage. There were longer-term problems, or at least a sense that there was more to life than the existence he was leading in Seattle that led him into the presidential campaign in the first place. In the end, while standing trial alone in Washington, he entered into an affair with another woman:

> I was deeply affected by it—I'd never come close to infidelity before—yet even so, it was essentially symbolic. I was telling myself I had no marriage in terms that I couldn't blink away. I was also responding to someone who was willing to say, "Regardless of what they are saying about you in the papers or in court or behind your back, I will take you into my arms." I needed that.
>
> In the midst of that brief encounter, everything went into a tailspin. I was convicted of more felonies, my wife heard from me of my infidelity and I was suspended from practicing law. . . .
>
> My wife came to Washington for the last days of the trial, and we returned home to Seattle in turmoil. Jeanne felt betrayed; worse, she didn't know what she wanted from me by way of expiation. I didn't know if I had anything to give her; worse, I wasn't at all sure I was interested in trying to put our marriage back together. We didn't talk; she cried and I yelled. Some of the children yelled, too.
>
> That was not, I told myself, what I was entitled to expect from these people in my family. I had been back East being beaten up by a bunch of paid assassins and in a few weeks I was going to be sentenced to prison. I was out of work, exhausted and feeling indescribable pressure.[6]

His description of what was one of the most difficult moments in his life draws the picture of private needs not met by private relationships. It is a clearer image of the dissolution of a marriage under public stress than we usually see, but there are many marriages of powerholders that do dissolve.

While the sense of significance that public power gives public officials can be reflected in the pride of their families, there are often great costs to the families (regardless of public evaluation of the powerholder's performance) in the time and energy shared with the family, and sometimes in the support and fidelity of and to each member of the family. Looked at from the perspective of the powerholder, those needs that cannot be met by the family may be met by others, or may go unmet. It is the unmet needs that should concern us the most because they may express themselves in other ways that matter in the discharge of public duties. Unfortunately, one can neither predict them, nor even diagnose them from a distance, because human beings have such wonderful ways of masking them to others as well as themselves.

FRIENDSHIP

If family relationships can be strained, so, too, may other kinds of private relationships. One of the most obvious consequences of power is that it attracts others to you. There is always someone willing to fill in the role of intimacy associated with friendship: people to listen to your problems; run the odd errands, from buying clothes and presents to conveying messages. Under those circumstances, it is hard to differentiate friends from acquaintances, because the acquaintance wants to be thought of as a friend. It is surprisingly easy to blind yourself to the reality that you are loved for your office or your fame. The more perceptive are more aware of the reasons for the attraction, and this can lead to a kind of cynicism. The less inward-looking are less aware, and haven't the time to notice anyway because their lives are so crowded.

What differentiates these intimate acquaintances from friends is that the relationship is almost all one-way: the acquaintance gives and the powerholder takes. The relationship will not extend beyond the power, but that is something to be tested only in the future.

As for friends among the staff, if the powerholder has been in office for some time, there is often a generational difference, where, in the words of one long-time powerholder, "you lose the common analogies, common history, the comfort of camaraderie with people who had been there at the beginning." As time goes by, the group that came into office with a powerholder is replaced by younger and younger aides. One reason the supporters move on is that the one-way relationship eventually becomes unsatisfying. The acquaintance gains what he or she wants to gain from the powerholder in association, or understanding, and then begins to seek it elsewhere from someone else, or in his or her own right. It can be part of their training, or just their way of seeking influence, involvement, or excitement.

Another characteristic is that the people who play supporting roles—whether old outside friends or inside aides—are not peers, and they are not treated as such. The real peer group is found among other power-holders. Two titans may not have the time to share in give and take, but they pretend they do. They presume a personal caring that extends beyond business. Although there is the possibility of considerable hypocrisy in such a relationship, it would be a mistake to presume the hypocrisy exists. There is, after all, real need for friendship and camaraderie. The civility between them is also a way to diffuse the natural enmity that might occur among adversaries, and the capacity to be civil—even to become friends—is valued and respected in the real world of politics.

An alternative to finding new friends is to bring along old friends, believing, as one former powerholder put it, "If they liked you when you were poor, they will be faithful when you are rich." It is a solution to the constant question of trust, but it is not without problems as well, although handled with more grace by some than by others.

Old friends, relatives, even long-time wives are reminders of the past, sometimes valued but often eschewed. Myra MacPherson makes the point that one reason there are so many divorces in Congress is that politicians come to believe their public images and do not want to be reminded of how much they owe their wives, who also have the unfortunate capacity to "remember them when. . . ." A former Hollywood powerbroker saw the same pattern of behavior in himself:

I'll never forget when my cousin came out to visit me from Dallas, Texas, and he walked into my Beverly Hills house and he says, "Boy, is this a long way from the candy store," which is where I grew up. I remember resenting it. Ok, I said to myself, it was in poor taste for him to do that, but I really resented being reminded of where I came from. Part of it is the congressional wives syndrome, that they are reminded of where they came from, and part of it is the change in the one with power, who now sees himself worthy of a more beautiful, talented, sharper person as his mate.

There are other problems with old friends and acquaintances that some handle better than others. Well-known people become "intimate strangers," to use Richard Schickel's term, even when they were acquaintances or friends before.[7] It leads to an awkward imbalance in the sense of intimacy: for those who "knew you when," you may think you have changed (or not), depending on your self-evaluation, and they may (or may not) be able or willing to see or credit the growth or stability. Those who never knew you, but think they do, are even farther removed from your sense of self. If you play to their perceptions of you, either out of a sense of politeness or because you need to sustain or believe in the image, you risk distancing yourself from the person you really are.

ILLICIT RELATIONSHIPS

If it is the pressures of power, particularly in politics, that make traditional relationships difficult to sustain, the logistics make illicit relationships easier: one never has to be anywhere at any particular time, which makes them at least more feasible than they might be for those who live in more structured ways. Free time is scarce, but because it is erratic, there are more opportunities to spend the odd hour as one wishes. The fact that illicit relationships are feasible, of course, is not a sufficient reason. What is more germane are the pressures and attractions of holding power. "Having affairs," noted someone experienced in both power and affairs, "was an extension of power. It was exercising power over a woman." Having gone through analysis, he also concluded that it was related to a lack of love from his parents, or at least an unsatisfactory relationship with them that led him to seek the love of others whom he then abandoned in one form or another. The subconscious motivations aside, he thought there was enough in the nature of power to stimulate the interest:

> The powerholder knows that he cannot have meaningful peer relationships in his work life. It is particularly true, for instance, of a college president. Colleges usually are in rather isolated settings. If you are a college president, you can't have friends on the faculty or in the administration. You've got to find friends outside in the community, and there may not be any community. So, since people need peer relationships—I think that's a pretty basic need—where do you find them? If you are fortunate enough to have a good marriage, you can find it there. But if you don't have a good marriage, you go looking for it.

I may not think of the women with whom I had affairs as peers, but I thought of them as people with whom I can have a peer relationship, because it is a relationship in which you can confide in the other person in a way that you can't do with any of your colleagues because you are not in a hierarchical relationship. It takes you outside the hierarchical system.

In the classic affair (as opposed to the one-night stand and the reversal of roles where the woman is the more powerful), the relationship for the powerholder may not be hierarchical in an organizational context, but it is essentially supportive. The woman accepts his position of power and dominance, and does not threaten it in any way (except with the fear of exposure, a fear she usually shares with him on an almost equal basis). She supports his power by succumbing to it, and usually in the more subtle reinforcing fashion of admiring him. Ultimately, of course, both parties can easily succumb to the dreams and images of power.

On the other hand, if one wants power but doesn't have it, one may seek solace in an affair. What makes the difference between those who have power and those who seek it, assuming there is a difference, is that the woman is more apt to be attracted to the man with power, and the man with power is more apt to have enough control over his time to respond. "I was lucky," a powerholder said. "I made free time for myself rather deliberately. I would simply disappear from the office at lunch hours, go see friends, or some lady that I was interested in, and no one asked where I was going because no one was entitled to. You still have to put in your 12-hour day."

Another side to the question of time is that while two hours in the afternoon may be sufficient for an affair, two hours at night (assuming the hours can be found with the participants sufficiently awake to enjoy them) is not really enough for a spouse and family. The lesser partner in an illicit affair expects less of the interaction than that which must be invested in a marriage. Beside the sex, he may talk over his problems, he may even listen to her problems, but that can pretty much take up all the time there is. They don't have to talk over "their problems," because once their problems emerge, the relationship usually ends.

If we could put aside, for the moment, the morality of these relationships—with the admission that it is a "bigger aside" for some than it is for others—the revolution in sexual mores in the last thirty years has spawned any number of books and articles recognizing the phenomenon of extra-marital relationships, giving them a kind of curious legitimacy. It can be, many have written, the better option: it can save a marriage that might otherwise break up because of the unmet needs; an illicit relationship may be better than no relationship at all; and so on. The very need for secrecy can be a source of excitement, although most would agree it is an excitement that can pale fairly quickly.

The question we must ask ourselves is, what makes affairs that involve powerholders different from affairs in which the participants are not marked by special standing? There might be greater risk involved—the risk of disclosure that could cost one a public career—but many powerholders tend to be risk-takers (hence their capacity for attaining power in the first place). On the other hand, emotion can easily blind anyone to the possibilities of anything going wrong. Almost every relationship—illicit or not—could be said to begin under the aegis of extraordinary optimism. There may be a greater trading on the public image by both parties than is the case with affairs of more private individuals. But again, relationships often develop out of the confused, or at least inaccurate, images that each partner holds of the other. Love, after all, always begins as an idealization of some internal image we attach to another person.

Perhaps, in the end, all that can be said about the differences between the affairs of the powerful in relation to the affairs of the less powerful is that they require less of the individuals involved than full-time relationships, and less—for those who have little time and energy to give—can be a value. They may trade on the fact of power, relieving both partners, but especially the powerful partner, of the need for explanations and preliminary expressions of interest. It is certainly possible to argue that those who hold power probably seek power more than others, and, by inference, need power more than others. This could bring us full-circle, back to the argument that powerseekers are motivated by some form of pathology or uncompensated need, but I think there is a degree of need or desire that can fall short of the aberrational, or at least the pathological.

Oriana Fallaci, the Italian journalist with a reputation for getting beneath the masks of her subjects, interviewed Henry Kissinger in 1972, and elicited an interesting and relevant sense of his strengths and his relationships with women—two separate, but not unrelated, subjects. With respect to the source of his success he argued that it was due to the fact that he was alone: the cowboy who rides into town unarmed, ready and willing to face the enemy. The comment drew a great deal of attention by the press and from President Nixon when it was published; both interpreted it to mean that Kissinger viewed the success of the Nixon foreign policy as essentially his rather than Nixon's. But the point for our purposes is that Kissinger saw himself as a loner, and he saw the image of a loner as romantic hero critical to his success as a powerholder.

With regard to women—he was at the time divorced for many years and widely regarded as a playboy—he thought that his Don Juan reputation enhanced a sense of his virility in the minds of others and countered any possible image of an aging academic. Also, he claimed, the obviously frivolous nature of the charge amused him.

Kissinger told Fallaci that women were a hobby to him, and their importance in his life could be measured by the amount of time he devoted to them. Clearly, he suggested, by looking at his schedule, anyone could tell he did not give much time to women. No one would to a hobby.[8]

The women Kissinger preferred to be seen with in those heady days of his preeminence in power leaned more to the glamorous starlet sort than the more serious woman he eventually married, which makes suppositions about his deeper needs somewhat chancier; but since he sought the public image of playboy, and since he also sought and exercised power, the armchair analysis by a distant political scientist many years after the fact is no more speculative than his reasons for projecting both images in the first place.

His affairs, however consummated they may or may not have been, were more public than most because they were not strictly illicit and because he wanted them to be that way. In his own mind, the source of his power was his loneness, his lack of connection to anyone, including— and perhaps, especially—women. He also admitted to being shy, which may have been more a cause for the loneness than the conscious image-projection, but the shyness aside, this consummate powerholder appears to have felt that the source of his power would be diminished by needing, or even by associating with, others in a meaningful way. It may be that casual relationships that do not lead to more serious commitments are, in the context of this discussion, similar expressions of the ability of the powerholder to stand alone. Others might question the value of such a strength, or even its need, but it seems to suit at least some who hold or seek to hold power in our culture.

THE ONE-NIGHT STAND

Power generates energy, not all of which is consumed in the process of carrying out the daily tasks. It can promote an exalted sense of self, a belief in one's invincibility, a confirmation of superiority. Of all the spoils of victory, none can be as attractive as sexual prowess, or at the very least, the image of it in increased sexual activity. Power touches the libido and, as one of my confidants noted, an affair releases it: "You get all steamed up in the process of work, and let off energy in sex."

In fact, he reiterated, it is not so much having the power as the drive for power:

> If they are looking for power, they are probably driven, and it isn't so much a function of having power, as being the kind of person who has a strong power drive, and it is as true when you are working your way up—even though you may never get there—as when you arrive.

That there is a relationship between sexuality and power is not hard to accept. Nor, for that matter, is it difficult to imagine that people seek solace in one area of their life when the other is threatened or exercised. Power is an aphrodisiac that works both for the dominant and the lesser partners. There is also the mythology each partner in a relationship has about the other. The belief that the loved one is more powerful, more beautiful, more caring, more whatever, is doubtless true of all relationships to one degree or another, but it is the dominant understanding in a one-night stand because no other knowledge intervenes. Not that there needs to be a lot of understanding, or even caring.

These are not relationships in any meaningful sense of the term. Most of them would barely measure up to dates for most of us, or even for such a one as Henry Kissinger. They are interactions that physically might, at best, be likened to mutual masturbation, but otherwise serve only to give the participants the knowledge that they went to bed with someone. Each side considers it another notch in the belt. The powerholder is less apt to remember whom he or she conquered because the lesser partner is not likely to be important professionally, while the lesser partner is more likely to have "slept up," as it were, and take whatever pride there is to take in that accomplishment.

While the male (assuming the greater probability that the powerholder is male) perspective in this powerplay presumes an image of macho conqueror, women are more apt to think of him as something of a public utility: predictably there to be had if one chooses; perhaps an interesting way to spend the night. For those who measure power by unpredictability, the certainty of the behavior renders the powerholder less powerful, and his power significantly less meaningful in the eyes of the woman. Both sides can view the other as "being had."

ABERRATIONAL BEHAVIOR

The preceding discussion has been based on the assumption that we are speaking of heterosexual relationships. Although the number of openly homosexual men and women is relatively small in political life, as in the general population, there are some acknowledged gays in power in both public and private life. Those who practice homosexuality as the norm in their lives do not fit in the context of what I would call "aberrational." The individuals whose behavior I do put into that category are those who pursue a sexual fantasy that is out of character with their role, their standing in life, and their normal behavior. Ultimately, I am addressing the problem of those who lose their self control, if not their careers.

I would make one other presumption about this group, and that is that it may well be that the behavior that scandalizes the nation when revealed in Washington is relatively common practice everywhere else, and the "aberration" lies in getting caught on the grand scale. Obviously, many men associate with prostitutes or it would not be such a stable profession. Similarly, many men may employ women under the cover of office work to assure themselves sexual access. The models of such relationships are firmly fixed in our movies and our minds.

Two things stand out, however, that distinguish the sexual pranks of our powerful leaders from those of their less visible brothers: they risk so much and can literally lose their careers over them; and, secondly, you would have thought they might have had better options than, say, a fan dancer, although the demeaning quality was doubtless intentional and a significant reflection of their own self-image. The risk, of course, is greater now than it used to be, primarily because the press has ceased to ignore it. As one powerholder put it, "Hey, you could be drunk on the floor of the Senate, and people wouldn't write about it. That's all gone." "There was no risk involved, and if there was, it wouldn't have stopped any of them anyway. The need is there. It is an addiction." In fact, a book by Shelley Ross on scandals in American political life suggests that personal scandals are more apt to be forgiven by the voters than corruption. "But while we accept apologies and embrace candor," she notes, "we loathe denials and cover-ups. And, ultimately, we draw the line at financial corruption and illegal activities."[9] Although embarrassing if made public, clearly the risk was not as great in the past as it is today. Probably even more salient, even to a "forgiving" public, is the hubris of the powerholder who has come to believe in his own invincibility. That egoism, alone, may be sufficient to disqualify risk as a factor in his eyes. In the eyes of others, of course, such hubris is also enough to disqualify that individual from power.

Highly publicized scandals emerge from time to time and analysts are trotted out to hypothesize on the whys and the wherefores, and we watch with a combination of pity and amusement, especially if the powerholder is someone with whom we are not sympathetic. I believe such crises are related to the experience of power and to the sense of inadequacy that great power can foster in some who might, under other circumstances, not feel inadequate. What does it provide? How does it work as a compensation?

At a very basic level, a sexual encounter is a concrete assurance of existence. It is a reaffirmation of the corporeal in the face of the ephemerality of great power. It may be degrading, but it is real. It can be touched, and believed in, and demonstrates a measure of power when everyone else around you swears fealty in which you cannot quite believe. The image that comes to mind is the Wizard of Oz: that small frightened man behind the mirrors and echoes of his image. When everyone around you seems to fall before your power, at some point you may wonder why it is you have such an exalted status and they do not. Why are you better/smarter/more powerful? Why are you different? It is a fundamental question that stems from the very earliest strivings for individuality, but, for those who rise very far in the world, it is a question that may gnaw—consciously or unconsciously—at their achievements. For some, the thrill of possible degradation is, if not an answer to the question, at least solace for the experience.

At the deepest level, these sexual encounters have no more to do with sex than does rape. From a psychoanalytic perspective, the cause of such aberrational behavior is a combination of an unhealthy narcissistic personality and the grandiose sense of being above the law: a feeling that the rules don't apply for those who are so special. In a thoughtful article in the New York Times, that followed on the emergence of the Gary Hart/Donna Rice scandal, Daniel Goldman cited Los Angeles psychoanalyst Judd Marmor's analysis that "there is a terrific seduction of the spirit that takes place when you are surrounded by admiring throngs, when the red carpet is laid out for you. . . . Unless you are aware of the blinding effect the adulation can have, your judgment can be impaired so that you begin to feel that you are immune to normal limits and penalties."[10] The psychological pressures combine to prove one's self on the one hand, and to disprove one's self at the same time. Therein lie the seeds of success as well as the deep urge to fail.

CONCLUSION

Power cannot be exercised without risk, risks cannot be taken without sometimes losing, and loss cannot be experienced without wanting solace. Solace, we assume, is found in private relationships. The combination of support and reality that private relationships can provide buoys those who have such relationships. Not all families work out that way, of course. The powerholder may be too exhausted, or too willing to believe his public image to want to hear anything less than praise. His or her partner may resent the other's success, or the changes required to play the role of wife or husband to a powerholder. There are limits to what one can ask or expect from another, although the ends of willingness are rarely clear or constant.

One aspect of consistency in the nature of relationships is determined by the consistency the powerholder is able to sustain within himself. The least conflicted person is the one who appears to be on the outside what he or she is on the inside. If the public persona is false, or takes special energy to be open, tough, or whatever the image might call for, the private persona will be strained. This is not to say that all aspects of one's character need to be revealed at all times, or to everyone, but merely to note that there are costs associated with being open, or even with being closed.

Another aspect of this question of identity and relationships concerns the degree of commitment the powerholder makes to the object of his power, and whether or not that object is significant enough to enlarge his or her sense of identity. In some respects, I think that this, rather than power *per se*, is what makes for greatness, but the capacity to lose one's self in a cause or an organization that can lead to power also reflects upon the need we do or do not have for others. The role of the priest, or the image of a celibate revolutionary, come immediately to mind. I also recall a man who was very much a father-figure to me when I was in my early twenties. His name was Stephen Galatti and he was the Director General of the American Field Service, an organization that then, in the 1960s, was an exchange program for high school students to and from the United States. It has since expanded into a worldwide exchange program, but it began as an American adventure driving ambulances in France in the early stages of World War I.

At the time, he told me, he was young, newly married, and idling about on the French Riviera, facing threats from his family that if he did not return to a more productive life, he would be disinherited. The outbreak of war was a serendipitous turn for the young American, enabling him to rush off to Paris to drive ambulances with a number of his chums from Harvard and other Ivy League schools. The Field Service played a similar role in World War II, and over the course of time Galatti became the head of the organization, devoting all of his time to it, and all of his energy.

When I knew him, he was widowed and in his mid-seventies. His son also worked for the Field Service, but the father's life revolved around the organization more than anything else. He used to tell the young students who came to America every year that if they ever needed him, no matter where they were, he was only twenty-four hours away. The year he died, he received an honorary doctorate from Harvard and was nominated for the Nobel Peace Prize.

On a personal level, Stephen Galatti had little small talk and, although he had a wonderful sense of play, his presence tended to cow others, particularly the young women who populated the organization staff at the time. He was revered by almost everyone he met. Being revered, however, did not necessarily make for meaningful interactions for him.

We used to talk about the aura of his greatness that so overwhelmed those around him, and I do not remember now whether we agreed then, or whether I came to the conclusion later, but it seems to me that his greatness—his power—was in direct proportion to his commitment to the cause of the organization: the cause of peace and understanding between nations. It was sufficient to enlarge his soul, his entire being, although it left him lonely from time to time. There was little consolation in the company of most others because they felt unworthy in the presence of his commitment. At other times, in other individuals, it was the stuff of which saints are made.

I have known others committed to the causes of the organizations they founded or formed, but only when they stretched their horizons well beyond the mundane battles that exist in every organization, did their commitment become ennobling, turning them into more than they might have been. There is also probably some cut-off mark of extrinsic value: peace is a more worthwhile goal than the production of widgets, although, as one observer pointed out, a company that produces widgets by giving employment to those with disabilities is also serving a valuable social end.

On the face of it, it seems improbable that this path to greatness is determined by the degree to which one sacrifices private happiness. If one's partner in a relationship becomes part of the public domain because of such a commitment, the spouse is usually carried at least a little distance along the same path. The most obvious constraint is that it places limitations on the spouse in terms of activities and, sometimes, in terms of interests. For those who are uncomfortable as speakers or as objects of public attention, it can be a very painful experience. For those who enjoy political issues, however, it can be a greater opportunity to share in the public spouse's work than would normally be offered. Ginny Thornburgh noted that when her husband practiced law she had little or no involvement in his work. When he ran for office and was elected governor of Pennsylvania, however, she had the opportunity to educate herself about a range of issues and offer her opinions to him, which he took as he would the opinions of any close aide, reserving final judgment to himself

Another aspect of the impact of power—or of place, in this case—on the spouse was reflected upon by another political wife who talked about the need to look assured, calm, and "always optimistic." Of course, she said, at the same time "You have to put aside your worries. You learn how to do it, because it is not going to help anybody bringing them out." There is a balance between looking like the mindless adoring wife, she noted, and wanting to show that she was a woman interested in and devoted to her husband: "You don't want to look like a manikin. . . . You are aware of people watching you. It is strange to know that you are being looked at . . . but like it or not, people were going to be looking at me all the time."

The most superficial changes were in some respects the most difficult to address. Before her husband entered politics, she was not the sort of woman who paid much attention to her clothes or her beauty. "As a matter of fact," she said,

> until we began to enter politics, I spent no time on them, and was ten pounds heavier than I am now, and only because it became clear that this was very important—that like it or not, people were going to be looking at me, did I mature and say, OK, you better handle this one. I don't mean I started spending a lot of money on clothes, but I started paying attention and dropped ten pounds, which to me, was never very important. Clothes are not important; and weight should not be important; and yet, it clearly was.
>
> I think it was a great maturity, or fortune, or whatever—to take it on and just say: let's get the darn thing done.

Clothes and outward appearances are not entirely superficial in their reflection of the inner person, and those sorts of personal changes required of the families of powerholders come at some cost. It does take maturity to pay that cost and not hold it up for ransom. How great the cost, how capable of change these private members of public families are, vary from individual to individual and circumstance to circumstance.

They can be quite significant, leaving the sense of an unpaid debt just beneath the surface for many years to come. Or worse yet, they can explode into public scandals.

How willing a spouse may be to change his or her appearance to advance the mate depends on how committed they are to each other and how committed both are to the powerseeker's goal, including how much the spouse wants to be part of the pursuit of that goal. Relationships are never static, and they are rarely even: one partner is usually more dependent on the other and, therefore, more willing to follow along. The perceived wisdom on the subject usually places the woman in the relationship in the more dependent position, because more often a woman's identity is bound up in her marital status and in her husband's identity, which suggests she would be more likely to bend to his interests than he might be to bend to hers. This is less absolutely true today than at other times, but it is still the norm for most people. If it is true that women value relationships more than men, wives would also give more importance to the marriage.

One's independence or dependency needs are formed early in life and other factors often intervene: the woman may have more power, or she may have more money and by extension more power. A person may be more dependent in one relationship than he or she is in another for many reasons, or for no reason other than the vagaries of love. If predictions can be made, or explanations offered, it is likely that the individual who is more secure in his or her professional success will be less insecure about the private relationship. But the obverse is probably just as accurate: a person who is insecure professionally is likely to become more dependent privately, and the relationship can alter with the circumstances, following the patterns of ups and downs in one's career. It is often suggested that a bad turn in a profession accounts for the tendency of many women to get married or have children. Relationships frequently break up when the career is lost for the same reason.

In the end, we assume that private relationships fulfill private needs, enabling individuals to address their public roles as more complete and secure persons than they might otherwise be. At least that is the ideal. In practice, we recognize that the presumption does not always work. Sometimes, it is the public world itself that destroys whatever private accommodation had been reached. Sometimes, the public role is sufficient to fulfill whatever needs the individual requires filling. For that person—and for the world he or she does not dare leave—losing power is a very serious problem.

PART
TWO

Losing Power

The synergism, the excitement, the awe of it—whether it is influence or power—whether it is doing for others, or being the focus, the center of attention—seldom does your mind or your body get that experience again.... Like war, it is not a duplicable experience.

KEVIN WHITE, former Mayor of Boston

The experience comes once, perhaps twice, or perhaps it lasts over the space of a lifetime career. In time, however, it is over, and the best becomes past. "Attention, like pleasure, is addictive," said one former powerholder, "and withdrawal is painful." The pain may be sharp and searing, or little more than a dull, unfocused ache. "They shine a search-light in your eyes for four years, and then it's over. They turn it off and you can't see a damned thing," said Linwood Holton, the former governor of Virginia.

The loss of power may even have biological consequences, as some research has suggested of leaders in other species who experience a chemical change in the brain when they lose power.[1] But the hurt of withdrawal is there, no matter what its cause, no matter how power passes. It does not matter if the powerholder was thrown out of office, came to the end of a legally limited term, or left of his or her own accord; there is a feeling of emptiness and a sense of having done something wrong. Even those who seek power to accomplish a goal—and accomplish it—even they leave office with regret, a fear of boredom, and a vague sense of shame.

It is a peculiar feeling, this sense of shame, because on the surface at least, for most people there should not be anything to be ashamed about. Yet, there it is. Putting the chemical balance aside, it is also likely that the disquiet reflects a combination of deeper, unexpressed causes buried beneath the surface—conflicts the powerloser is not quite prepared to face. One of the most obvious causes of discord comes from the desire to retain something that must be relinquished—usually with grace and a measure of civility that is rarely heartfelt. It is hard to let go of things that are dear, that have become part of your very identity. And it is harder yet to move on to another stage of life, a stage that is frequently associated with decline. Giving up something important to one's sense of self, and being unsure of what the future will bring, combines with the inability to express regret and foreboding to increase the angst of powerlosers. For the individual, losing power is akin to losing anything else important in life, and it needs to be mourned. Unfortunately, mourning the loss of power is not considered appropriate behavior, so the emotions are, in some part or other, repressed.

The powerholder stands at the far border and does not want to look beyond. It is not just a question of relinquishing the known for the unknown, although that would be natural. It is not death, although it is as impenetrable from the high country of power as death is from the perspective of the living. It could be an experience of growth, but no one knows for sure. What is known is that those who have gone that way before are viewed with a measure of pity and disdain because their day in the land of power has passed. Like alumni returning to school, or former legislators coming onto the floor of the legislature, they are greeted, but they are not really welcomed beyond the first "hello, how-are-ya." Returnees have no place and are only a distraction to those who are at home, a reminder of bad things yet to come when present tenants must leave their home for the unknown. Ira Jackson recalled the concern Kevin White expressed for him at a going-away party the Mayor gave his administrative assistant when he was leaving to take a job with Harvard at the age of twenty-seven:

> White said, "You poor bastard, you've done more at a young age than I even had the opportunity to do, and it's all downhill from here." And he wasn't saying it in a hurtful way, I think. He just said, hey, you know, I played a role in Quincy Market, busing, his running for vice president, little city halls, Mick Jagger concerts, Rolling Stones, racial conflagration, and you know, I was a lucky son of a bitch and he was worried about me.

How grievous the experience is depends on a variety of factors such as how one handled other losses in life, whether the leaving was voluntary or not, what kind of opportunities lie ahead, and where all of this fits with the life cycle: when the young lose power, as did Jackson, they can have every expectation that it is not so much a loss as a lateral step in a promising career. Well, almost every expectation. The nagging doubt that you have gone as far as you are ever likely to go is never entirely absent.

The quality of one's performance in power is clearly a factor. Those who can look back and say, "I did everything I wanted to do," or "I believed in everything I did," surely face the future with a brighter demeanor. It is not unusual, however, to be more aware of the failures than one is of the successes, and to dwell on the might-have-beens.

Those who hold power for significant periods of their life clearly recognize that they will lose some part of themselves in the process of losing power. So, too, does the organization one leaves, whose members often feel anger because they will be left behind. No matter how adult the membership, a leader's leaving is like a parent leaving a child. The anger may be overt or covert, but it will be expressed somehow to relieve the betrayal, even if it was the leader who was betrayed.

As the sense of power winds its way into one's experience, one senses the loss of a kind of armor that was a shield against intrusions. Great power is carried about as if it were couched on a velvet cushion. It is treated with respect and awe. Losing it opens the individual to the frailties of the human experience. Having power can be a defense against fears of insignificance and irrelevance as well as mortality, but most certainly power provides structure, and structures are important walls that protect us against a host of fears. The loss of these structures weakens the defenses that give personality form and meaning. Whether we fear the loss of the defenses, or dread the more inchoate fears beyond, we usually know enough instinctively to try to ward off the change and guard against the loss.

HOW ONE LOSES POWER

For some, the loss of power is the realization of how badly they had exercised it. As a former corporation president put it:

> I was down. Depressed. I thought I had lost it because I had not handled it right. I think having power means having the ability to stay in power as well. I was very good at getting it; very bad at maintaining it.

To the extent that the loss of power is a failure to maintain it, it clearly matters, and it is immaterial whether it is lost because of the envy of

others, a general *coup d'état* in a company, a takeover, a change of administrations, the state of world markets, or the loss of your own bid for
reelection. Or worse yet, if it is lost because of your measurable failure
to produce profits, sales, or the resolution to a problem. The only
acceptable reason for not maintaining power is if it is legally limited
because of years in office or age, and even then the loss still puts you on
the losing side as a lame duck before the actual transition, and makes you
the embodiment of past history when you are out.

One woman I interviewed recalled with a rueful smile her husband's
experience in 1981, on the day Ronald Reagan was inaugurated:

> I am talking to him on the phone and we were watching the
> Reagan inauguration on television and I'm saying, "Bill, they're
> coming towards the White House. You're the only person there still
> in his office." And he won't leave! He kept saying "This election
> didn't mean to wipe me out, it was just Jimmy Carter. The public
> didn't mean to make me leave!" He had a very hard time
> adjusting.

The capacity of the human spirit to adapt and survive is critical to life
itself, but when the loss is not internalized as your loss, it becomes
incomprehensible and unreal, as appears to have been the case with Bill.
On the other hand, when there is no question that the loss is due entirely
to one's own behavior, it becomes an arrow pulled taut, ready to pierce
the self esteem of the powerholder, creating doubt as well as pain. Losing
power is, to put it bluntly, embarrassing.

Losing power is losing in everyone's eyes. Several months after Kevin
White left office (while he was still vacationing in the Caribbean), he
spoke by telephone to his former deputy mayor, Micho Spring. "She said
I shouldn't come back," the Mayor recalled. "I said why? and she said, 'I
cannot define it, but I think if there were statues of you they would be torn
down with a big rope.' That there's sort of a sense of freedom of opinion.
There is a deep hostility that never surfaced while you were mayor."

The curious thing about this image is that the sense of the mayor's
being ousted was widely felt, despite the fact that White was not actually
overthrown. He chose not to run for reelection, even though his polls
suggested he would win reelection, given the choices most likely to be
available. It has become part of the myth of Boston history that Kevin
White lost to Ray Flynn, a perception of reality often reinforced in the
city's media, which is as unmindful of the reality as everyone else. It is
another aspect of the sense of shame associated with loss, and part of

that peculiarly public sense that a new administration should make a clean sweep of the predecessor's legacy.

Sometimes the decision not to run for reelection is a way of avoiding likely defeat, although it cannot make the transition out of office much easier, given the probability that everyone will be quite aware of the reason. Losing power because you lose a battle, or worse yet, because you did not choose to fight the battle, reflects on one's character and sense of identity. Adam Yarmolinsky, who was ousted from a position in the Johnson administration because of a powerplay in Congress over the passage of the Poverty Program, described it this way:

> I think it had as much to do with my own basic insecurities. It brought them all out. Another person—someone more secure than I . . . would have reacted differently. I think if the same thing were to happen to me today, I would have fought it. I didn't fight it. In fact, my first reaction was to tell Shriver when he came in with the news at the end of the day—one of those long days—Shriver came in and, not uncharacteristically said, "Well, we've just thrown you to the wolves and this is the worst day of my life." And my reaction was to say, "Don't feel bad, Sarge." It was not the right reaction. I think if it happened to me today, I would say, "Well, tough, but let's see if we can't do something about it. Pull yourself together."

The belief Yarmolinsky has now, that he should have reacted differently then, reflects the intensity of the experience at the time, his inability to let go of it, and the lessons he learned from it about himself and about power. What he learned—as have others in similar positions—is that power can legitimately be fought for and held. The presidential campaign of Gary Hart in the 1988 campaign was fraught with a number of odd turns by the candidate, but one of the more understandable was his assertion upon reentry in the fall of 1987, that he did not want to give up without knowing whether or not he could have won. Although the former Colorado Senator seemed beset by a number of internal problems, that decision, albeit somewhat quixotic (especially in retrospect), was one of the more mature he made, judged by the experience of others who learn that it is sometimes more important for their sense of self-esteem in the long run to stay and fight than it is to give up and get out. Staying to fight may not be the gentlemanly thing to do, but it might be the right thing to do.

Perceptions of winning and losing can be tied to greater events—to destiny—and the capacity to make that judgment depends to some extent on the circumstances, the personality of the powerholder, and one's intellectual framework. It is axiomatic in politics, for instance, that a candidate claims victory by dint of the force of his personality, and explains defeat by noting that the issues were against him. No matter how hard we struggle to explain voter behavior, the truth of the matter is that it is an exceedingly complex issue, and, while exit polls are revealing, they do not provide the whole truth. It is likely that candidates (as well as many others in the public and private arenas) require uncertainty to save themselves from serious damage to their sense of well-being.

Perhaps those whose ideological framework is dominant can depersonalize winning or losing. "People who are in the process because they are ideologues," said one legislator, "are more concerned about expressing their point of view than accomplishing any particular goal." In American politics, particularly, those who fit that description are few in number. Even within that group, many are likely to experience a shift in allegiance from commitment to ideology to commitment to personal involvement and being part of the process. But for those who remain pure, losing on an issue is a more protected loss than losing because of who you are. The same comfort can be drawn by those who lose in the battle over an issue in the world of business—as long as the issue is clearly the cause, and not just the excuse for the domination of one faction over another.

Whatever the cause of loss, the more you want to be part of the process, the more painful the loss when you are ousted. And the less ideological you are, the less able you are to excuse defeat because of issues and attitudes.

THE THINGS THAT ARE LOST
WITH THE LOSS OF POWER

Many things go with the loss of power, from the proverbial key to the executive wash room to one's sense of identity and well-being. Telephone calls are not as easily made, and certainly not returned with the alacrity they were before. One is relieved of all of the social obligations that accompany power, but the transition to uncluttered lunch hours and free evenings still comes as something of a shock. Being "free" is a more positive characterization of one's status, which might just as easily be described as not being needed, not being wanted. Carla Singer described a conversation with a friend who had just left a position similar to hers in the television industry:

You are devastated. The phone stops. This friend of mine said it's amazing, two weeks ago, he was being invited to all these places for dinner. And today, nobody calls him. Can you believe, he said, last week this guy wanted me and my wife over for dinner. Now, my friend said, I'll never hear from him again. I said, You're right.

Along with the loss of filled time comes a loss of significance. After all, the fact of being wanted cannot be entirely separated from the effect of feeling important. This is particularly true of those who held power in the public sphere. Almost everyone I interviewed in politics said the loss of significance was the biggest and the most enduring loss. Harry McPherson recalled an experience that brought it home to him when he was arguing a case before the Civil Aeronautics Board on a muggy afternoon in May:

And here I was, arguing passionately, or at least loudly, on behalf of ———— Airlines, and two of the five members of the Board were quite asleep on this balmy afternoon. A third, who'd been appointed by Johnson, was looking at me with squinted eyes, trying to remember what—who the hell I was. He knew I had something to do with . . . but he couldn't remember. And the other two were impatient for the thing to get over with.

Suddenly, I did a sort of—I felt like Topper—remember the movie? I felt like this phantom person over here looking back at McPherson. And right in the middle, I suddenly looked back at me and thought: McPherson, a year ago you were desperately trying to figure out the size, the shape of the table at Paris with the North Vietnamese, and we were having big trouble with the South Vietnamese being included, and the LFLB being included, and all that—trying to get peace talks underway. And you were working your tail off on a subject of consummate importance—stopping the war. And here you are. What the hell are you doing? What are you doing with your life?

Related to significance is the loss of opportunity to make a difference, or even just to belong to the community that matters, that makes the difference. As one former public powerholder still in the midst of transition to private life put it:

Some of us were given enormous authority and opportunity in the public sector to exercise leadership, to take a problem and turn it on its head, to change the face of an issue, to turn around an agency and to do it in a way that obviously, visibly affected—and

immediately affected hundreds and thousands of employees who
are directly accountable to you, and hundreds and thousands of
citizens who rely upon your services ... in a way that affects
virtually everyone. To have that opportunity to virtually exercise
leadership, I think, is something for which there is no analogous
afterlife, or equivalent public or private sector experience. So,
that's the toughest part of it. That's the toughest part.

Beyond significance there is the question of happiness. If what makes
you happy is doing the things you do best, and what you do best is being
a public servant—effecting compromise, making things happen—when
that opportunity is denied, so, too is the sense of accomplishment and
engagement. So, too, is excitement and a certain *joie de vivre*. As one former
public official put it:

It's never the same. Regardless of what any public official would
claim that he or she doesn't miss it. I assure you that life is never
the same. It can't be! And money is incidental. I mean I am making
a great deal of money now—more than I ever made in public life.
But money and peace—peace in the sense of when the telephone
rings now it's a friend. It's not a migraine or an ulcer. So, I can
take a vacation whenever I want to take a vacation. I can do
whatever I want to do. . . .
    One doesn't get the zest. If one is in government at all—I never
had a boring day in 20 years. Frustrating days, sure. Days filled
with anxiety—a lot of laughter—challenge—you can run the gamut
of emotions. But never boring. It can't be boring! It's a great, great
business.

A perceptive former White House aide tried to put his sense of loss in
context:

When we got out we all laughed about the absence of the White
House car and the absence of the White House telephone operator
who could find anybody. I walked out of my house after a month's
vacation and there was nothing out there, and I walked up the
street and got on a bus and went to work as a lawyer. And we all
laughed about that. That's not the deprivation. You recognized
while you were riding in the White House car that this is a facility
that is made available to me for the short period in which I am
going to be here, and it is helpful. I can read the stuff, the papers
and things on the way to work. I don't have to worry about driving
the damn car. I don't have to wait for the bus. Somebody can drive

me. That was a help, and when it is taken away what you can't help but miss badly is the sense of significance.

The help can be more significant than drivers or other basic support services. Ginny Thornburgh described her husband's sense of leaving of the governorship in terms of the staff support to which he had grown accustomed:

> He has all kinds of things that he wants to do, and he doesn't have the research support, the first draft speech support, the "here's an issue give me three options" support. I think that's been the most painful thing for him—not having that network of people who are with you and [with whom you] work on developing an idea together.... We miss this network. We miss them psychologically and spiritually.

The services are lost, but more significantly, the people who provide those services are lost: that community of supporters who are with you when you do well and even when you fail. They are the small cadre of those a powerholder sees every day, who make his or her career and well-being their own. There is also the larger group who are not part of day-to-day life, but who still cherish their relationships with you. The distant friends remain, but even if the magic does not go out of the relationship, their very distance means that they can offer that sense of community only intermittently.

Ira Jackson described his sense of community loss this way:

> By the time I left ... the 3,000 people who were the Department of Revenue had become family to me. I never worked so closely and collaboratively with and almost spiritually with any group before, and probably since, in my life, and it was home. I mean it was home! My office was adorned with art work from my four kids. I had left my personal imprint and signature all over the place, both because—reflecting my personality and values and their achievements—I had become the Department of Revenue, and the Department of Revenue had become me to a degree, and so that was a metamorphosis of some tremendous proportions personally, and somewhat institutionally.

Without that feeling of community, a sense of loss and loneliness is inevitable, particularly if the feelings were intense, as they almost always are, because the world of power is always embattled. "Thousands of people used to speculate on my every wish and prayer," a former powerholder noted. "I'm totally irrelevant now." Having said all that, however, he went on to say that "You also feel—you feel excessively self-indulgent to have even this conversation [I am having] with you:

> It is A, undemocratic, but B, it is egotistical, self-centered. It is not wholly unique, but it is such a small, tiny group of people you would be able to engage, or find relevance—it's not something that would come up at a cocktail party."

At another level, the loss of power means a loss of the idealization of what that power represents. It means letting go of something deeply valued, whether in the public world, as the chief executive officer of a corporation, or the president of a voluntary association. It is an internal conflict associated with loss that becomes intensified because there is an anger that can be neither expressed, nor dealt with openly. What could you say? "I want to be in charge! It matters to my sense of identity, my sense of what it means to have value." To whom would you say it?

THE AWKWARDNESS OF INCOMPETENCE

There is another side to the loss of the minor perks of power that is often trivialized and laughable, but with the sort of laugh that comes from the recognition of pain that is part of the human condition.

It stands to reason that there are skills acquired by powerholders in the exercise of their role. Some powerholders are doubtless more talented than others, but there are things to learn about the role, and although acquiring one skill does not necessarily mean losing another, it generally works out that way. If, for instance, you grow accustomed to giving a speech by scribbling a few words on a legal pad and getting back a triple-spaced typed address; if you never write a letter or an article yourself—you can forget how to spell. If someone else always places your long-distance phone calls, you may never learn how to do it yourself (to say nothing of the constantly changing long-distance phone procedures we have witnessed recently). These are simple tasks, but they become the responsibility of others to perform them for powerholders. A former governor once noted that when he went back to his law practice, and his clients noted his poor spelling, they looked at him with an expression he described as saying, "And this fool was our governor?"

The difficulty lies not just in the loss of those very nice services, or even the loss of community or significance, but in the conflict it promotes of believing yourself to be a capable and accomplished person on the one hand, and on the other hand, finding yourself in your eyes, and worse yet—in the eyes of others—incapable of performing very basic skills associated with normal living. I used to have an office near a former governor who would often, on a quiet afternoon, knock on my door and offer to do a favor for me if I would place a long-distance phone call for him. We kidded about it at the time, given the difference in dimensions of the favors exchanged, if there really was to be an exchange. Now, I wonder about the period before he knocked, and if he tried to dial the call himself, or how he selected me—the least threatening of the professionals on the floor—to come to his aid. If exercising power requires exhibiting competence, being incompetent is a sharp blow to the self-esteem of the former powerholder. It also provokes a diminishing sense of one's ability in others.

Herbert Harris, a psychoanalyst who headed the department of psychiatry at the Massachusetts Institute of Technology before he retired, suggested to me that his own research led him to believe that the telephone comes to represent something more than an advanced technology to those who have lost power. It is another way of being cut-off. In Freudian terms, it is an extension of self and connected to castration fears that are more likely to rise in the period of transition following the loss of power.

Another story, related by an aide of a former public executive, reveals another side to the discontinuity that comes with the loss of power at the most basic level of social intercourse:

A delivery boy came to somebody else's office and there was nobody outside to sign for something, and the guy said "Would you sign for this?" And he [the former powerholder] went through his usual—which he's done all his life since I've known him—"Where do you come from? How long have you lived in the city? What do you do?" And the guy thought he was out of his mind. I mean nobody who signs for a delivery questions your curriculum vita! And I thought to myself—I didn't say a word—but I looked at somebody else in the room, and I thought this delivery guy has no idea who he is. That's part of what's going on here. And he [the former powerholder] is presuming that he [the delivery person] does. Otherwise he wouldn't have the license to ask. . . .

I think at the beginning, when he just left office, I think he kept talking about it in terms of perks. You know, "I've been in public life and we had helicopters and cars and all this stuff, and aides since I was 30." Well, there is a lot more. That's an easy answer.

What is lost is a level of communication that is based on the assumption that the person being addressed knows to whom he is speaking: knows his work, his problems, his interests. The public person is being polite by expressing interest in the private person. It is not just an awkward misreading of the situation, it is mortifying to find that not only are you not on the same wave length, but that you are no longer part of the common knowledge, part of the world.

Some never get over the image of themselves in the past and face a future of increasing public forgetfulness. They are particularly vulnerable to slights and invariably strike their new acquaintances as overly-sensitive, insecure individuals, becoming caricatures of their former grandeur. The presumption of power without its presence is a ludicrous sight and the butt of much humor. The fact that it is so humorous is in itself an indication of the underlying psychic quality that is being exposed. It makes the former powerholder appear vulnerable to the need of attention, deference, and a whole host of other requirements for identity to the outsider.

It would be a shame to leave this discussion without retelling some of the stories associated with loss, because they are amusing, and also because they are revealing. One of my favorite (which may be apocryphal because I have heard it about two individuals) is of a former Cabinet secretary who wanted to go somewhere the first day he was out of office, went out to his car and got in the back seat.

On the other side (but still within the arena of discontinuities) a story was told of the late Senator Robert Taft, who left a restaurant one evening and was recognized by the doorman who began calling "Senator Taft's car. Senator Taft's car." "It's a nice car," the Senator said, "but it doesn't come by itself."

Car stories seem to predominate, perhaps because they truly represent power to the American individualist. Barbara Bush was reported to have told her husband that if he did not win the presidential election in 1988—and he insisted upon driving away from the White House—she, for one, was not going to get in the car with a man who had not driven a car in eight years. When Linwood Holton retired as governor of Virginia and left Richmond, he bought a new car and the family did go with him, but he got lost three times on the way home.

There are lots of stories of former powerholders who rarely carried cash when they were in office and were stuck at toll booths and restaurants with neither a cent in their pockets nor an aide to rush in to cover the bill. This requires a bit of bargaining, although, if the former powerholder is well known, things are easier. Easier, but still awkward.

As easy as it is to forget how to spell, imagine how much more likely it is for returning attorneys to forget the law, for professors to forget the citations they used to know, or to be unaware of the latest literature on a subject. Everyday knowledge requires everyday usage. Those who journey to higher realms can fall with a thud in their own and everyone else's eyes when the forgotten lore requires someone else to step in and take over.

FINANCIAL SECURITY

Having great power is not the same thing as having great wealth, although there are similarities. For one thing, when you have power, you have many of the perks of wealth: opportunities to travel and vacation in luxurious ways and places; deference from supporters, friends, and strangers eager to respond to your every wish; and so on. Certainly, it will come as no great leap of imagination to understand that having a nest egg (preferably a large nest egg that can sustain the old perks) is easier than facing an uncertain future without one.

The problems for those who lose power, and do not have an income to fall back upon, are more complex than the loss of things money can buy, however. For many, there is the need to learn the ropes of American private enterprise. As one former legislator put it:

> I was twenty years in the legislature, so for almost a quarter of a century, at the end of the week, or two weeks, or month, someone said "Here's your check. We have taken out the withholding tax and everything else." I had no need to employ a secretary as such. If I employed one, the legislature, or someone else took care of the details. I didn't have to make out quarterly tax forms. I didn't have to pay unemployment compensation tax, or workmen's compensation tax, or rent an office, or hire people. I had none of that experience.
>
> So the answer to your question, after 24 years of living a particular way, I not only went into a brand new occupation, it was an occupation that said OK, find an office, find a secretary, get some stationery, buy a typewriter, get a desk, order the telephones. You do this all yourself because you don't have an administrative assistant to do it for you. It is a somewhat unnerving experience to do it for yourself at the age of 50. I left the legislature at 49, and the following January I turned 50. So, after a quarter of a century or more, of different jobs of working one way, I was out in the free

market system trying to make a living from the ground up. And I was somewhat nervous.

A younger man, who left a position as the head of an important state agency, had a similar experience:

When I was on the private side, I knew I had to start over. The thing that I think was the most devastating at first was the fact that—My God—it's not just budgets on a sheet now! In order to buy a chair that costs $250, you have to pay for it out of your own checkbook. And that set in very quickly. So we didn't buy $250 chairs. We bought them used, where we could find them, at good reasonable prices.

I haven't minded the idea of starting over ... but I wasn't as good as I probably should have been to leverage from the Agency up past that. I also looked back at it, and there wasn't much else to do within the state at the time. I had one of the best jobs in the state. Probably one of the three or four most highly paid jobs, at $55 grand a year. I was about the same salary as the Governor. I knew I had to still be producing income. I couldn't spend a lot of time crying about that.

Some have more experience than others in starting over, and those who seek power are probably a bit more likely to fall into the experienced category because they are more apt to be risk-takers who have had to start over more than once in their lives. John Buckley, the former sheriff, said that when he left office at the age of 50, with kids of college age, all he knew was that he was going to start over:

There were a couple of people who mentioned I could go to work for them, but it was nothing I really cared about. So, I always start my own business. Since I was out of college, I've had maybe 10 of them. And every one has been dramatic, and all of them hard. Sometimes when I've spoken [to a group], people have said, "Next time we want you to talk about how you changed careers." I always say it is very difficult. With much difficulty!"

Why, the reader might wonder, does a former powerholder have to start from scratch? Why not join an existing organization, coming in at a level commensurate with the public power where the perks of private industry are similar? The answer is that most enterprises, in most cases, cannot bring in someone accustomed to power without disrupting the distribution of power that already exists within the organization. And by the same token, once an individual achieves power, he or she will not want to be subject to the rule of others. Once you become the mother or father, it is harder to go back to being a child. The same problem occurs for those who retire from the business world and think they will cap off their careers with a stint in the public sector. The rules are very different. The collegiality that characterizes the use of public power is often unsettling for those used to stricter lines of authority, and it is a rare individual who makes an easy transition either way.

It is easier for the former powerholder to start his or her own organization, usually as a consultant or a lobbyist, assuming it is legal to do so. It is, for instance, lawful for a former member of Congress to become a lobbyist immediately upon losing office, but not for a former member of the administration. And what is legal in some states is not permissible in others.

Not everyone who is legitimately able to become a lobbyist will find it attractive, however. There are psychological costs in moving from the giving side of the table to the asking side. Kevin Harrington raised the point himself:

> If I could make a good living as a lobbyist, what about all the speakers and senate presidents who have preceded me? How come they didn't do it? How come they would settle for jobs that paid—what—$40—$50,000 a year—clerk of courts, or whatever? Why not get out and make big money?
>
> You're talking about power. The answer is very, very simple, at least in my experience. They can't bring themselves to go back and ask a favor where they had exercised all that power. When they used to say come and people came, and go and people went, do this and people did that, and so forth. The answer was no and that was the end of it. The answer was yes and something happened. Now, they are out. They can't go back to Mary, or Harry, or Sally or Charlie and say "Will you do me a favor, support this bill, or vote against this bill?" They can't bring themselves to do that.

Having been on the side of dispensing the goods and services that public power has to offer, many cannot step down to the lesser role of supplicant. Power—and the prestige that accompanies it—are more important than money, as long as there is a base that is more-or-less equivalent to their legislative incomes. You rarely "need" more than you have, after all, so foregoing the increased income is not, in itself, a loss.

TRANSITION: THE ACTUAL PAIN OF LOSS

Harrington cited another lesson he learned early in his career in the Massachusetts state house:

> In 1959, the first time the Senate went Democratic, I was a freshman member of the Senate, and I was the first Democratic chairman of a committee then called Labor and Industries.... There was a great veteran House chairman named Mike Carroll from Lynn. And at the end of the year, Mike Carroll died of a heart attack. And I always remembered getting on the elevator in the morning when the newspapers had announced that he died. There were three people—three guys on the elevator. I don't know who they were. And the elevator door closed, and this was the conversation—this was what they said, and how quick they said it:
>   Someone said, "I see where Mike Carroll died."
>   The second fellow said immediately, "That's too bad, he was a good guy."
>   The third fellow said, "Who's going to be the new chairman?"
>   That quick! That was the obituary! It was all over. He's dead. Who's next. I said to myself, Whoa, whoa—you know, you better get ready Harrington because you're going to be out of here one of these days. You better start to think about tomorrow. And a lot of them don't.

Dying with your boots on, of course, alleviates a lot of the pain, but the story stuck with Senator Harrington throughout his career. Death aside, one can be eased out of office in a polite transition, or one can be tossed out the door on one's ear. There is a lot to be said for both alternatives from the perspective of the organizations and, perhaps, from the experience of the powerlosers. American political institutions usually transfer power slowly, several months after the election itself. It is an extraordinary display of the overriding consensus of our democratic traditions, but it is not the only way transitions can occur. In England, for instance, when the government loses an election the change takes place the next day. Adam Yarmolinsky described the experience told him by Roy Hattersley, a minister in the former Labour government:

> There is no transition period. After the election, you come in the next day—which you did—and at the entrance to the building, the clerk says "May I have your pass, please Sir." And he said, "Well, how do I get out of here when I leave?" And the clerk says "We

have a temporary pass for you good for the rest of the day." And he goes in and packs up, and his assistant said, "Perhaps you would like to have a dispatch box as a souvenir." You know, they use these great boxes, and the clerk says "That will be two shillings to change the lock." He said the only thing that he got out of it was—his driver, who was a retired sergeant—said he wasn't supposed to do this, but he might like to have the flag as a souvenir.

Of course a major difference between the American and British governments is the existence in Britain of a senior civil service that remains in office regardless of the party in power, and has more responsibility for running things; and the Parliament, to which the retiring minister can return if he has retained his seat in the election.

The British transition is designed to serve the best interests of the government and the nation, rather than of the individual powerholder, as in its own way does the American system, because when a president leaves office so, too, do all of his top aides in every department and agency. Without some overlap, it would be too abrupt and disjointed. Although it is clear that the pace of the process is designed to serve the purposes of the state rather than the individuals who run it, the difference raises the question of whether or not it matters to those involved. Is it, for instance, easier to make a quick break than to go through a drawn-out procedure?

The answer is probably variable, depending primarily on the psychological make-up of the powerholder and how loss was handled before, but also dependent on the options before him, the manner of losing office, and where he or she is in the life-cycle. To those accustomed to change, "pain" may be too strong a word. As one observer put it, "It's been a shift, but then we've made all kinds of shifts." Very few suggested the loss was not difficult, even for the experienced, and the reaction to it may be more a reflection of varying tolerances for pain than a difference in the nature of the experience. It is also quite likely that women have an easier time of it than men, because our identities are not bound so tightly into the job in the first place—whatever a woman achieves is a plus—and because women are raised with an expectation of passing through several discontinuities in life: marriage, children, children leaving home, and a career before, sometimes during, and frequently after. A man's identity, on the other hand, is not bound to these changes, but is linked to the assumption of a single, upwardly moving career. Shirley Williams recalled the loss of her last election in a way that may have masked some of the disappointment, but certainly reflects a very different attitude than that likely to be found in a man in a similar situation:

> I remember a friend of mine—a woman friend of mine who had been a friend all my life—who was staying in my house the day I lost my seat. And you know, it was all over the television that I was the most senior minister to lose a seat. I was in a very marginal seat, as women often are. And she was very worried. She felt that I've got to cheer her up and so on. And the next morning she was lying in bed and she heard me singing, and she said to herself "It's going to be all right." She came down and I was singing around the place, and she said, "God, I didn't expect to see you singing!" And I said, "It's just wonderful. There are sixteen things I can now think about doing."
>
> That's not special to me, except that I've always wanted to live about ten lives. I only had one, and that one life was politics, and I loved politics, but there are at least five or six other lives which I would loved to have pursued if there had ever been time. Here I am in an academic world, pursuing a different life. And I've got other things up my sleeve I'd like to do when I get out of here. So, I don't think I did feel the loss of power particularly strongly.

Still, for most people—women as well as men, particularly if they have never gone through the experience of loss before—it is hard and it takes time.

Generally speaking, it takes about a year and a half to recover from the loss of power. That is the period it seems to take to make the adjustment from being a public person—a powerholder—to being a private individual without formal power. That is the period of time it takes to recover the basic skills so clearly lost in the period of awkward incompetence, to adjust to a new set of expectations, and to settle into a new pattern of behavior with new relationships.

One might wonder whether or not eighteen months is a long or short period of time, or whether it is bounded by some dimension of inevitability in human development. Would it be faster, for instance, if the loss of power were recognized to require a transition and could be mourned more openly? Clearly, the variables of age and experience in loss matter somewhat, but they never entirely compensate for the time it takes.

If the experience of power has any impact on one's sense of identity, clearly its loss leaves one feeling more naked and exposed. Yarmolinsky recalled another British public official who said the first thing he did when he got out of power was buy an umbrella. "This is British," said the

American. "All the time he was in power, someone held the umbrella." Power is an umbrella in its own right, with or without the frequency of rain: whoever walks beneath the umbrella of power has his spirit protected by the public persona. The transition from power is the period of time it takes to learn to survive in the rain.

According to Abraham Zaleznik, a psychoanalyst at the Harvard Business School who has studied leadership and power, there is a danger of the powerloser rushing from one umbrella to another too quickly. He will move quickly to elude the depression that hangs over him as long as there is nothing to distract him from his role as a powerholder.

One of the most intelligent and perceptive—and most unhappy—of those I interviewed described having less control over his life when he was out of power than he did when he was in office:

> If I were in a government job, I would feel that whatever I do on the job is an effort sufficiently significant to absolve me from any obligation to participate in other public activities. As a private lawyer, I find I need an extraordinary amount of time in pro-bono activities and have less time for myself than I ever had. So, I am always under pressure. I find it hard to turn down appeals for areas where I have worked. I can only do it when I find I have absolutely no more time.

His search for significance is a search for meaning for his life, for the person he has become after many years of public service. The only thing that makes him happy is doing what he does best, which is being a public servant. Without the opportunity to be one, however, he almost does not exist. He cannot find pleasure in other things, but rather finds himself getting angrier, instead of more mature, as he gets older.

The transition from being a powerholder to someone outside of power is a necessary condition for survival. One either tries to find a way back to power, as this driven public servant has, or one must come to terms with "the melancholy of all things done," which he has not.

The capacity to find a new identity is clearly more difficult for those who never had a firm grip on who they were to begin with. Jack Flannery, whom I had known in power and out, and who during the course of this study described himself as my best example of a failure in surviving power, explained it this way:

> If you find your identity in what you do, if you are not quite sure who you are, or what you are, or what you are up to, and you find yourself chief of staff to a governor, through whatever process—do you then begin to define yourself to yourself in those terms? If you

do, what happens after you lose that job? Who are you then, if your identity is so tied up with your occupation? If your occupation changes, then you've got to either reinvent yourself, or fall back on resources that, in my case, were absent.

He started to say that he felt a lot less important now than he did then, but he stopped himself and said, "No, that isn't even so. When I look back on those years and realize I was important—at the time—I don't know that I noticed it so much, or realized it, or said wow to myself." Power is something more often perceived in the eyes of the beholder or seen in remembrance of things past. Flannery, like many others, did not recognize it when he had it, but lost his identity when it left him. It took him seven years, and several careers, to find himself and put the past into perspective, and then, quite suddenly and sadly, he died at the age of 53.

CONCLUSION

Although I could not write about the loss of power without emphasizing its painful aspects, there are obviously those who leave power with a sense of relief and look forward to the challenges of whatever awaits them with an emotion more akin to excitement and pleasure than despair. It is likely that the majority are putting a good face on a bad reality, but relief from the pressure, the time commitment, and the energy it takes are real and among the rewards of moving on to another stage in life.

Kevin White described the moment before loss of power as being like a "super nova": the power burns most brightly just before it goes out.

The loss of real power occurs most often at the pinnacle of its perception, and its perception and decline are swift. The examples in history are many.

A group came to see me that were supporters of mine . . . and all they were saying to me was "Just come out and see us. You don't have to do it our way. Just listen to us and then do what you think is best. Just do for us what you did elsewhere. But just listen!"

What less could they have asked you to do? "Just listen to us!" And I couldn't do that. When I got through, I didn't have the power to perform in the terms that they thought I could. Their view of my power was so blown out of proportion that I didn't have the ability to deliver on what they thought I could do. I found out that for all of my office, my personality, my Quasimodo's hump that fascinated people—and I wished I could leave out of the room when I came in—was the fact that I was really no more than the chief operating officer of a subsidiary, of a parent company that was being run by Eddy King, or Frank Sargent, or Mike Dukakis, who was held by a holding company headed by Ted Kennedy, and that made it a very difficult thing for me to fight.

And so I saw this as trying to recreate power. Not over the people I served—they were almost mesmerized ... but something was conveyed to them that I had it to such degree that the only way of getting rid of me was to shoot me.

All of the attention is focused on the powerholder. There are memories of greatness, a legend develops of the mythic proportions of one's power, and then, in a flash, it is gone. Standards of civility require the loser to contain all the emotion associated with the burst of glory and the darkening gloom within his breast, bow graciously to his or her successor, and step across the border to the land of those without power, into a land where there is also no memory.

Ira Jackson looked back on the experience of others as well as his own and said

There is no institutional memory. There is no back bench. There is no curiosity. A guy like Kevin White dominates the city in a way that is equivalent to, in my small way, the way I dominated an agency, and maybe galvanized the attention of the public. But he shaped the city. A much more complicated thing than a revenue system, or refund process, or even attitudes toward state government. This town acquired his personality, and now ... I don't think he's talked to Ray Flynn in maybe three years. So, he is obviously not even on a park bench, to say nothing of a back bench. And he doesn't even get a footnote. The historians in the year 2000 will give him a major footnote, but now he doesn't even get a footnote.

Those whose ambitions still rage within their breasts will suffer more than those who, in some measure at least, recognize that they have gone as far as they are likely to go because they have reached the zenith of their world, because they are of an age to retire, or because they have done all they could do in that particular place, at that particular time. One former powerholder talked about being haunted by the Rocky Marciano image:

A lot of people told me to leave years before I did. You know, any success: just grab it and run. You're a fool if you don't because it's going to catch up. I left, not responding to that kind of common

sense, but rather because I did what I could do. I was done. I was done. I had done all that I could do. Maybe my dreams were too modest, but I fulfilled them to the extent that I could....
Leadership is mostly driven by creativity, and when the creative juices are either exhausted or inappropriate—you know it's time.... Whatever the hell it is that drives you, well, then you are no longer a leader. You are a manager.

It is the best of times to leave when you know when you are done. It is the worst of times to leave when you know there is more left to do, or when you will be left without anything else to do. For those who are driven by creativity, or even by the rawer emotions of aggression, yesterday's triumphs belong to the past and offer little comfort in facing today and, even more, facing tomorrow. It does not matter that you headed an organization yesterday. It brings no sense of accomplishment today. It does not help you accomplish anything today. It does not even help you fill the day.

Those who seek power may be like organizations that require a goal to keep going. Once that goal is achieved, they need to develop another or they face extinction, replaced by other associations that meet more current needs. Losing power requires a readjustment of one's goals. It is seldom enough, in the long run, to spend the rest of one's life drawing comfort from the past because, just as winning power makes one a winner, losing power—no matter how—has the capacity to make one a loser.

Perhaps the novelist who searched for a long time into the heart of power said it best:

It was hard for anyone outside to find within him that pure and simple feeling. He cared, less than many men, what his own feelings were. He had felt most temptations and passions, but not that kind of self-regard. And yet, he wanted something for himself. When he said, he wanted to get power and 'do something with it,' he meant that he wanted a justification, a belief that he was doing something valuable with his life. He also wanted a justification, in an older and deeper sense. He wanted something like a faith, a faith in action. He had lurched about until he found just that. Despite his compromises and callousness—or to an extent intertwined with them—he had believed in what he was doing. Those round him might suspect him, but there, and there alone, he did not suspect himself.[2]

PART
THREE

CHAPTER
8

---- ■ ----

Surviving Power:
Life After Power

I f power puts one in the very center of a universe, equal to the stars, with
planets, moons, and satellites spinning around in a constant, eternal
manner, losing power is like being jettisoned into outer space. There may
well be life out there, in some form or other, but it will not be the same.
It will never be what it was. Every powerholder knows that, and if there
is not outright fear about what lies beyond, there is concern and a certain
measure of unease. There will be a period of transition—typically a year
and a half—before the former powerholder can even begin to know
whether or not he or she has survived the experience and is again able
to live for the future instead of the past.

If power has any impact on identity, it will have left those it touches with
a host of wants and rewards that differ from those of individuals who have
not shared that experience. Even if the powerlosers return to the land
from which they came, they will not be the same. They will be different
people inside the body of the old familiar person who crossed the border
nigh these many years past. Everyone changes in some ways, but what is
most typical of those who hold power is the curious discontinuity that,
while they change on the inside, they feel a need to appear to have
remained the same on the outside. Everyone wants to know that old Joe
remained true to his origins.

There are conflicting pulls upon the psyche of the Once Powerful. There
is the need to let go of the past, and the need to feel that the past has
meaning, that it was not an experience isolated unto itself that has no
bearing on the rest of one's life. There is the need to bring something of
value into the new life, some justification for the past that makes the
future possible. There is the need to leave a legacy and assure one's self
and one's family that all the sacrifices it took to acquire and hold that

power were not in vain. In public figures, there is often the irrevocable loss of the wealth that was never made because of dedication to political gain, the loss of time for family and friends, the loss of intimacy, the giving as well as the taking, and the loss of joy in shared experiences. And finally, there is the loss of time for one's self and for awareness of the world around us.

Public people are driven by public events. It is how their days and their nights are occupied. The higher they rise, the greater the need to keep in touch and stay on top of things. They have little time for solitude or inner reflection. And, of course, they have no time for leisure activities, unless that is one of the ways they are tied to the never-ending need to stay in touch with others.

In the back of everyone's mind is the hope that there will be a return on the investment both for the individual and the enterprise to which he or she has devoted so much energy. The latter hope is easily frustrated by one's successors, but the need to believe that the experience has meaning never fades. It is akin to the very human need to believe that there is some order in the world. John Ehrlichman described the danger of having it come to naught this way:

> You write that off—the sacrifices—like a failed business or something. All those sacrifices to no apparent end. And then you have to decide, well, do I stay in the game and redeem that somehow? Or do I write it off and start new.
>
> I had the advantage of going into bankruptcy, so to speak, so that I was starting fresh regardless. But I think a lot of these guys hang around Washington consulting, or they do whatever they do, in an effort to somehow or other amortize all of that sacrifice.

Amortizing the sacrifice and staying in the arena is one way of finding the value of what is past, and using it to make the next steps easier or more meaningful, but it can be a delaying tactic rather than a genuine transformation to a new life. It means translating power into influence, which can be very rewarding in its own right, but only if the individual can come to terms with having access rather than choice.

In the long run, of course, the surest reward of power is internal. Some manage to catapult from one success to another, regardless of age. Some do not. How well one lands depends on a great many variables, most of which are beyond anyone's control. The variable most within control (unlike age, external opportunities, political and economic factors of the day, etc.) is how the individual reacts to the situation. There is a talmudic story that the greatest gift God has to give man is freedom of choice. So concerned is God that man appreciate it, He preordained everything in order that man be free to choose how he reacts.

If it is a question of choice, one person newly out of power described it as "sorting out now how I should use the rest of my life." Something, she added, she did not do when she was younger and "so busy living." The questions she asked were this: "What can I do next? How do I seek that?" Finding the answers can be painful, even more painful than the actual loss of office, but there is a great reward to be found in at least framing the question.

AGE: THE PHYSICAL DETERMINANT OF EXPECTATIONS

Age is a major factor in expectations. A youthful powerholder will expect to go from one success to another, although deep in the recesses of the mind there often lurks the fear that the early success was really a fluke, and that someday someone will find that out. Whether imbued with a tremendous sense of personal efficacy or not, an older powerholder cannot have the same hope to return to power, particularly if the power is of a higher order. At some point—even though age is a relative term and society is in such a state of flux that traditional models no longer necessarily apply—the fact that one is past one's prime must be recognized (although "prime," too, is a relative term, depending on the world in which one lives: some worlds promote the young early, and some late).

The young who gain and lose power have the advantage of not knowing they may never achieve such prominence again. By the time they realize the best is past, they will often have adjusted to life without power. They can also be filled with a strong sense of competence that will carry them quite well through life, not needing to prove themselves again, sure that they could succeed if they really had to go back. The young who let go of the ambition to be "successful," having demonstrated to themselves that they have the ability to gain and exercise power, may actually be quite happy, assuming they can find pleasure in other things and do not stay awake nights wondering if they could or should have done more.

Losing power later in life requires coming to terms with one's own mortality, something we would all rather like to avoid. It requires acceptance of things that are passed, and an image of one's self that is more or less at peace with the internal conflicts that shape one's personality. It requires a capacity to let go of the things that drove one before: the issues; the organizations; the loves and hates of life in the world of power. How much one lets go of the world may depend on the culture in which the former powerholder lives: some environments lean to the spiritual; some to pleasure and private pursuits; some merely offer a quieter, less structured existence in the same environment. It is a period when the survivor must come to terms with the myths of the world about the later stages of life, and the myths in his own mind about himself and his place in the world.

These requirements for the survival of power are really characteristics of human development in general. What makes them "more true" for the formerly powerful is only a question of degree. Everyone who grows old must learn to adjust to the inevitability of death and the need of society to continue. It is just a more obvious adjustment for those who have scaled the highest reaches of society and merged their lives with the world in such a way that makes the leaving of it all the more painful

EXPERIENCE IN LOSING

It may be that knowing intellectually that loss is inevitable is sufficient—like male obstetricians knowing about pregnancy and the birth process—but all of those who had the opportunity to see the loss of power firsthand in their families, or in their own experience, spoke of that opportunity as a great advantage over those who had no experience of it. One ruefully noted that he learned a lot about defeat from his father's experience. "When you do not get as many votes as there are relatives in the district," he said with a smile, "you know you are in trouble." Another thought of it as a formative observation:

> I knew it was not forever. A lot of people, in my opinion, come into power and think they are going to be there forever. And they're not! Of course, some die in political office, but most are defeated. . . . People lose, or people reach for a little higher level and they lose, and they are out. But I don't think that most ever think they will be out.

It doubtless takes first-hand experience, however, to really learn the lesson:

> I was defeated the first time. I've seen people—the first time they ran they were elected, and they were reelected, and reelected, and reelected. And all of a sudden they were defeated and they were absolutely crushed because they'd never been defeated. To be

defeated the first time, hopefully, in a small, minor office is the best. . . .

It's a schoolyard fight between two boys . . . the first blow to the nose is really a stinging thing, and tears come to the eyes, and so forth. Five minutes later, you get hit in the face five or six times, but by that time it's numb. A rough analogy, but suffering a couple of political defeats early on is kind of healthy, I think. It trains perspective. Of course, some walk away. Some quit. Some dig in and they get tougher. They change their tactics. They adjust.

The advantages of an early defeat, whether in electoral politics or the private world of organizations, is first and foremost the opportunity to learn how to overcome it. Secondarily, there is the added probability that very few people beyond yourself and your immediate rivals notice. The world is still large enough to start over. The higher the powerholder advances on the ladder, the smaller the world, the greater and more public the fall. Yet we have seen some individuals make remarkable comebacks: Richard Nixon, perhaps, being among the most sturdy of comeback-politicians. For all of his drawbacks as a political figure, his capacity to conquer the seemingly insurmountable is impressive.

Putting embarrassment aside, the higher one goes, the more one's identity is wrapped around the role, the harder it is to step aside. One longtime Washington observer noted the phenomenon of those elected and appointed to a high-enough office to merit an "honorable" linked to their name:

Somehow or another, in a program or a verbal introduction, if there is some kind of recognition, and they are not recognized for having been a senator or a cabinet secretary, it is devastating. And never believe that they won't stand up in an audience and say, "I was. . . ." Or, they'll write a letter to the editor, or a letter to you—"You forgot to say. . . ." It is really pathetic. But it is pervasive.

One observer noted that the British system, while more brusque in the first instance, is less severe and a little easier to bear in the long run: "You train all your life. You have all these positions. And then you are dropped. At least in the British system they send you to the House of Lords, or put you back in Parliament," noted one observer. The United States, in contrast, sends its former leaders back to the bucolic life, expecting, in some mythological way, that they will be like Cincinnatus and return to the farm because they have served their time and no longer need or want public attention or involvement.

LETTING GO

Some argue that if you really held power, and not just influence, but held it to the extent that the power enveloped your sense of self, to the extent that you are not even aware of having it, then, in that case, you do not miss it when it is gone. According to Kevin White, the loss of power becomes something like the loss of a great love affair: "When it goes— and it is really over—when you look back, there can be warm memories but at the same time there is not a tremor. Not even a tremor!" Looking back on his years of power, he thought that those who hold it the most suffer the least breakdown when it is gone. All biographers agree that Napoleon was a calm man at St. Helena. The former mayor thought the former emperor would have accepted the notion of loss of power. "He understood its delights so he was never tempted to fantasize over any substitute for the real thing. What makes you calm is that you know what it is and you know that you cannot have it back." He would have been disappointed, said the mayor, but then he would have settled in:

> Most men try to reorder it, they try to restructure it, they see it through a distant prism. That's human nature. But are they pacing the island?

Those who wield influence, the former mayor argued, always look over their shoulder in the expectation that they will regain access. But for those who are touched by real power, "there is no afterlife," and they do not "pace the island." They may go over the events of their lives in their minds, considering the options they might have applied, the opportunities they might have taken, but they do not hunger to return to the fields of battle. Most of those I interviewed, in fact, stated unequivocally that they would never submit themselves again to the process of attaining power. Not quite the same thing as saying they would not like to have power, but sufficiently limiting as to preclude the opportunity for power from their expectations.

Still, one former powerholder said, it took him five years "to get the bug out." Although more or less settled into another life, the thought that there might be a return burned like a little night-light.

> Just that I might do something political. The realist in me said there would never be anything in politics. As far as elective office

is concerned, it was all over. But for five years, I think, it really got inside of me. . . . It did take a long time to get the bug out, longer than I thought.

An influence-wielder, who now practices in Washington, talked about the transition, the sense of significance, the opportunity to participate as an Elder Statesman from time to time. But, he concluded, "You know, what you do is look for another opportunity, and you hope very much that you can reach the point—that there will coincide a future administration in which you would be asked to play a part, and your financial situation would make it possible to do it."

"But," as one former powerholder put it,"while nothing takes its place, I don't think I would go back because I do think it's a young person's game." The price of achieving and maintaining it is just too high. Or perhaps it is that, with the exception of those who remain in the arena as influence wielders, the descent from its heights is just too steep. A man who had risen far in the world by his own standards, and headed a national voluntary association, said to me once that if he lost his position he would commit suicide, because he had been at the top and could not stand the thought of being lower. That may be an extreme view of the problem, and one that not even he might pursue, but it does suggest something of the problem and the difficulty—sometimes the terror—a powerholder perceives when it comes to having to create himself all over again in another image.

Several relatively young men stated forcefully that they did not want to put themselves or their families through the upheavals of the transition to private life again: they set their courses, achieved some economic stability, and they did not look forward to risking any of it again, however fondly they recalled their years of public power.

Many powerholders stay in power because they do not know what else to do, or where else to go. Having a profession to fall back upon is better than not having a profession, but it is a marginal difference. An attorney who returns to a law firm from a public career often finds himself the "new boy on the block," less familiar with the law than first year law school graduates. More likely, he or she is brought in to be a drawing card to potential clients. It is an awkward thing for those who view themselves as public servants. The period of awkwardness can be compounded by a long period of adjustment during which they draw large sums from the firm and add very little in return. Still, it is an identity and it can provide economic security and even some interest. According to one attorney:

It is somewhat easier for a lawyer—for most lawyers—to do it.
They have a place to go. And lawyers by nature tend to invest what
they are doing with a lot of energy and attack. And then, once it is
over, to move on to something else. That's what I was doing then,
and this is what I'm doing now. It helps something. And when you
get a really interesting case that requires an awful lot of work and
mental energy, and combat, you get really fired up and it takes on
its own significance. And the fact that you get paid a lot more for
it—that helps.

Other attorneys also spoke of the opportunity available to them to put
together a "package of extra-curricular activities" that is usually more
feasible when linked to a law practice than a business career, but it does
not make the practice of law any more exciting or rewarding.

A professional role is a reasonable alternative, as is a serious hobby like
writing, painting, or love for a sport like golf or fishing. Leisure activities,
like a dedication to a sport as either a player or a fan, appear to be more
common among corporate leaders than among political leaders—some
notable exceptions notwithstanding, such as the love of golfing by such
figures as Dwight Eisenhower, Gerald Ford, and Tip O'Neill. It may be that
politics or public events fulfill a need for testing one's self out of desire
rather than necessity, an emotional need that the business world—based
as it is on material rewards—cannot match.

Such personal satisfactions aside, those without either a professional
or an amateur identity to slide back into have a more complicated
transition to overcome. There is a sense that the skills acquired by a
successful government employee are essentially public relations skills,
and former political figures are usually slotted into such peripheral roles
at corporations as government or public relations directors.

The problem of letting go of power extends to deeper levels than issues
of vocation or avocation. Separating one's identity from the role is
perhaps the most critical factor in survival, but it is also likely to be one
of the hardest things to do, especially if the power is held firmly over a
long period of time, because everyone else will confuse the person with
the role. Many try to defend themselves against the inevitable loss of
power and public identity by reminding themselves of their private
identities and keeping a distance from the beginning. The wife of a former
powerholder noted that they would "both look at each other and say,
'Hey, just remember how you were raised.' I don't mean to say we
humbled each other or ourselves, but we did keep reminding ourselves
that this was a great opportunity and that good fortune had come to us,

but we mustn't buy into it totally. And that, I think," she concluded, "has eased our exit."

A former governor described it this way:

It's not easy when you leave public life, I'll tell you. It's not easy. When you are in office, you press a button and you have somebody do what you want them to do. And people are—not subservient—but they are aware of the fact of who you are. It is very easy to become arrogant, even though you don't realize you've become that way. And the use of the public power—it certainly has a psychological affect on everything else that you do.

From the perspective of another former powerholder the problem is not identity, but the nature of the circumstances: having power is a better thing than not having power.

In my opinion, it's the biggest single reason why political people don't leave public office: You just don't know what to do. Well, sometimes it's financial, but sometimes they recognize that whatever else they do, it is never going to be like being governor, or mayor, or speaker of the house, or whatever. They suspect the boredom, and they don't want to walk into it. Or they are unsure. Basically, what it comes down to is that they just don't know what they want to do, and it keeps them in forever and a day.

It is a scene we have observed many times in many places: the head of the organization who stays not because he enjoys it, or the organization's survival depends upon him (frequently it is hurt by his too-long presence). He or she stays because they have devoted every waking minute to the job and cannot imagine how they will fill their days without it. They have lost the ability—assuming they ever had it—to sustain interesting and rewarding private relationships. They have neither the skill nor the energy to work their way up in another career, should they be young enough to pursue that option. They cannot imagine other identities for themselves, other issues that would capture their minds and their energy. They are trapped at the top and they are not sure there is a net to catch them from falling all the way down. Any net, any other activity, in fact, would be less satisfying than their life's dream, which is now behind them. The problem is that any other life cannot be comprehended. After a lifetime of convincing one's self that this is the best of all possible worlds, it is clearly a letdown to move to another world knowing that the best is past.

Letting go of the world one has created or led is a little like letting a child leave home. We acknowledge it as the mature, proper thing to do—better in the long run for everyone concerned—but in our hearts most of us know it really is not better for us. As one former public official put it:

> What do you do next? People like myself say I'm jumping, and I hope there is a net there or something. But you have to do that because you have to break away from it.

Letting go requires time and the healing that comes with time and, if possible, a "therapeutic" environment of support: people who will tell you they are glad to see you; that you did a good job, and that it is hard to let go of the past, but you need to look forward to the future. It helps to have people who can realistically talk over your options with you.

Leaving power knowing that it was the time to leave, that nothing more could be accomplished, nothing further gained, is the best of all possible options. One rarely has such an unambiguous opportunity, however. It is quite likely that knowing the limits of one's power is a never-ending search for most of us, most of the time. It would truly be a gift to be able to say, unambiguously, that this is the time, this is what I can do, and no more. Ira Jackson, who was nine months out of power in state government when we talked—too short a time to know how his transition would work out, too soon to know whether Michael Dukakis would be elected president and he would be called back to serve in a national administration—put it this way:

> Knowing when to get out—especially if you are perceived to have had a successful engagement—and thinking about whether to go back. You know—high expectations, both personally and externally. And you wonder whether you don't just savor the memory. I don't know. . . .
>
> What do you do for an encore? It's not so much that you're going to earn a living, that you're going to have self-esteem, but how are you ever going to do anything that is going to be this much fun, this meaningful again? Luckily, I've had a couple of turns at doing things that met my criteria of progress and personal satisfaction, but this one—this latest chapter—it's tough. It's tougher.

It is helpful to be able to plan for the future *before* leaving power rather than afterwards. It is the same rule that argues it is better to look for a job while you have a job, rather than look for one from the ranks of the unemployed. As with the unemployed, there are more powerholders and they are not as distinguishable as the pool of current powerholders, who can often offer something immediate to balance a promise for the future.

Another element in planning for the future is timing in terms of the current job. Unless the power is held for a limited term, there is always doubt about what else might have been accomplished, what new heights might have been scaled. It is like the gambler knowing when to quit: if you lose the $100 you were willing to gamble right off the bat, you give it up and accept defeat. If you win $500, and then lose $100, that hurts. It is the unknown, the potential that might have been that rankles most deeply in the soul.

The National Governor's Association provides some advice for retiring governors, the main thrust of which is that planning for it while in office is critical: for a smooth transition for the incoming governor and his or her staff; helping the outgoing staff find employment elsewhere; finding oneself a home (preferably away from the state capital); buying a new car and making sure one's license is up to date (although one former governor suggested it might be better to lease a car and hire a chauffeur to drive it); seeing what help will be available to one's spouse and school-age children in their transition (no particular answers, just the note that it should be addressed); and arranging for help in handling the government-related work that still remains (although a former governor remarked to me that he put two telephone lines into his new home only to find that they never rang—the advice from the Association notwithstanding).[1]

The most significant benefit of planning is that it helps bring the future into focus.

PRIVATE OPTIONS

Moving from a powerful job in a large sphere to a powerful job in the smaller world can provide a great deal of satisfaction, as long as the powerholder can adjust to it. Adam Yarmolinsky, who went through several transitions as professor, lawyer, back to public life, back to law, and now is the provost of a state university, described his journey this way:

> It would be easy for me to feel that what I am doing at this
> campus is so much less important than what I was doing at the
> Pentagon. And I could feel awfully sorry for myself if I wanted to.

On the other hand, I don't look at it that way. I think of it as an extraordinarily responsible job in which there are thousands—hundreds of people and thousands of students—relying on me, and in this context, I have just as much opportunity to use whatever talents I have.

It may be significant to note that he did not move directly from the government to being provost. The satisfaction he finds now comes after the experience of dissatisfaction with teaching and the isolation of the academic community, and the practice of law. If nothing else, he learned, over a long career, what does not work for him. If power is a finite commodity in all organizations, part of the pleasure of power is to have more than others (and not be subject to the rule of others), and to be able to use it to accomplish some goal. While the ivory tower is not in business for the sake of business, being at the business end of it is probably closer to the experience of power than being at the scholarly end.

Moving to a university is an option that many pursue, or think of pursuing. Other virtues of the university world, from the perspective of the refugee, are that it is prestigious because it deals with ideas and the future, and secondly, that it is not hierarchical, which is to say that power is perceived to be distributed in a collegial fashion with no one having significantly more than anyone else. This, of course, is not necessarily true, but it is ambiguous enough for anyone to believe it who wants to believe it.

While many move to university settings, few remain for very long if they have the opportunity to leave. For all its perks, sitting in the ivory tower can be a lonely life. Any life is lonely compared to the centers of power, but the intellectual world is more isolated than most, presumably because it leaves room for the mind to flourish. As one former powerholder/former professor put it:

> Perhaps the most miserable time in my life was when I left government and finally went to Harvard to be a professor. I tried to behave as if I had power. I didn't. I was in considerable demand for a while, for consultancies and things, and I made too much of that. I didn't buckle down to the job of being a professor. . . .
>
> But I was not cut out to be a lonely scholar, and that's what they wanted me to be . . . and I was not willing to be it. . . . I didn't appreciate it. I wanted to be back in power.

One man told his secretary that she had to be on call twenty-four hours a day in case the White House telephoned. It never did (at least not after the normal working day), but he could not imagine when he left Washington that his contributions would be so easily forgotten. It is very hard, indeed, to come to terms with not being needed; it is an inconceivable notion to those who immerse themselves in the center of things and come to think of themselves as indispensable.

Although both Kevin White and Jeane Kirkpatrick spoke of being most excited by ideas (rather than by the world of power), it is not irrelevant that she found herself best able to pursue them in an academic setting, free of the bickering she associates with "court politics," while Kevin White was intellectually challenged by ideas in the political setting, where there is a rough and tumble immediacy about ideas, and bright, committed advocates stand ready to advance them.

Another problem for former powerholders in the academic setting is that they are not usually good at it. There is a genuine difference in the intellectual approach taken by those who practice politics (in whatever form, whether public or private) and those who deal with theory. Politics is about specifics, compromises, and what is possible. Academics talk about theories, Basic Truths, and what makes one thing similar to something else, rather than what makes it different. Former practitioners tend to think and talk about their experiences, tell anecdotes, and bring in guest speakers for the benefit of their students. Those who come from the world of the real to the world of theory often find errors in the arguments used to explain the theories. Minor errors, to be sure, but errors nonetheless, and because of them they tend to discredit the theories.

While it is a rare practitioner who feels at home in the world of theory, it is an equally rare practitioner who can ignite the minds of his or her students once the glitz is gone. Students may be attracted because of their ambitions and belief that the former powerholder could help them—all of which may well be true—but they are rarely attracted as students are to others who teach in our universities who can ignite the mind with untold possibilities.

There is also the problem of relations between those who come to the university by virtue of their politics and those who come because of their scholarship. Each side looks down a little on the other. The academics see the former powerholders with the double standard we typically apply to all politicians: as people who have somehow or other compromised themselves. And practitioners see the scholars as insecure persons afraid to test themselves in the real world. As one former powerholder in a university put it:

There is envy all over campus for a man who had been confident enough and well-informed enough—I think confident is the key word—to put his or her name forward for elective office and do it, and obviously have done it well. And although it's hard to know how that is computed, there is definitely admiration there, whether it is stated or not.

The failure of a former powerholder to repeat success in an academic setting, however, is as future problem. The first issue in letting go is having a place to go to. As one public powerholder put it, "The big problem is where do you go? Am I going to move to ——— University and take over the Center for Policy of Whatever? The world gets very small." Not everyone leaving office has a policy center in their area of expertise ready and waiting for immediate occupancy. And even fewer are acceptable as teachers at a major university today unless they also possess a Ph.D.

STAYING IN THE ARENA: INFLUENCE

An easy step is to move from the office but stay in the area, in an effort to wield influence on the issues that have grown dear to the heart. When you become a person thought of as influential, as opposed to holding a specific influential position, the identity lasts longer than power. You become associated with—and identified by—issues, hopefully, by important issues. One can have influence on going in and on going out, assuming that relationships with other powerholders were established and sustained after leaving office. Actually, just the knowledge of how the system works: what goes into reaching a decision, what an office handles or is not capable of handling, and so on, are valuable bits of information that can keep a former powerholder in the realm of decision-making, assuming he or she is willing to sit on the other side of the table as a supplicant or an observer instead of a distributor of largess. The biggest problem is whether or not he or she is willing to be a supplicant, an outsider; and the second biggest problem is whether or not those now in power are willing to let the Ghost of Power Past in the door.

It is at that point that questions of behavior become relevant. If the powerholder behaved with civility toward others while in office (was not abusive, arbitrary, etc.), he or she is likely to be treated civilly by the Establishment upon losing power. If the power was abused in the eyes of others, the potential for remaining influential declines markedly. It seems almost too obvious a point to make, but it would be a mistake to omit making it because it is important. It is a necessary condition for those who need, or think they need to stay.

Wanting to be influential must be balanced against the emotions that come into play on all sides when someone from the past seeks a role in the present. Most of the complexity is not too difficult to imagine, but part of it is that once you know how decisions are actually made, how intimate and insulated the process, a former participant feels awkward about the gulf that exists, knowing it cannot really be breached. However eminent the personage on the outside, he or she will be judged as much by inferiors on the inside who are "in the know" as they will be by a peer replacement. Some do not care to submit themselves to such a review.

What is left the former powerholder is his or her reputation, and it can be squandered, like any fortune, by spreading it too thinly, or by trying to employ it in losing battles. Accepting the circumstances of the outsider, and accepting the notion of a new peer group (one not solely composed of the world of the powerful) and a new identity for one's self, all this is key to holding on to the past organization or issue. In fact, it is key to the notion of surviving power.

Another potential reward for those who can stay in the arena is simple economic gain, although most of those who leave public power do so too late in life to amass really large fortunes. Still, the money does provide many of the comforts of life, and it is also as good a measure as there is of a former powerholder's position. As one former powerholder noted, people who pay for his advice tend to take it. Before—when he was in office—those who came to him for help added his views on how to go about achieving their ends to the calculations of others. In his present position of consultant, they were more inclined to accept it. Although he is offering advice as influence rather than power, there is satisfaction in having it taken. And there is certainly a measurable satisfaction in making money, albeit of a lesser magnitude. If nothing else, the very "measurableness" of money is satisfying, assuming you come out on the upper end of the scale.

USING THE SKILLS

If it is true that there are skills that are learned in using power, the best of all possible things is to be able to practice these acquired skills in the future, not to tuck them away in the attic along with the dreams of a future that might have been. Kevin Harrington described it this way:

The point is that the experience of power—the experience I had—changes forever one's perspective, and whether I deal with the business world, or the academic world, or so many worlds I deal with today, it is interesting when I sit down with a potential client or a group of people, I pretty much know where they are going almost before they know where they are going, because I saw it so many times in the legislature. Seeing the onions come in, so to speak, with all of the layers of the onion.

Former California Governor Pat Brown talked about the public issues he concerns himself with today as the head of his own institute. In his case, he uses political skills in working with people, and the knowledge and commitment he made to issues while in office. He created his own institute that provides him the opportunities he wants to stay involved and to "amortize" the experience of his public years. According to the former governor, the Edmund G. Brown Institute of Government is focused on four things:

we're working on minority crime ... completion of the water project ... the method of treatment of the mentally ill ... and mass transportation.
    I work with other groups, too, in the infrastructure of government. I work with the California Council on Environment and Economic Balance that I started after I left the governor's office.

Several governors, including his own son, have been elected and served since the senior Brown left office, but he has probably been more successful than most former governors in positioning himself in the world of public advocacy and public interest. If one has the resources to do it, it is a more active position than an academic post might be, and less time-consuming than actual government service. It has a broader horizon than business, in which he also engages, and it is well-insulated from the vagaries of an electorate. It is an almost unbeatable combination, assuring both the feeling of having profited from his years in office, and a sense of significance in the issues to which he devotes himself.
    Governor Brown and Robert Finch, former Secretary of the Department of Health, Education, and Welfare (who also served as Lieutenant Governor in California) both play supportive roles, from which they derive enjoyment, in electoral politics at the local, state, and to some extent, the national level. The position of elder statesman provides much of the deference that accompanies power and participation in serious public

matters. Of course, the mantle of elder statesman does not necessarily devolve upon every former powerholder, even those who held significant posts. More than a few are put on the shelf, or at least feel that way, particularly if the only direction they look is back.

In order for former powerholders to use many of the lessons they learned of power on issues of significance, others must come to them. They are not in a position to command that problems be brought before them. If they seek to wield influence, they are dependent on the recognition that no one is bound by their views, no issue determined by their responses, and their advice must be solicited.

For those who derive satisfaction from the task—rather than the recognition—the knowledge they possess is power. Said one traveler from the world of power:

> Somebody called me recently because their child is leaving school and has no job—a child with mental retardation. I was able to give him a name and the address and phone number of the director of a workshop, and I said, "I don't know whether he has an opening, but this is a very caring man and I suggest that you call." And that helps: to be able to have this vast network of names and numbers helps.

Using the skills of power depends, to some extent, on the willingness of others to be deferential in recognition of the former authority, if not the present knowledge or status. If others are unwilling—or unknowing— the former powerholder is not without resources (he or she did, after all, have the skills to acquire power in the first place), but he may be without the heart to undertake the effort because it can take a lot of effort. On the other hand, it can also be a rather simple and effortless task to bring together people who can help each other, or to offer a different idea on a subject you have studied for years. If you have been involved with an issue for a long time, you also have the benefit of being articulate on it (because you have said the same thing over and over again), which makes you sound so much more intelligent than those who are grasping for a way to conceptualize their concerns.

PRIVATE PERSON/PUBLIC IMAGE

Achieving power gives one status, position, and identity, but in leaving power these attributes become both an aura and an albatross. At one level, being identified as a public person becomes a disqualification for filling another role. Micho Spring, five years out of power as deputy mayor of Boston, acknowledged that a comfortable part of the role was that people knew who she was. "I used to say," she continued, "the further I isolate myself at the top, the harder it will be to translate that into another job afterwards, if that's what I want to do. In many ways, that is still accurate." She, like many other former powerholders, chose in the end to start her own firm, retaining the position of power, even if it is over a vastly diminished empire. Perhaps she would not be a "captain to another captain," but on a daily basis—to the crew—she is indeed the captain. She also thought that to many people it would not matter what she did, she would still be thought of as the Deputy Mayor:

> I have the feeling that if I were to become president of Gillette next year, I would still be introduced as the former deputy mayor. That's a much more interesting title. I don't think it matters what else I do. People will always want to bring that up because that's kind of the sense of relevance. I think that will be part of my identity forever.

Unless, of course, you are forgotten. Robert Finch noted that whether a powerholder is elected or appointed, there is a tendency to get a distorted sense of his public image, "an enhanced view of his popularity, what his mandate is, and the feeling that he can serve or be reelected indefinitely, or something more important." One reads the polls, but the polls reflect relative choices. Still, it is the only measure there is. Once out, however, one is frequently dropped from the list of choices. Then, the former powerholder must come to terms with his popularity among those whom he meets on a regular or even on an infrequent basis. According to Finch:

> My image was all very largely distorted by the false sense of the ability that you have in appointive office, or elective office—[the idea] that you can hang on to your power in some perverse way, and you can be appointed to something, or you will be elected to something else if you choose to be. . . . It is very hard to get a realistic assessment of where you are at any given time, or in any given election or administration.
>
> And then, that brings you back to those who come through in high places in one administration . . . who get Potomac Fever. They stay on and decide to do something else in Washington, as opposed to those who go back, for whatever purpose. Some go back and think they need to be reanointed. Some are bored

because they want to pursue something else. . . . You get a whole different set of decisions that flow from their view of their popularity as to what it is they might want to do in one setting. . . . That is one of the reasons I stepped out of a large law firm when I got back, because when you are playing that kind of game, you are really not in control. So, I took the next step out, which is to control my time in a very small firm.

The public image is a role that can be played while in office, but it can become something of an albatross when out of office because of the danger of being type-cast into certain kinds of roles, or frozen into a particular emotional posture—or worst of all, being thought a fool by those who do not care, one way or the other, who you were yesterday, because they did not know who you were then, and do not care now. When fame or notoriety give one a public image, there are some benefits: quick service and good tables in restaurants, and so on, which can be a kind of solace for the years put in that are past; but it can also be a barrier to other things such as privacy and the capacity to develop another identity. Too public or notorious an image, of course, can overcome many restraints. John Ehrlichman spoke of the rebirth he underwent when he eventually retreated to Santa Fe after serving time in prison following Watergate:

> One of the more interesting aspects of the freedom that I found here was the freedom to walk through the open doors as they presented themselves, without any fear of consequences. There was no downside to anything I wanted to do, and that must be what a bankrupt feels like, once he comes out of bankruptcy and gets rid of all of his debts. There is no more financial burden. And that whole . . . feeling of liberation from social constraints—I don't know how to describe it—is something I have never experienced before. It was all new. It was like being nineteen on shore leave. I did all sorts of things: I was invited to France by the French government. . . . all these good, amazing things that I would probably never have thought of doing. It turned out to be a very rich kind of transition.

For most people, the freedom to completely rebuild their lives comes at too great a cost and is not realistically available. There are marginal opportunities, marginal licenses given to step beyond the norm, but the public image weighs heavily. For some—the survivors—the private image is firmly fixed, rooted in a set of values, or a sense of place. Others are not so fortunate. According to Ehrlichman,

Other people are blown by the winds. I think an awful lot of quite successful people have never had to stop and ask themselves, where do I want to go, and what are my life goals? Or what do I want to do tomorrow? They want to open doors all their lives. And at each open door there is a mommy to tell them, "Straighten your tie, or take this job, or don't take this—whatever." I think the mommies may not necessarily be their mommies, but they may be a boss or somebody in position of authority.

Many of those I spoke to stressed the importance of being able to turn inward, to retain or create a sense of self. David Braun said that he finally learned that "what makes you happiest—assuming you are capable of being a happy person—is accommodating to what you are at that moment in time. Not spending your time wishing and hoping for something else:

> I remember dancing in high school and always looking around to see if there was a prettier girl. There is always a prettier girl. . . . There is always someone richer than you. If you are going to let that drive you crazy, you will never be happy. You find what pleases you and you plumb it. I never understood that. Including relationships. And sometimes it's too late, and you find out about that when the opportunity is gone. Your kids get grown and you can't do that anymore. You had to do it when they were 4 and 5. When they're 22, you can't do it anymore. So, it's very important that you know those things when there is still time. Now, at 56, there is still plenty of time for a lot of things, but not that anymore.

Another factor for those who wait to be asked back is that they lose all control over their own lives. Waiting by the phone for the call from the White House, accepting all engagements in the hope that they will lead to something of significance, is a sad, familiar pattern. Those who wait never look for alternative sources of happiness, and make themselves even less powerful than those who never held power in the first place. You wait, you defer things in the hope that something else will turn up. You look for opportunities. Most of all, you are never content, nor are you in a position to recognize or take pleasure in the things you have.

We are all familiar with former powerholders whose egos appear to be without restraint, and who demand deference to their erstwhile position from everyone. They are a sad, sometimes ridiculous sight. Why, a thoughtful person might inquire, don't they see themselves as others see them? How can they be so wrapped up in position that they fail to perceive the impression they are making?

From the perspective of the former powerholders, of course, it is a different story. To some extent, they are protecting the office. To a larger extent, they are protecting themselves, and can feel quite vulnerable if their public role is not remembered. What they are protecting, ultimately, is their identity. The public role was the purpose for their existence. Not to have the role recognized is akin to not existing.

And having the role recognized—and one's performance in the role as well—is akin to drinking nectar. John Buckley, who was often described while in office as the most liberal sheriff in the country, reflected thus on his public image almost ten years later:

> It's nice being on the sideline for a change, and watching the great parade of madness. There is a certain satisfaction in looking back at it. I think another thing that has surprised me is the respect that I have from people I didn't think of, like ———— [a current public official] telling people I was different; but I believed in and loved what I did. I only see him maybe once or twice a year, but he holds me in great respect, partly, I think, because I took the stands that he couldn't take. Remember, we'd been asking him for support against the death penalty, and he says, "You know, personally I agree with you, but in my district I couldn't take that stand." In his district—no one's going to defeat him! But he is going to bottle up the death penalty this year for the Governor so it won't be embarrassing, they won't have to veto it, which is fine, because he won't do it forever.
>
>   But anyway, I think the fact [is] that he is one of the best politicians. And then there is Tip O'Neill. He was talking about my great victory in 1974 over his friend Walter Sullivan—great victory—like it happened last week! I think he was a little concerned that I might be thinking of running against him, which would have been more hopeless! I think that pleases me.

Being remembered with respect and a measure of love is a reward that can fill the heart. Clearly, not everyone will be remembered so kindly, but most of us have a capacity to believe that we did what was best at the time, and that can compensate for a great deal.

Jeffrey Sonnenfeld, of the Harvard Business School, notes that the chief executives he studied were less likely than their subordinates to prepare themselves for retirement. They were also less likely to find pleasure in other things, and they were more likely to stay involved—or at least to try to stay involved—in the activities of the firm:

> Such work-intensives as chief executives of corporations come to look forward to never-ending missions and enduring status. It is hard to obtain the immortality they seek, if indeed (it is) at all possible.[2]

If it is difficult for those in the private sphere, it is that much more difficult for public officials who are known to a wider spectrum of the population. For many, it is a "never-ending mission," the chief objective of which is to secure their immortality.

PRIVATE PERSON/PRIVATE IMAGE

Having another identity, another role to go to, is the easiest transition from power, although one that cannot be popular before events require it. For many years these people have lent their identities to other causes and to the public image of who they are. Retrieving that identity for private use makes them uncomfortable. As public leaders, they are imbued with strengths beyond compare. The problem of survival after power requires the emergence of an alternative self-concept, one they can live with in comfort, one in which they can even find pleasure.

One of the easiest solutions (albeit one not available to most powerholders) was Micho Spring's, who left office when she was three months pregnant. Having gone through transitions from office before, she knew it was going to be difficult, and that it was going to take time. For a woman, the role of expectant mother and mother is a traditionally acceptable role that brings its own rewards, as well as absolution from the need to maintain a public career.

Unfortunately, there are very few powerholders likely to have the options of motherhood and all that it entails in truly re-orienting one's emotions as well as one's identity, although even that opportunity is more a passing phenomenon than a long-term solution. "One of the real downfalls of the task-oriented thing," said one former powerholder,

> is dulling the feelings. After a while, you spend so much time doing things . . . you don't attend to your emotional needs. . . . You get so caught up in what you are doing that you don't spend time with old friends because there is too much going on.

To the extent that private satisfactions are based on relationships with family intimates, or with old friends, they require some kind of nurturance to survive. Many persons who rise to power were never good at private relationships in the first place. Some are particularly inner-oriented and need less in the way of intimacy. One observer mentioned a powerholder whose best friend lived in another state. When the powerholder left office and moved not only to the same state, but the same city, he saw his friend only once in the first year out of office. The powerholder did not feel any less close to his friend, he just did not need to see him.

Such a self-contained figure is not quite so common among those who seek public office. Typically, there is the man (more rarely the woman) who spends ten, twenty, or thirty years as Mr. Mayor, Mr. Whatever. Everyone he meets talks to him in the context of his title. They tell him their problems and what they think he wants to hear. They are solicitous of his person because he carries the greater weight of public responsibility. They accede to his wishes out of respect for the office. It is the optimum role of the father, but there is no role beyond parenting to help us model an alternative part to play.

One rises to the head of the family (public or private), and when the children are gone, or a new leader emerges to take that place, there remains only the role of grandparent, or elder statesman, someone who may be called upon from time to time to offer an opinion, but who is never sure of involvement, certainly never sure of having the advice taken. The part is sufficient for some. It is more likely to be sufficient if they can turn their energy to other things, and offer the views they are called upon to express without much attachment to the outcomes. If it is not sufficient, former powerholders—like parents whose children leave home—suffer from an empty nest syndrome.

The energy required of powerholding can be tremendous. Much of it is fueled by the power itself, but shifting to a lower gear is a necessity when one leaves office. One man recalled that his secretary once told him he made more than 600 speeches in a single year, "That's almost two a day! And she said, 'Yes, and I'm missing some of them.' And I said that's incredible. And when I think of it, I think of all the energy. And now, it's like I am on vacation." It disappears "like smoke," he said. "As an old guy, what you end up with is yourself in the mirror." Survival requires either shifting to a lower gear, or redirecting the energy to something else.

Power is associated with control. Surviving power means being able to live without control over the lives and ideas of others. Those who were in public life need to let world events go by without them, without the need to link their lives to the issues which mark the age. It is a far more difficult thing to do than we think, stemming from the very core of fear of mortality.

There is a discontinuity in the transition from power, during which the former powerholder feels as if he were "walking around inside" himself, recognizing the separation of the private from the public self. The survivor must come to the point where the inside once again merges with the outside. He or she must come to the point where the public image can be called up for special occasions, or for casual interactions with strangers, but where it does not dominate. The survivor of power must, at some point, give up defending the public image from attacks and, most of all, from a sense of neglect. He will always recall the past, but he should not dwell in it himself, or require it of others. Kevin White said that the public—over time—forgives its leaders. The survivor, too, must come to forgive himself for "all the changes of the seasons missed in that passion that people call the pursuit of power." What he has become, what he has shared of the human experience, is who he is. What he has not shared does not diminish his authenticity.

Losing power leaves the individual less protected than he or she had been, but it does not leave holes in the personality like parts of a puzzle that can no longer be found in the box. The outer wrappings are gone, but the individual who has held power is left with a sustaining sense of his ability. He knows that, if he chooses to, he can take on the burdens and the pride of leadership. In any group he chooses to join, he knows that he could become its leader, even if he does not choose to, even if its other members are unaware of his capacity. There is a sense of competence that comes with the experience of power that never really leaves even while the former powerholder lets go of that restless longing for confirmation of his strengths that was fueled in the past by ambition, aggressiveness, or even by uncertainty as to who he was.

But do we ever really "let go?" Is not life characterized by striving, and do not those who have striven hard all their lives to achieve something have striving and struggle embedded in their characters in such a way that they cannot let themselves be satisfied by the sense of competence and the assurance that comes with success? Just as yesterday's triumph gives little comfort to those whose faces are turned toward today and tomorrow, so, too, must the motivation that drives them keep churning in some inner recess of the soul. It is not enough to have won elections in the past if you are not likely to win them in the future. That loss will always burn more deeply into the identity of some than the victories ever did.

While the characteristics of the personality that drove one to achieve power in the first place do not disappear with the loss of power, survival requires that they be channeled in some other direction, or that the former powerholder transform himself, turning the drive to attain power into the achievement of other ends. There are only a few paths that can be taken: *up*, to some higher, perhaps transcendental end, although "up" might also include a larger mountain in the world of the powerful; *laterally*, to a similar role in another sphere; *inward*, to discover new talents and joys; or *downward*, to lead a quieter life in a smaller sphere, conscious that it is "down" and content to let others take the lead.

Moving Up—Putting aside the political need in both the public and the private sector to be seen upholding traditional religious values, there are a surprising number of men and women who succeed in the world while sincerely seeking a spiritual path. The seriousness of their purpose usually gives them a higher standing among their peers who recognize their broader horizons. Whether or not these serious individuals can, upon retirement, give themselves over entirely to the search for their spiritual end is not clear. Some merely exchange institutions, replacing the temporal with the eternal. Some maintain the same level of spiritual commitment, but it does not fill their hearts in sufficient measure to overcome the loss of power. Some succeed, and for them, surviving power is another step toward a larger end. The paring away of the structures of power is a process they can use, to reveal an inner self that has been altered by the experience and made stronger for the next step toward the ultimate end. Believing in a higher end can relieve one of fears about the future, even the fear of death. More immediately, the breadth of focus can lessen the pain of personal loss, helping the individual put the experience and himself into perspective in relation to the larger questions of life and the meaning of life.

A *Lateral Move*—To a large extent, a lateral move is more of an exchange than a survival, but it is a way of overcoming the loss of power in the first instance. Given the value many of those I interviewed placed on having experienced loss earlier in their careers, the process is unquestionably a valuable asset in their next job. Moving from the public to the private sphere—or the other way around—is a genuine lateral move to the extent that it permits the individual to recreate himself as another person in another realm. It also preserves the structures by which the individual has defended himself, preventing any venturesome intrusions into his sense of self. It is an escape from the need to come to terms with one's self, but it works as long as internal problems do not arise.

Inward to Other Satisfactions—There is a sense that the exercise of power is akin to the exercise of freedom, but the experience of those who have held power is of a far more circumscribed adventure than they had ever thought possible, bounded as it is by ritual and the wide dispersal of authority. While the freedom associated with exercising power may be more illusory than real, the greater challenge and opportunity for freedom is that which comes after, when those who have left power—knowing that they are capable of great things—can choose how to use their strengths and how to employ the person they have become. The survivors are those who rebuild their worlds on the strengths that they have revealed to themselves, while retaining enough curiosity to see how far those strengths will really take them.

Downward—America, like ancient Rome before it, values the example of Cincinatus who retired to his farm after holding great power. We admire someone who can find pleasure in simple things. Yet it is one thing to know that it is valued in general terms, and another to feel it for one's self. Letting go of the images and expectations of worldly power could be a giant leap into the unknown except that it does not happen all at once. The former powerholder needs time to find other things to care about, the kinds of things most of his fellow citizens worry about and take pleasure in: the family, the house and garden, the town. He needs to narrow his focus, and, ideally, he needs to derive pleasure from the new environment in which he finds himself, however intimate that world may be. The former powerholder needs to recreate himself.

Rebuilding, or recreating one's self outside the world of the powerful, depends on two things: knowledge of one's strengths and weaknesses, and the willingness to take risks. Recreating one's self as an autonomous whole—not just as a participant in other worlds—is within everyone's grasp as long as they are willing to reach out, knowing that the process will take time and that it will lead them only toward themselves and those few with whom they share their lives.

Not everyone survives power. Some lose themselves in the experience. Some become enlarged by the experience but find themselves at sea when it is over, unable—sometimes unwilling—to touch land anywhere because it will mean the end of their journey. Unless there is another image of themselves that they can fit into, it can be the most difficult adjustment they ever make, and those who fail to make it can become bitter and behave in self-destructive ways. Those who enabled them to function when they were in power are no longer there and, left to their own devices, many lose the one thing they had retained until then: their reputations.

Perhaps it is right that "the pursuit of happiness" comes after life and liberty in the hierarchy of natural rights. It is an objective that can be most securely sought after only after the pursuit of other goals, when one can draw comfort in the knowledge that everything else has been done that could be done. It is critical to survival to continue the search for happiness (in the sense of joy and fulfillment) when other goals have been met or lost, because of all the things we might pursue, only inner happiness is an end in itself.

Notes

CHAPTER 1.

The Powerholder's View of Power

1. Tip O'Neill with William Novak, *Man of the House: The Life and Political Memoirs of Speaker Tip O'Neill* (New York: Random House, 1987), p. 213.

2. See Norbert Elias, *Power and Civility: The Civilizing Process*, vol. 2, translated by Edmund Jophcott (New York: Pantheon Books, 1982), part 2, chap. 1, "The Social Constraint toward Self-Constraint."

3. Ibid., p. 258

4. See, for example, O'Neill's *Man of the House*, op. cit., p. 309

5. Charles A. Vigeland, *Great Good Fortune: How Harvard Makes Its Money* (Boston: Houghton Mifflin, 1986), p. 127.

6. Peter Woll and Rochelle Jones, "Bureaucratic Defense in Depth," in Ronald E. Pynn, ed., *Watergate and the American Political Process* (New York: Praeger, 1975), p. 233.

7. Rosabeth Moss Kanter, *Men and Women of the Corporation* (New York: Basic Books, 1977), pp. 222–24.

CHAPTER 2.

Crossing the Border

1. Daniel Goldman, "Politics as an Ego Trip," *Boston Globe*, December 20, 1987, p. A22.

2. William Glaberson, "Life After Salomon Brothers," *New York Times*, Sunday, October 11, 1987, Section 3, p. 6.

3. Most notably the work of Matina Horner, e.g., "Femininity and Successful Achievement: Basic Inconsistency," in J. M. Bardwick et al., *Feminine Personality and Conflict* (Belmont, Calif.: Brooks Cole, 1970).

4. Jack Newfield, *Robert Kennedy: A Memoir* (New York: E.P. Dutton, 1969), "When the crowds mobbed him in Manila or Cracow [the tours he made just before he ran for the Senate in 1964], he would mumble to aides, 'It was for him, it was for him." p. 31.

5. Ibid., pp. 26–27.

6. See Michel Crozier, *The Bureaucratic Phenomenon* (Chicago: University of Chicago Press, 1964).

7. C. P. Snow, *Corridors of Power*, 1964, in Omnibus Edition, *Strangers and Brothers* (London: Macmillan, 1972), vol. 3, p. 74.

CHAPTER 3.

Exercising Power—the Unexpected Experience

1. Rosabeth Moss Kanter, *Men and Women of the Corporation* (New York: Basic Books, 1977), pp. 51–55.

2. See, for example, the work of Howard Raiffa on decision theory at the John F. Kennedy School of Government, Harvard University.

3. James G. March and Herbert A. Simon, *Organizations* (New York: John Wiley, 1958).

4. See Donald A. Ritchie's biography, *James M. Landis* (Cambridge: Harvard University Press, 1981), which describes the lengths to which the bureaucracy will go to protect itself and its administrators.

5. Those who make the argument for play include Nietzsche, Schiller, Sartre, Boehme, Huizinga, Marcuse, and Norman O. Brown.

6. Richard E. Neustadt, *Presidential Power* (New York: John Wiley, 1960).

7. Bob Woodward, *Veil: The Secret Wars of the CIA 1981–1987* (New York: Simon and Schuster, 1987), p. 293.

CHAPTER 4.

The Structures of Power

1. The term "rainmaker" is used in law firms to describe the well-known members of the partnership whose major function is to draw important clients to the firm.

2. David R. Mayhew, *Congress: The Electoral Connection* (New Haven: Yale University Press, 1974).

3. Christopher Matthews, *Hardball: How Politics Is Played—Told by One Who Knows the Game* (New York: Summit Books, 1988), pp. 136–138.

4. Tip O'Neill with William Novak, *Man of the House: The Life and Political Memoirs of Speaker Tip O'Neill* (New York: Random House, 1987), p. 131.

5. "Tales from the Top: Inside the White House with Eight Former Presidential Aides," *Washington Monthly*, April 1987, p. 24.

6. Harry McPherson, *A Political Education* (Boston: An Atlantic Monthly Book, Little, Brown), p. 123.

7. Ibid., p. 162.

8. Said by Haldeman at a conference on the Nixon presidency at Hofstra University, October 1987.

9. Ruth Marcos, "He's staying on as Attorney General, but many other Justice officials may not"; and Barbara Vobejda, "The low-key Education secretary will retain his post," *The Washington Post National Weekly Edition*, November 28–December 4, 1988, p. 32.

10. James David Barber, *The Presidential Character: Predicting Performance in the White House* (Englewood Cliffs, N.J.: Prentice-Hall, 1972).

CHAPTER 5.
Men and Women

1. J. M. Bardwick, "Notes about Power Relationships Between Women," in A. G. Sargent, ed., *Beyond Sex Roles* (St. Paul: West, 1977).

2. Jane Meredith Adams, "The Disillusionment of Success: How Women View the Work World," *Boston Globe*, November 10, 1986, pp. 53–54.

3. Ibid.

4. C. O. Sylvester Mawson, *Roget's Thesaurus of the English Language* (Garden City: Garden City Books, 1936), revised ed., p.298.

5. Rosabeth Moss Kanter, *Men and Women of the Corporation* (New York: Basic Books, 1977), pp. 211, 230–37.

6. Quoted by Richard Saltus, *Boston Globe*, February 8, 1988, pp. 33, 35.

7. H. Garland, K. F. Hale, and M. Burnson, "Attribution for the Success and Failure of Female Managers: A Replication and Extension," *Psychology of Women Quarterly*, 1982, vol. VII, no. 2, pp. 155–62.

8. Judith Briles, *Women to Women: From Sabotage to Support* (Far Hills, N.J.: New Horizons, 1987).

9. Judy Foreman, "New Frontiers of Women's Psychology," *Boston Globe Magazine*, September 22, 1985, p. 13.

10. American Council of Education, reported in *Boston Globe*, March 28, 1988.

11. Helen Rogan, "Top Women Executives Find Path to Power Is Strewn with Hurdles," *Wall Street Journal*, October 25, 1985, pp. 35, 44.

12. Carol Gilligan, *In a Different Voice* (Cambridge: Harvard University Press, 1982).

13. Ibid., p. 63.

14. Ibid., p. 17.

15. Ibid., pp. 62–63.

16. Jean Lipman-Blumen, *Gender Roles and Power* (Englewood Cliffs, N.J.: Prentice-Hall, 1984), p. 30; described by Virginia E. O'Leary, "Women's Relationships with Women in the Workplace," in B. A. Gutek, A. H. Stromberg, and L. Larwood, eds., *Women and Work: An Annual Review*, vol. 3 (Beverly Hills, Calif.: Sage Publications, 1988), p. 192.

17. In public life, Norway is the only nation in which women have achieved

equitable or majority representation in power, and it will be interesting to see what scholars eventually conclude will be the significance of that difference.

18. Jeanne Kirkpatrick, *Political Women* (New York: Basic Books, 1974).

19. Xandra Kayden, "Politics and Sexuality: A Speculation," *Harvard Political Review*, Spring, 1976, vol. 4, no. 3.

CHAPTER 6.
Private Relationships

1. Hedrick Smith, *The Power Game: How Washington Works* (New York: Random House, 1988), p. 113.

2. Ibid.

3. Myra MacPherson, *The Power Lovers* (New York: G.P. Putnam's Sons, 1975), pp. 432–43.

4. Robert E. Lane, *Political Life* (New York: Free Press, 1959).

5. Harry McPherson, *A Political Education* (Boston: The Atlantic Monthly Press, Little, Brown, 1972), p. 87.

6. John Ehrlichman, *Witness to Power* (New York: Simon and Schuster, 1982), pp. 413–14.

7. Richard Schickel, *Intimate Strangers: The Culture of Celebrity* (New York: Fromm International Publishing, 1986).

8. Oriana Fallaci, *Interview with History*, translated by John Shepley (New York: Houghton Mifflin, 1976), pp. 42–43.

9. Shelley Ross, *Fall from Grace: Sex, Scandal, and Corruption in American Politics from 1702 to the Present* (New York: Ballantine Books, 1988), p. xx.

10. Daniel Goldman, "Sex, Power, Failure: Patterns Emerge," *New York Times*, May 19, 1987. pp. C 1, 5.

CHAPTER 7.
Losing Power

1. Biochemical studies on animals such as monkeys suggest that leaders have higher levels of serotonin in their brains than do their followers, and the serotonin subsides to normal levels once the monkeys are no longer in leadership positions.

2. C. P. Snow, "Corridors of Power," *Strangers and Brothers* (London: Macmillan, 1972), vol. 3, pp. 270–71.

CHAPTER 8.
Surviving Power

1. "State Services Management Notes, No. 3: The Departing Governor: Transition out of Office," National Governor's Association Ofice of State Services, Washington D.C., July, 1986. They also publish a case study by former Governor

Washington D.C., July, 1986. They also publish a case study by former Governor John Carlin, "Gubernatorial Perspectives on Transition: The Carlin-Hayden Transition in 1986," September 1988.

2. Jeffrey Sonnenfeld, *The Hero's Farewell: The Retirement and Renewal of Chief Executives* (New York: Oxford University Press, 1988), p. 275.

Acknowledgments

The seeds for this book were sewn in my first exposure to politics in Robert F. Kennedy's 1964 campaign for the Senate, as I watched him and his aides go about the business of handling a public personality. The seeds came popping out of the ground when I came to Harvard as a graduate student in 1971, after several years in Washington. I was made very conscious of the difference in the way people responded to me (and I to them) as I traveled back and forth between the long halls of the federal government and the streets of Cambridge. It is a path I have seen many people take with varying degrees of confusion and pain. A few years later, I organized a dinner at the Institute of Politics on the transition of going from public to private life. But it sometimes takes a long time—and many intervening people and events—to realize what it is you know and how much you care about it.

A number of persons and institutions helped me along the specific paths to the book: James Q. Wilson has always encouraged me to write about the world of politics and about people that I knew, helping me realize that my perceptions were not always apparent to the rest of the world. Other friends who were important in the formative stages of this book were Donna Bojarsky, James MacGregor Burns, Gunner Erickson, Devon Gaffney, Milton Gwirtzman, Herbert Harris, Bert Hartry, Eunice Howe, Douglas and Sherry Jeffe, Karlyn Keene, Margot Lindsay, Seymor Martin Lipset, Theodore Lowi, Virginia O'Leary, Evelyn Pitcher, Nelson Polsby, Elliot Richardson, Victoria Sackett, Marge Schiller, William Schneider, Peter and Tjasa Sprague, and Abraham Zaleznik.

Arthur Singer, at the Alfred P. Sloan Foundation, made the book financially possible with the critical initial support of his organization and the later help from the Earhart and Bradley Foundations. My agent,

Robert Ducas, and my editor and publisher, Erwin Glikes, both believed in the book and really made it possible by staying the course.

The Institute of Politics at Harvard has always been a major factor in my ability to function as a somewhat unorthodox scholar. Those on its staff who have been very helpful on this project include Lisa Belsky, Ann Doyle, Nancy Deitz, Dennis Galvam, Ann Kenny, Yin Lam, Mary McTighe, David Runkle, Ginny and Dick Thornburgh, and Sonya Wallenberg. Long ago, in the late 1970s, I was the co-leader of an Institute study group on the subject of the private side of public life; in 1981, I ran a seminar at Brandeis University on public careers, and in the fall of 1987, I ran another study group at the Institute of Politics, specifically on the topic of this book. All of the students and guests who participated helped me put what I was learning into perspective, and along the way, they—and many of the people I met who pass through the Institute—have been interesting, informative, and a lot of fun to know.

In the long run, of course, the book is about the people who consented to let me interview them on a very personal and sometimes painful side of their experience. Even those whom I had counted as friends for many years—to say nothing of those whom I had never met before—were taking a chance on me and, to some extent, on themselves, in exploring a topic many never before put into words. I am very grateful to them indeed. All quotes, unless otherwise noted, are based on interviews with me, conducted in person between 1987 and 1989.

Index

Aberrational behavior, 17, 122–124, 145, 148–149

Access, 7, 9, 98–100

Accomplishment, sense of, 90–91, 122, 178

Adams, Jane Meredith, 211

Age; *see also* Physical attributes; Power
  as a factor in expectations, 106, 125, 159, 183–184
  youth of staff aides, 91

Aides, 28, 47, 51–54, 88–91, 141
  bias, 50–51

Allen, Richard, 74

Alliances, 62

Ambition, 25–27, 132–133, 136, 178, 204; *see also* Power, drive for

Arnold, Benedict, 54

Arrogance, 58

Authority
  dealing with, 35
  establishing, 94
  versus influence, 90–91
  versus power, 11–13

Autonomy
  as a measure of power, 57, 78, 87, 97
  public versus private, 92, 94

Bakker, Tammy Faye, 124

Barber, James David, 101, 211

Barwick, J. M., 209, 211

Belsky, Lisa, 216

Bennett, William J., 93

Biden, Joseph, 134

Boehme, Jacob, 210

Bojarsky, Donna, 215

Boland, Eddie, 84

Bork, Robert, 87

Braun, David, 58, 200

Briles, Judith, 211

Brown, Edmund G. (Pat), 196

Brown, Norman O., 210

Buckley, John
  leaving office, 73–74
  on power, 4
  public image, 201
  starting over, 170
  successors, 95

Bureaucracy
  change, 60, 91, 119–129
  distribution of power, 68
  protecting leaders, 58
  women, 117–118

Bureaucratic behavior, 113, 118–119

Burford, Anne, 74

Burns, James MacGregor, 215

Burnson, M., 211

Bush, Barbara, 168

Bush, George, 92, 93

Califano, Joseph, 72

Carlin, John, 213

Carroll, Mike, 172

Carter, Jimmy, 16, 96, 115, 137

Carter, Rosalyn, 137

Casey, William, 75

Cavazos, Lauro, 93

Celebrity status, 32

Church, Frank, 115

Civil rights movement, 21, 103, 109

Civility
    as a characteristic of the culture of
        power, 13–17, 63, 142, 194
    in dealing with the loss of power, 158,
        177

Clifford, Clark, 99–100

Commitment, 150–151

Communication, 48, 65, 95, 168

Communities of power, 19

Competence, sense of, 58–59, 183, 204;
    see also Confidence

Competition, 25–26

Confidence, sense of, 58, 67–68, 76; see
    also Competence

Constituents
    attitude toward legislators, 79
    competing, 62
    expectations, 66, 76
    legislative leaders, 82–83, 84

Corruption, 70, 75

Crozier, Michel, 209

Daley, Richard, 8

Defeat, experience in, 184–185

Defenses, 36

Deference
    and autonomy, 37, 63
    as a characteristic of the culture of
        power, 13, 169
    differences in attitude between men
        and women, 111–117
    the lack of, 64, 168
    staff aides, 90

Deitz, Nancy, 216

Dine, Thomas, 115

Disloyalty, 53, 96

Dole, Elizabeth, 137

Dole, Robert, 137

Doyle, Ann, 216

Ducas, Robert, 215

Duffy, Joseph, 120, 121

Dukakis, Michael, 61, 95, 190

Egeberg, Roger, 59

Ehrlichman, John
    coming into power, 29–30, 41–42
    on authority, 11–12
    on influence, 10
    private relationships, 140, 212
    surviving power, 182, 199–200
    trust, 54

Eisenhower, Dwight D., 188

Elias, Norbert, 209

Eller, John, 39, 83

Emerson, Ralph Waldo, 37

Envy, 70, 108–111, 122, 194

Erickson, Gunner, 215

Executive leaders, 84–88
    power, 81, 84

Expectations, 65, 67, 183–184
    differences between men and women,
        103–107, 173–174

Failure, 49, 149, 159

Fallaci, Oriana, 145, 212

Fame, 37–38

Family
    associations of power, 33–34
    impact of power on, 131, 133, 136,
        137–141, 203
    justifying power to, 182
    women with power, 104, 106, 112–113

Favors, 31, 62–63, 96, 167, 171

Fear
    differences between men and women,
        107–111
    of success, 31

Femininity, 107

Feminist
    movement, 21, 103–104, 108, 122
    perspective, 122, 134

Finch, Robert
    appointed power, 86–87, 97, 98
    picking your own team, 59
    surviving power, 196, 198–199

Fitzgerald, F. Scott, 8
Flannery, Jack, 45–46, 52, 95, 175–176
Flannigan, Frip, 7–8
Flynn, Ray, 160, 177
Ford, Gerald, 115, 188
Foreman, Judy, 211
Freud, Sigmund, 57, 212
Friedan, Betty, 109, 110
Friends, 25, 44, 80, 141–142
Frustration, 6, 19, 59

Gaffney, Devon, 215
Galatti, Stephen, 150–151
Galvam, Dennis, 216
Garland, H., 211
Gilligan, Carol, 113–114, 117, 128, 211
Glaberson, William, 209
Glikes, Erwin, 216
Goldman, Daniel, 149, 209, 212
Goldwater, Barry, 136
Goodwin, Doris Kearns, 27
Gratification, 57; *see also* Satisfaction
Gutek, B. A., 211
Gwirtzman, Milton, 215

Haldeman, H. R., 41, 210
    executive power, 85
    relationship with Nixon, 52, 53
    staff power, 89
Hale, K. F., 211
Hamilton, Alexander, 53–54
Hardesty, Sarah, 105
Harrington, Kevin
    achieving power, 43–44
    getting tired, 72
    legislative power, 82–83
    losing power, 171, 172
    motivation, 26
    physical attributes of power, 12
    staff power, 89
    using the skills, 195–196
Harris, Herbert, 167, 215
Hart, Gary, 134, 149, 161
Hartry, Bert, 215
Hattersley, Roy, 172–173

Helms, Richard, 75
Holton, Linwood, 157, 168
Homogeneity, 49
Hoover, J. Edgar, 45
Horizons, 43, 151
Horner, Matina, 128, 209
House, Col. Edward, 52
Howe, Eunice, 9–10, 215
Huizinga, J., 210

Identity
    changing, 153
    and gender, 104–105, 107, 113, 122–126
    and ideology, 162
    and loss of power, 174, 185
    private, 31, 58, 202–207
    private versus public, 23, 64, 115, 150,
        153, 175–176
    professional, 187–188
    protecting, 158, 168, 202
    public, 36–37, 181, 185–186, 197–202
Illicit relationships, 143–146
Incompetence, 166–169
Independence, 46, 91–92
Individuality, 36, 38
Influence
    after power, 177, 194–195
    appointees, 95–98
    measuring with favors, 62
    outsiders, 78, 98–100
    versus power, 7–10, 182
Insecurity
    and envy, 68, 109, 193–194
    in others, 56, 110–111
    in powerholders, 53, 54, 152
Isolation, 19, 34–35, 64, 128–129

Jacobs, Nehama, 105
Jackson, Ira
    coming into office, 30–31
    controlling one's own agenda, 85–86
    creating one's own group, 60–61
    leaving power, 158, 163, 165
    ritual, 63–64
    transition out of power, 177

Jeffe, Douglas, 215
Jeffe, Sherry Bebitch, 215
Jefferson, Thomas, 53
Johnson, Lyndon, 18, 72, 89
Jones, Rochelle, 18, 209
Jophcott, Edmund, 209

Kanter, Rosabeth Moss, 49, 209, 210, 211
Kayden, Xandra, 212
Keene, Karlyn, 215
Kennedy, Edward M., 177
Kennedy, Jacqueline, 135
Kennedy, John F., 37, 52, 134, 135, 136
Kennedy, Robert F., 136, 209
    on coming into power, 36–37
    measuring character, 135
    supportive relationship, 52
Kenny, Ann, 216
King, Eddy, 177
Kirkpatrick, Jeane
    civility, 14–15
    on coming into power, 30
    internal politics, 96–97
    parenting, 57
    surviving power, 193
    women and power, 115, 116, 123, 212
Kissinger, Henry, 145–146, 147
Knowles, John, 69
Kramer, Albert, 52, 68–69

Lam, Yin, 216
Landis, James M., 210
Lane, Robert E., 135, 212
Larwood, L., 211
Lasswell, Harold, 131
Leadership, 13, 27, 35, 43
Legitimacy, 35, 64, 76, 99
Leisure, 188
Limits, 5–6, 36, 58
Lindsay, Margot, 215
Lipman-Blumen, Jean, 118, 211
Lipset, Seymour Martin, 215
Lowi, Theodore, 215

Loyalty, 92, 96; see also Trust

MacNamara, Robert, 45
MacPherson, Myra, 133, 142, 212
March, James G., 210
Marcos, Imelda, 124
Marcos, Ruth, 211
Marcuse, Herbert, 210
Margolin, Burt, 79, 80
Marital status, 104, 112–113, 120–122
Marmor, Judd, 149
Masculinity, 107, 121
Matthews, Christopher, 81, 210
Mawson, C. O. Sylvester, 211
Mayhew, David, 79, 210
McPherson, Harry
    cultures of power, 18
    influence, 88
    leaving power, 72
    public versus private power, 136
    relationship with staff, 88, 210
    significance, 163
McTighe, Mary, 216
Mecham, Evan, 74
Media, 70
Meese, Edwin, 74, 93, 138
Meir, Golda, 115
Mentor, 94
Miller, Jean Baker, 111
Minorities
    in relation to dominant cultures, 17, 103, 108, 120
    subject to envy, 69
Moore, Jonathan, 52
Morality, 76, 134, 144
Muskie, Edmund, 81–82

Neustadt, Richard E., 41, 66, 210
Newfield, Jack, 37, 209
Nietzsche, Friedrich, 210
Nixon, Richard
    imperial presidency, 115
    overcoming defeat, 185
    relationship with Haldeman, 52, 53, 85, 89

relationship with Kissinger, 145
trusting staff, 54–55
under pressure to quit, 74, 75
North, Oliver, 118, 120
Novak, William, 209, 210

O'Brien, Tom, 8
O'Leary, Virginia E., 211, 215
O'Neill, Thomas P., 7–8, 73, 84, 188, 201,
   209, 210
Organizational maintenance, 56, 62

Parenting, 35, 57, 171
Peers, 25–26
Perez, Leander, 45
Pieczenik, Steven, 131
Pitcher, Evelyn, 215
Planning, 183, 190–191
Polsby, Nelson, 215
Power
   abuse of, 80
   achieving, 77
   appointed, 67, 85, 88, 92, 95–98
   benefits of, 29–33
   borrowed, 95–98
   collegial distribution, 15, 78, 90, 117,
      171
   corporate, 22, 43, 77, 92–95, 105
   cultural changes, 20–22
   culture of, 19, 60, 132
   definition, 4, 106
   drive for, 84, 126, 131, 147; see also Am-
      bition
   elected, 9, 22, 78, 84, 92, 99
   executive, 84–88, 92–94
   legislative, 79–84
   pathological view of, 131, 133–134,
      136, 137, 145
   physical attributes, 12–13
   public versus private, 92–95
   realization of, 27–29
   sex role differences, 106, 110–111,
      127–129, 173
   staff, 88–91
   temporary phenomenon, 22–24, 184

transition out of, 160, 162–167, 172–
   176, 186–191
Powerlessness, 38, 43, 45, 126
Privacy, 71
Process, 61–62
Pynn, Ronald E., 209

Raiffa, Howard, 210
Rainmakers, 78, 98–100, 210
Randolph, Edmund, 53–54
Rayburn, Sam, 84
Reagan, Nancy, 137
Reagan, Ronald, 15, 92, 137, 160
Recognition, 35–36
Reeves, Richard, 131
Regan, Donald, 74
Reputation, 75, 207
Reward
   emotional, 188
   in holding power, 56–61, 91
   legislative, 81
   rainmakers, 100
   in retrospect, 201–202
   significance, 47
   staff, 88
Rice, Donna, 149
Richardson, Elliot, 215
   culture of power, 13
   limitations, 42
   trust, 52
   working with the author, 12, 119–120
Risk, 148, 150
Ritchie, Donald A., 210
Ritual, 61, 63–65, 68
Robertson, Pat, 131
Rockefeller, Nelson, 10
Rogan, Helen, 211
Ross, Shelley, 148, 212
Runkle, David, 212

Sackett, Victoria, 215
Saltus, Richard, 211
Sargent, A. G., 211
Sargent, Francis, 45, 52, 68, 95, 177
Sartre, Jean Paul, 210

Satisfaction; *see also* Accomplishment;
  Gratification
  after power, 188, 190
  in relation to accomplishment, 30, 81
  from the task, 188
Scandal, 124
Schickel, Richard, 143, 212
Schiller, Johann, 210
Schiller, Marge, 215
Schneider, William, 87, 215
Security, 54
  financial, 169–171
Self-reliance, 51–56
Shepley, John, 212
Shriver, Sargent, 161
Significance, 47, 163–166, 175, 200
Simon, Herbert A., 210
Singer, Arthur, 215
Singer, Carla, 114, 162–163
Smith, Hedrick, 131, 212
Snow, C. P., 44, 209, 212
Sonnenfeld, Jeffrey, 201, 212
Sprague, Peter, 215
Sprague, Tjasa, 215
Spring, Micho, 121, 160, 198, 202
Spring, William, 121
Stability, 93
Standard operating procedures, 68, 113
Status, 7, 32, 99
Stereotypes, 108
Stromberg, A. H., 211
Sullivan, Walter, 201
Sycophants, 48–49

Taft, Robert, 168
Temporary, 22–23
Thornburgh, Dick, 61, 65, 93, 137–138,
  216
Thornburgh, Ginny, 65, 137–138, 152, 165,
  216
Thurman, Strom, 45
Tokenism, 21, 108, 120

Tower, John, 15
Truman, Bess, 137
Truman, Harry, 137
Trust, 48–51

Uncertainty, 46, 50, 162
Unintended consequences, 42

Vigeland, Charles A., 16, 209
Vision, 87
Vobejda, Barbara, 211
Vulnerability, 71

Wallenberg, Sonya, 216
Washington, George, 53–54
Watt, James, 74
Wealth, 33, 169
Westerfelt, Esther, 108
Wexler, Anne, 13, 21, 106, 120
White, Kevin
  expectations, 66
  getting tired, 172
  leaving power, 157, 158, 160, 176–177,
    186, 193, 204
  power versus influence, 9, 100
  relationship with staff, 51, 52
Widnall, Sheila, 108
Williams, Shirley, 20, 104–105, 129, 173–
  174
Wilson, James Q., 215
Wilson, Woodrow, 52
Wirth, Timothy, 89
Woll, Peter, 18, 209
Woodward, Bob, 75, 210

Yarmolinsky, Adam
  on coming into power, 45
  losing power, 161, 172–173, 174
  power and parenting, 57
  surviving power, 191–192

Zaleznik, Abraham, 175, 215